May you be blessed by your visit to The Pond.

Lucy Allen

the POND

Lucy Allen

ISBN 978-1-68197-813-0 (Paperback)
ISBN 978-1-68197-814-7 (Digital)

Copyright © 2016 by Lucy Allen

All rights reserved. No part of this publication may be reproduced, distributed, or transmitted in any form or by any means, including photocopying, recording, or other electronic or mechanical methods without the prior written permission of the publisher. For permission requests, solicit the publisher via the address below.

Christian Faith Publishing, Inc.
296 Chestnut Street
Meadville, PA 16335
www.christianfaithpublishing.com

Printed in the United States of America

POND REFLECTIONS

Dan Allen, my husband's grandfather, may very well be the instrument God used to bring about this book. Nearly a hundred years ago, he purchased and developed the land where my husband and I lived for thirty-five years. Nestled around us were cousins, aunts, uncles and other family members that made our community very unique to say the least.

A few years ago we learned that our home was in the path of what was to be an interstate through our county. Although our home wasn't purchased by the Department of Transportation, my husband and I began to think about moving. The interstate would run directly behind our house and the connecting road was a stone's throw away—so much for living in the country! Our home was directly across the road from our church, so moving away was a decision we struggled with and prayed about often. God did answer our prayers!

We were blessed to be able to purchase a home with a few acres and a pond! My husband had always wanted a pond. Little did I know how God would use that pond to be a source of peace and a solace to my heart.

I often sit by the bay window as I read my morning devotions. I truly feel that God has opened a door using the pond and it is with faith that I step through. I have wondered just what my spiritual gift might be, and as I wrote down the first few "reflections" I felt that I had found that gift.

My prayer is that as you read, these pieces with speak to your heart, your soul.

If you do not know Jesus as your Lord and Savior, may I direct you to read the Gospel of John to begin your journey, remembering that "For God so loved the world, He gave His only begotten Son that whosoever believes on Him will have eternal life." (John 3:16).

Look back at the work whosoever…that leaves out no one.

Blessings!

THE POND

A place where inspiration lives and grows
A place where my Savior continually shows
His majesty, His goodness, His creation
From daybreak to sunset
Stories unfold within me
I can't explain it
It's as though God is whispering to me
In that still small voice
Saying
Listen and I will tell you
Things you never knew
Watch and I will show you
Your gift
And He did
The pond has forever changed my life
God's spirit swells up inside of me
Each time I look toward the pond
Stories are created from within me

LUCY ALLEN

Unexplainable
Amazing and incredible
Only God could have given me the will and the passion
To move
To write
To create
To search and find
The gift I have longed for
Searched for
And yes
Finally found
By
The Pond
May the words in this book inspire you
May they give you a reason
To pause
To search
And maybe for the first time
To see your Creator
The one true God
Who made it all

—Kathy M. Crouch

A BEAUTIFUL MYSTERY

As I rounded the bend in the driveway, my view was of the pond, shrouded in gray. Clouds like gray silk floated above and a gray mist was rising from the water. Even in these somber colors the pond was a thing of beauty and mystery. Tomorrow the scene will be changed, possibly as bright as today's grayness has been.

I love mysteries, and God has provided a number of them in His Word. The one I want to focus on here is the mystery Paul speaks of in 1 Corinthians 15:51, *"Behold, I shew you a mystery; We shall not all sleep, but we shall all be changed."* Of those that are in Christ, all will not die! Look on to verse 52, *"In a moment, in the twinkling of an eye, at the last trump: for the trumpet shall sound, and the dead shall be raised incorruptible, and we shall be changed."* Again, a thing of both beauty and mystery.

Such a change is hard to imagine, but look at Philippians 3:20–21 as it speaks also of the change of a believer, *"For our citizenship is in heaven; from whence also we look for the Savior, the Lord Jesus Christ: Who shall change our vile body, that it may be fashioned like unto His glorious body, according to the working whereby He is able even to subdue all things unto Himself."*

Not only does the heart and life of a Christian change once we are saved, but Christ, in the twinkling of an eye, a moment, shall change the bodies of those still living at the time of His second coming to a glorious body! That takes my breath away! This is what we call the Rapture; when the dead in Christ shall rise, and those that remain will be caught up to meet Him in the sky. This truth comes from 1 Thessalonians 4:16–18.

A mystery certainly, but in faith, we believe we shall be changed.

Are you certain of your standing with Christ? If you desire the certainty of this glorious change and forever abiding with the Father and the Son and Holy Spirit, you only need to believe on Him, Jesus, the Son of God. John 3:16 is the place to go in the Bible to read this for yourself. And remember, "whosoever" is You!

A BIRD AND A LESSON LEARNED

When I sit down to read my Bible, I ask God to open my eyes and show me something new and fresh that He has for me. It's amazing how God does just that.

This morning I was sitting on the porch, reading today's devotion and noticed a bird flying up to the laundry room window. She seemed to be flying back and forth, trying her best to find a corner or ledge to build a nest. She'd fly at the window then back down to the ground. After sitting there a few seconds, she would try it again. I thought, "crazy bird, how many times are you gonna try that?" Then it hit me; that's exactly what I do. I am like that bird, hardheaded and stubborn ... beating my head against a wall, trying to handle something myself instead of handing it over to the Lord.

Try after try, until finally He says, "Come on, give it to Me. I've been here all along just waiting for you to give it up." After all, He tells us to cast *all* our burdens on Him, as we see in 1 Peter 5:7.

Casting all your care upon Him; for He careth for you. Will you give up and let Him care for you?

A DIAMOND IN THE PROCESS

The day dawned bright and beautiful. Not a cloud to be seen, the sky an endless canvas of blue stretched over the pond. Perfection! There is nothing like a day such as this, so bright and pond water so still the sky is reflected as if in a mirror. The air about the pond fairly shimmers with excitement, almost knowing how the beauty of the morning has moved me. Like a glittering, flawless diamond the morning lay before me full of promise.

As the Lord gave me this comparison of the day to a diamond I felt His prodding to further explore this process. I made a few notes to help me gather my thoughts. Let me share them with you, and this is exactly how I wrote them down.

Diamond = perfection from pressure
Formation of diamond = Jesus purifying =
Perfection of the Saints

A diamond is formed by pressure deep within the earth and delivered to the earth's surface by volcanic activity. This is a very simplistic explanation and works best within this lesson. Oftentimes, we as Christians are formed by pressure deep within our hearts then our joy bubbles up as by volcanic eruption! At times we feel we have been through the fire in our Christian life and knowing that fire purifies

I would like to bring to your attention Hebrews 10:10,14, "*By the which will we are sanctified through the offering of the body of Jesus Christ once for all. (14) For by one offering he hath perfected for ever them that are sanctified.*" How beautiful is this picture? Jesus offered Himself…Once!

First John 3:2–3 speaks to the perfection of Saints: "*Beloved, now are we the sons of God, and it doth not yet appear what we shall be: but we know that, when he shall appear we shall be like him; for we shall see him as he is. And every man that hath this hope in him purifieth himself, even as he is pure.*" As Christians, we recognize Christ has a sanctifying influence on the life of the believer due to our belief in His imminent return. In the last sentence of the verse selection I would like to point out using the Believer's Bible Commentary's statement that, "The Lord Jesus never had to purify Himself; He is pure. With us, it is a gradual process; with Him, it is a fact." A gradual process not unlike the process God designed for the formation of diamonds!

A diamond is strong, beautiful, and a picture of perfection—all of which we can be when we are in Christ. Philippians 4:13 puts it very plainly, "*I can do all things through Christ which strengtheneth me.*" I might also add that we can *be* all things as well, but only in Him.

A GENTLE SAVIOR

This morning as I looked out over the pond, I spied some of the most gentle of all creatures, deer, all four of the female persuasion. The does were all standing on the pond dam casually munching on leaves or grass and just strolling in the general direction of the back yard. I froze, hoping that they hadn't detected my movements as I'd stepped out onto the carport. The morning was pristine, just before 7:00 a.m. with birds chirping and a woodpecker hard at work off in the distance.

As I was watching them, one by one they stepped off the path and disappeared into the woods. Just like that, they were gone. Gentleness was the word that kept circling in my mind.

In Matthew's gospel, Jesus says, *"Take my yoke upon you, and learn of me; for I am meek and lowly in heart: and ye shall find rest unto your souls"* (11:29). Meek could be substituted with any of these words: *quiet*, *gentle*, and *submissive*. In this connotation, yoke refers to the Old Testament law, thereby giving us the picture of Jesus's yoke being light in comparison. The yoke of Jesus relieves us and calls us to rest in Him.

There are many lessons to be gleaned from this one verse, but in concentrating on the gentleness of Jesus, remember that the Bible also describes Him as the Lamb and a shepherd. Both descriptions denote gentleness.

We see great hope in this verse, Revelation 7:17, *"For the Lamb which is in the midst of the throne shall feed them, and shall lead them unto living fountains of waters: and God shall wipe away all tears from their eyes."* Hope and a promise from the gentle Lamb of God, Jesus!

Max Lucado paints a wonderful picture of our gentle Savior in the following quote:

"Our Saviour kneels down and gazes upon the darkest acts of our lives. But rather than recoil in horror, he reaches out in kindness and says, 'I can clean that if you want.' And from the basin of his grace, he scoops a palm full of mercy and washes our sin."

Do you need His gentle cleansing today?

A GLIMPSE OF HEAVEN

As the seasons begin their subtle change, the patterns of light and shadow from the sun are altered from what I've seen through the summer. Now that the days are getting shorter, the forest area on the opposite side of the pond from where I sit, fairly explodes with the soft, golden sunlight of late afternoon. As the rays of the sun are divided between the tree trunks, it adds depth that I've not noticed before. It is almost as if they are rooms…rooms bathed in that soft, golden light, welcoming one home. Similar to what you might see in a Thomas Kinkaid work of art.

My immediate thought was of the verse from John 14:2, 3, *"In my Father's house are many mansions: if it were not so, I would have told you. I go to prepare a place for you. And if I go and prepare a place for you I will come again, and receive you unto myself; that where I am, there ye may be also."*

What a promise! What an awesome home-going to look forward to! What will that mansion be like, you might wonder. In ancient culture, the father's home had rooms added on for extended family members to live, creating a tight and loving family community. I love this description from Matt Slick: *"Christ is saying that He is preparing a place for us in Heaven where we will dwell with God in close communion with Him and that there is room in heaven for all whom God calls to salvation."*

To put this thought into current day terms, "Have you made your reservations?" Do you know if you have a mansion reserved for you? I pray that assurance is yours today. If you are unsure, read the Gospel of John and meet Jesus Christ, our mansion builder. Salvation is simple… believe in Him and you shall be saved and your room reserved!

A GLORIOUS SIGHTING

Yesterday, as I was arriving home from being with my daughter while her husband had surgery, I saw the most glorious sight! If only I could paint the picture of it here, for words would not do it justice.

It was about 6:30 p.m., and I was headed down our driveway facing the pond when I realized just ahead the sky had darkened somewhat. Behind and around the darkness were lighter clouds brightened by the sun that they were hiding. The sun appeared to light the center of this mixture of light and dark with rays of sunshine reaching through the clouds as if to earth. I could only think that this must be what the sky will look like when Jesus comes back to earth. I couldn't keep my eyes off the sight! *Glorious* is the only word I could think of to describe the scene. I kept looking and thinking that it was so beautiful and the next thing I was going to see was Christ descending. It was Rapture worthy!

I kept thinking about the verses in 1 Thessalonians 4:16, 17: *"For the Lord himself shall descend from heaven with a shout, with the voice of the archangel, and with the trump of God; and the dead in Christ shall rise first: Then we which are alive and remain shall be caught up together with them in the clouds, to meet the Lord in the air; and so shall we ever be with the Lord."*

I'm also reminded of the song "Glorious Day" by Casting Crowns:

LUCY ALLEN

One day the trumpet will sound for His coming
One day the skies with His glories will shine
Wonderful day, my Beloved One, bringing
My Savior, Jesus, is mine

Glorious day, Oh, Glorious day!

A GOLDEN CROSS

As we approach the Easter season, my mind goes back to a spring afternoon at the pond when I saw a most amazing sight! After getting home from work, I decided to sit out by the pond for a bit and enjoy the last of the day. As the sun began to set, I looked up and beheld a perfect cross of sunlight. The cross was shining bright and golden, while all around it the clouds had turned a mixture of pink, orange, and gold. I was speechless as I stared at this beautiful sight. I grabbed my cell phone and took a picture for later proof of what I'd seen. I knew I'd just witnessed the cross after the resurrection for it could not have been so glorious otherwise.

I would like to explore what the cross might have been like at the time of the crucifixion of Jesus. Consider that there were no chainsaws, only roughly made axes or hatchets to use to cut the trees to form the cross. It would seem plausible to expect the cross was very rough, probably having splinters here and there. Physically, a very heavy item to bear recalling that Simon of Cyrene was drafted to carry the cross the remainder of Jesus's journey. In my imagination, it is actually an ugly piece. Even the place had an ugly name: The Place of the Skull. John 19:17: *"And he bearing his cross went forth into a place called the place of a skull, which is called in the Hebrew Golgotha."*

Our Redeemer, Savior, Shepherd and lover of our souls crucified upon that ugly heavy cross on the hill called a skull! Once nailed to that cross, He was lifted up between two thieves, and His garments became the winnings of a game of chance played by Roman soldiers as His mother looked on in horror. We cannot even imagine such shame, humiliation and loss. But even in this solemn scene on the horizon is waiting…HOPE!

HOPE arrived on the third day as it was discovered that Christ was not in the tomb. He had risen! He was changed, His earthly body no longer restricting Him. In my mind, I see Christ as almost luminous in His appearance, maybe with a golden shimmer outlining His silhouette similar to what I saw on the cross in the sky. Matthew 28:3 supports my vision: *"His countenance was like lightning, and his raiment white as snow."*

Jesus was subjected to this horrific death so that you and I might have eternal life. Philippians 2:8, *"And being found in fashion as a man, he humbled himself, and became obedient unto death, even the death of the cross."* An ugly cross, ugly place and an ugly death… for *me*! But now, thousands of years after the crucifixion, because of His resurrection, to me that cross has become beautiful. Just like it appeared in the sky, golden and gleaming assuring me of my *hope* in Christ Jesus.

Just as the Living Christ turned an unsightly cross into a thing of beauty, so too can He turn your life from bad to good. Turn to Christ of the cross; come to Him just as you are and allow Him to beautify your life!

A LESSON FROM A BEAVER

It seems there is never a dull moment around the pond. We thought a beaver might have taken a liking to our pond. My husband and our son discovered this was the case as they were walking back toward the house after hunting in the surrounding woods. Making their way around the westerly edge of the pond they located what they were certain was a burrow. Within the week that beaver gave us a bit more proof of his existence by gnawing and felling a hardwood tree just at the edge of the pond.

I have thought about that old beaver, how easy it had been for him to just slip on in. We didn't even know it until damage had been done. Satan can move into our lives just as easily if we are not on our guard! Most often, just like with our beaver, we are not aware of a problem until we see damage. Unlike our tree that cannot be repaired, Jesus makes repairs in our hearts, minds and lives.

Heed the warnings of Satan as we find in 1 Peter 5:8: *"Be sober, be vigilant; because your adversary the devil, as a roaring lion, walketh about, seeking whom he may devour."* In Ephesians 6:11, *"Put on the whole armour of God, that ye may be able to stand against the wiles of the devil."* To be sober means to be serious minded, to be intelligent concerning the strategies of Satan, but how do we do that? Studying God's Word, praying for wisdom and the ability to discern what is of God. Remember that Satan shows himself as an angel of light, sometimes without being steadfast in prayer and studying the Bible it could be hard to distinguish Satan's attack.

My second thought is on the armor of God; notice that the scripture says the *whole* armor of God. We must be completely armed, just a piece or two just won't do. Know that the devil is certain of your weakness and that is where his strike will be! To remind yourself of the pieces of God's armor read Ephesians 6:11–18.

In closing, I chose the scripture from James 4:7, which says simply, *"Submit yourselves therefore to God. Resist the devil, and he will flee from you."*

Penned by an unknown author, this verse is from a song titled "Resist the Devil":

> God promised to deliver and set us free,
> And give us power o'er the enemy.
> The Word of God will make the devil flee:
> God's word is stronger than he'll ever be.

A LIFE LETTER

Today's scripture is from 2 Corinthians 3:3, which says, *"Foreasmuch as ye are manifestly declared to be the epistle of Christ ministered by us, written not with ink, but with the Spirit of the living God."*

We have all written letters, yes, letters on paper long before the technological age hit. Be they love letters, letters between friends separated by distance, or those dreaded letters known as the "Dear John" letter. I'm afraid that the art of letter writing is fast slipping away.

This scripture says to me that I am a letter—a letter from Christ. This verse, like many others in the Bible, can be personalized by inserting our name into the verse.

As Christians, we are called to live a life apart from the world, to be in the world but not of the world. The way we live our life is our letter to others. I was recently reminded just how the world watches those of us that profess to be followers of Christ. Sitting here looking on the pond it is easy to imagine that this little bubble of life is my world when in reality, it's far from that.

This verse has challenged me to be better at living my life "to the letter." My prayer for all who read this is the same…how does your letter read?

A MIRROR IMAGE

The pond is very still in the late afternoon with the sun shining from the west now over the treetops. In a while, that sun will drop below the tree line and we'll hear the songs of the bullfrogs and crickets, but for now, it's quiet and still. Still like a looking glass, I see reflected in the water the trees and bushes along the edges of the pond.

What or whom do I reflect? As I look out, I think about how God the Father sees me. I am not worthy to approach Him in my natural state, full of sin and ugliness, but because I have Christ in me, it is Christ that is seen, not me! I know this from Galatians 2:20, *"I am crucified with Christ, nevertheless I live; yet not I, but Christ liveth in me; and the life which I now live in the flesh I live by the faith of the Son of God, who loved me, and gave himself for me."*

The truth is this: when the Father looks on me, He sees righteousness, yes righteousness! Unbelievable you say? Think on this scripture from 2 Corinthians 21: *"For He hath made Him to be sin for us, who knew no sin; that we might be made the righteousness of God in Him. "* God made Jesus to bear my sin, even though He (Jesus) knew no sin, so that I might be made righteous.

Webster describes *reflection* as "something that shows the effect, existence, or character of something else." In short, I reflect Jesus, to God the Father, and my prayer is that I also reflect Him to others.

We must check our reflection every day.

A NEW YEAR

As I write, we are fast approaching the end of the year. Just a few more days and 2015 will be past and we will be looking ahead at 2016 with much anticipation and wonder. The beginning of a new year is both frightening and exciting. We have the words of David as he says in Psalm 65:11, *"Thou crownest the year with thy goodness; and thy paths drop fatness."* I like to consider this thought as I contemplate the upcoming year. God crowns the year with goodness and where His feet have passed, plenty flows there like a stream.

I recall the October of 2014 and our imminent move from our home of thirty-five years to where we now live, at "the pond." Much like the anticipation of the New Year, we had those thoughts of certainty and comfort surrounding the old house, but waiting for us a few miles away was a little anxiety, fear and, yes, excitement. I have to admit I was a bit nervous at the idea of snakes in and around the pond. Spiders are not creatures that I love, but living near water, they were going to be a part of my life. It seemed no sooner did I knock down a spider and its web than it would be back. Never have I lived where the forest was so close...what was going to be lurking about in those woods? Instead of being fearful, I should have focused on this verse from Psalms. How easily I could have substituted words and had a verse like this, *"Thou crownest our new house with thy goodness; and thy paths around the pond shall drop fatness."*

We who are God's children should not fear the unknown. Deuteronomy 31:8 says, *"And the Lord, he it is that doth go before* thee; *he will be with thee, he will not fail thee, neither forsake thee: fear not, neither be dismayed."* How are we to not give in to fears? By having our hearts fixed on Jesus, the One who says, "fear not." Look at Psalm 112:7–8 for this truth: *"He shall not be afraid of evil tidings: his heart is fixed, trusting in the Lord. His heart is established, he shall not be afraid."*

Closing with the following quote, I pray will help us put the New Year in the right perspective.

As the old year retires and a new one is born, we commit into the hands of our Creator the happenings of the past year and ask for direction and guidance in the new one. May He grant us His grace, His tranquility and His wisdom!

—Peggy Toney Horton

A REPENTANT HEART

The atmosphere is a mist of mixed frozen precipitation creating almost a fog effect as I look out across the pond. What snow has fallen is a covering of white, as is the ice clinging to the leaves and pine needles of the surrounding trees. This brings to mind the scripture from Psalm 51:7, *"Purge me with hyssop, and I shall be clean; wash me, and I shall be whiter than snow."* This comes from King David after his affair with Bathsheba and the death of her husband, Uriah, the death that David himself arranged.

Perhaps the ups and downs of David's life are similar to our own. David was chosen by God to replace Saul as king of Israel and he knew that God was in control. Even so, he didn't always make good decisions and right choices. However we see in Acts 13:22 that David was a man after God's own heart as we read, *"And when he had removed him, he raised up unto them David to be their king; to who also he gave testimony, and said, I have found David the son of Jesse, a man after mine own heart, which shall fulfill all my will."*

David exhibited several characteristics that any of us as God's children should. First, he was faithful, and we find evidence of this in I Samuel 17, in the story of his defeat of Goliath. Look in verse 37 as David answers as to why he should go into battle against Goliath: *"David said moreover, The Lord that delivered me out of the paw of the lion, and out of the paw of the bear, he will deliver me out of the hand of this Philistine."* He had faith and confidence that God would deliver him. Secondly, he loved God's law. Psalm 119:47–48: *"And I will delight myself in thy commandments, which I have loved. My hands also will I lift up unto thy commandments, which I have loved; and I will meditate in thy statutes."* The third point is that David was thankful as we see in Psalm 26:7: *"That I may publish with the voice of thanksgiving and tell of all thy wondrous works."* With my final point, I circle back to where we began—with the fifty-first psalm. The psalm, in its entirety, is a pouring out of David's broken and contrite heart. *"A broken and contrite heart, O God, thou wilt not despise"* (vs. 17) is his prayer.

From David we see that with faith, thanksgiving, obedience and repentance, we too can be called men and women after God's own heart. For the heart that is truly repentant, there is the promise of God to no more remember our sins. Hebrews 8:12: *"For I will be merciful to their unrighteousness, and their sins and their iniquities will I remember no more."*

Take a few moments to read all of Psalm 51 and make verse 10 your prayer for today. *"Create in me a clean heart, O God; and renew a right spirit within me."*

A SOUL FULL OF JOY

Some days, when I come home from work, the call of the pond is stronger than others; today was one of those days. God had not pointed me in any particular direction for today's devotion, but He led me to the pond nonetheless. I scanned the bank for movement and saw none, studied the sky for unusual clouds, but there were only gray skies. I listened for birds calling, frogs croaking or peepers peeping, I heard nothing. I will admit I was a little disappointed. Then my eyes rested on the long cold fire pit and the chairs that circled it. That sight brought a smile to my lips and a wonderful memory of family time well spent. So, even though the things I'd gone in search of were not there today, when my eyes fell on the fire pit, I was moved to joy. Oh, how this reminded me that sometimes I look for the wrong things for inspiration, motivation and happiness. None of these things can the wildlife, the sky or nature sounds provide in and of themselves. We must look to Jesus for our joy.

David writes in Psalm 43:4, *"Then will I go unto the altar of God, unto God my exceeding joy: yea, upon the harp will I praise thee, O God my God."* David recognized where his joy came from.

Jesus wants us to have His joy. Let's look at John 15:11: *"These things have I spoken unto you, that my joy might remain in you, and that your joy might be full."* Man's idea of joy is to be as happy as he can be leaving God out of his life. The Lord taught that real joy comes by

THE POND

taking God into one's life as much as possible.[1] Even in our trials, we should be joyful because, if you are a child of the King, regardless of the situation you still have Him in your heart. Isaiah paints a beautiful picture in 35:10, *"And the ransomed of the Lord shall return, and come to Zion with songs and everlasting joy upon their heads: they shall obtain joy and gladness, and sorrow and sighing shall flee away."*

Can you, like Habakkuk, say, *"Yet I will rejoice in the Lord, I will joy in the God of my salvation"(3:18)?* I think a fine way to close this lesson today is with the quote by Sidlow Baxter describing this verse. *The literal is "I will jump for joy in the Lord; I will spin around for delight in God." Here is the hilarity of faith—joy at its best with circumstances at their worst! What a victory! May it be ours!*

May we as children of the King jump and spin in never-ending joy!

---

[1] Believer's Bible Commentary

A STRAIGHT PATH

This afternoon while sitting on the screen porch which overlooks our pond, two doves flew in and landed just a short distance from where I was seated. They poked around a few seconds and then began to make their way to the water's edge. Their path was not straight. It had a prominent zigzag pattern to it. I couldn't help but consider my own path...to the Living Water. It was a bit zigzaggy as well. Although not a straight path did they make, they arrived at their desired location as did I.

I'd like to go to Matthew 7:13–14, which says, *"Enter ye at the strait gate: for wide is the gate, and broad is the way that leadeth to destruction, and many there be which go in thereat: Because strait is the gate and narrow is the way which leadeth unto life, and few there be that find it."*

Matthew says the gate to life is straight, but notice he didn't say that the *way* to that gate would be straight! We all have a different story of how and when we were saved. Yes, I am sure there are those who did have a straight path to salvation. I would guess more would be like me in that sometimes I got off that path and if you could see the form that path took, it would be that familiar zigzag pattern. The important thing is that I found my way back on the path and like the doves, arrived at my destination, the place of eternal life!

May I encourage you today that if you find you have taken a step off the path, or you feel far from God, read John 15:16, and He will remind you that you are a chosen and ordained member of His family.

    Ponder these words from songwriter Charles Converse:

> Do you know that you were chosen
> Long before the world began
> That by God you were selected
> And appointed for His plan?
> Something in your inmost being
> Tells you this is surely true.

ADRIFT

Once I got home from work today, I changed my shoes and headed out to Silas's pen to check on him and his water supply since we've had almost two weeks of over ninety-five-degree heat. Silas is our German shepherd, and he is eighty-five pounds of pure love! He is most certainly attached to his "Dad," but when Dad's not home he's sort of my dog. Don't get me wrong, he loves me too; it's just that my husband has spent more one on one time with him over the past nine years, and they are very close.

Silas loves to wade out in the pond till his belly gets wet, but that's as far as he's going…at least for now. He also loves playing ball. We throw his tennis ball, and he chases it so hard, grabs it, and then takes off back toward us. Just when you think he's going to drop that ball at your feet, he zings right on by! Sometimes, like this afternoon, he dodges me altogether and runs down to the water's edge dropping his ball in the pond. Most often, the ball is close enough he doesn't mind retrieving it to play again. Today, however, was a different story; and that tennis ball right now as I sit writing this has floated almost out to the center of the pond. It looks lost and abandoned, floating aimlessly on the water.

Have you ever felt that you were like this tennis ball? Floating aimlessly, just bobbing about in life without plan or direction? Did you know that our heavenly Father has a plan for each of us? He tells us so in Jeremiah 29:11, *"For I know the thoughts that I think toward you, saith the lord, thoughts of peace, and not of evil, to give you an expected end."* In Psalm 139, we see that God knit us together in our mother's womb – He has known us since before we were conceived. But what joy remains to be when we read in John's gospel: *"I am the good shepherd, and know my [sheep], and am known of mine"* (John 10:14–15).

So during the times you feel afloat and lost, remember He who created the earth and everything in it, has a plan for your life. Search His Word and pray for His direction in your life. "He who has begun a good work will complete it until the day of Jesus Christ" (Phil. 1:6).

ANGELIC GUARDIANS

They stand silently around the margin of the pond, stretching up toward the sky as if trying to stay rooted in the earth and still have fingertips in the heavenly realms. Straight and tall, bare of leaves now, these dozen or so hardwood trees stand as mute sentinels guarding the edge of the property. Their white color is easily noticeable against the green backdrop created by the pines interspersed among them. As I study this scene I find myself thinking about God's angels standing in protection around His children as these trees encircle the pond.

The first verse that comes to mind is Psalm 91:11: *"For he shall give his angels charge over thee, to keep thee in all thy ways."* God has assigned angels to each of us, we are guarded by angels! I imagine them encircling me every minute of every day. Perhaps even as you read you can think of a time in which you wondered how you escaped injury or trouble. Could not one of those powerful protectors have put forth a hand on your behalf?

Looking also at Matthew 18:10, we find, *"Take heed that ye despise not one of these little ones; for I say unto you. That in heaven their angels do always behold the face of my Father which is in heaven."* Jesus is warning here to not despise His little ones, or even anyone who belonged to the kingdom. Their guardian angels were constantly before God. In my own words, this would be something like, "Don't mess with my children for their guardians report directly to me."

I find the fact that God loves me enough to place me into the care of His angels incomprehensible. I read it and believe it but it is mind boggling!

It is important to recognize that the mission of angels is service. Hebrews 1:14: *"Are they not all ministering spirits, sent forth to minister for them who shall be heirs of salvation?"* According to the Believer's Bible Commentary, these angels serve those who are saved from the penalty and power of sin but not yet saved from the presence of sin, that is, those believers who are still on earth.

There is a spiritual world around us that we cannot see and there are evil spirits waging unceasingly against God's elect as we see in Ephesians 6:12: *"For we wrestle not against flesh and blood, but against principalities, against powers, against the rulers of the darkness of this world, against spiritual wickedness in high places."* Knowing this, why should we be surprised that God has placed us within a hedge of protection?

Take a moment now to thank God for His protection that we experience as His children.

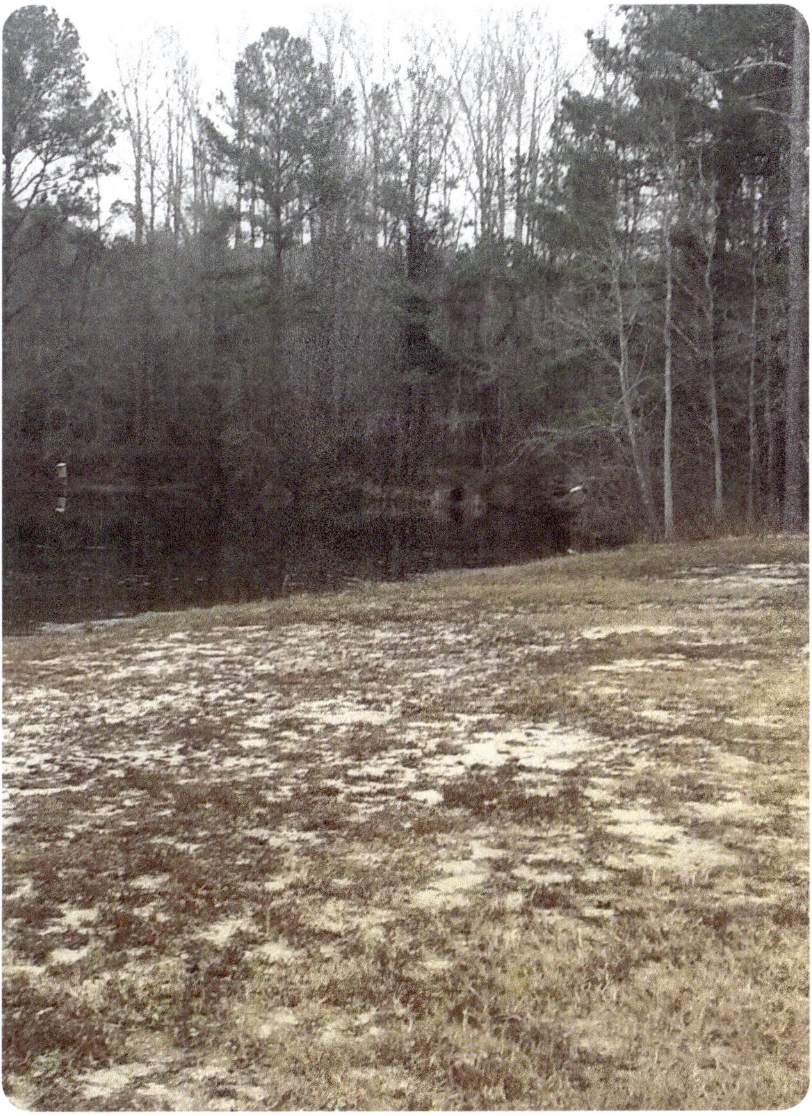

ARE YOU WASHED?

This evening finds me sitting inside in the cool air gazing out toward the pond expecting the Lord to show me something to write about. He does not fail me. I see a bluebird bathing in a small pool of water that has collected in a rut created by a hard rain washing a bit of the bank away. What I hear in that still, small voice is washing. The bird is washing himself, but He reminds me that I can't wash myself… physically yes, but spiritually, not at all. But, in His mercy, grace, and love for me (and you) He has provided a way for me to be cleansed, by the blood of His son Jesus!

Let's take a look at 1 Corinthians 6:11, which says, *"And such were some of you; but ye are washed, but ye are sanctified, but ye are justified in the name of the Lord Jesus, and by the Spirit of our God."* Now, just prior to this beginning in verse 9 Paul tells us what kind of people will not inherit the Kingdom of God. As verse 11 begins with *and such were some of you*, he is referring to the characteristics of those described in the prior verses. Notice that he uses, *but,* and the definition is *to introduce something contrasting to what has already been mentioned.* What a wonderful thought! We were like those already mentioned BUT! But we were washed! As Christians, we view the act of baptism a symbol of washing away sins, rising from the water a new creation. *"Therefore if any man be in Christ, he is a new creature; old things are passed away; behold, all things become new."* Second Corinthians 5:17 is where we find this scripture.

THE POND

Are you a new creature in Christ? Have you had your sins washed away? If you haven't taken the step to invite Christ into your heart, I encourage you to read the Gospel of John as he tells us who Christ is and of the love He has for us all.

Along with the washing, we are sanctified (set apart) and justified. Think of justified as "Just as if I never sinned!" What an awesome God we serve! As author Francis Chan puts it, "God loves us with a *crazy love*."

BASS LESSONS

The temperature is already in the mideighties on this July morning and the dragon flies are buzzing and spinning low over the pond. So low in fact that it's very possible many of them will end up as bait for the largemouth bass that live in the pond. Often, the bass can been seen as they breach the water's surface to snag this tempting treat. What, you might wonder, makes this a problem? You see, the bass, whose eye is on the prize—the dragonfly—is mighty susceptible to the shiny lures used by the bass fisherman as well. Old largemouth doesn't distinguish the difference until he's snagged!

How often do we get snagged? Is it easy to tell the difference in those things that are right, and the ones that "seem" right? There are several scriptures we can look at on this: Proverbs 14:12 says, "*There is a way which seemeth right unto a man, but the end thereof are the ways of death.*" Proverbs 16:2 says, "*All the ways of man are clean in his own eyes; but the Lord weigheth the spirits.*" Also take a look at Proverbs 12:15 and 30:12 for additional study.

How do we keep from getting snagged by temptation or that thing that seems right? We must stay in the Word, walking with Christ daily and allowing Him control of our lives. The Psalmist says in chapter 8 verse 14 after speaking in previous verses about wisdom," *Counsel is mine, and sound wisdom: I* am *understanding; I have strength.*" From this, I see God saying to us, seek Him and we will find good counsel, wisdom, and strength. He also tells us that He is understanding. In a few words, He is our all in all!

THE POND

A fine closing to this is found in Proverbs 2:5–6 and says simply, *"Trust in the Lord with all thine heart; and lean not unto thine own understanding. In all thy ways acknowledge Him and He shall direct thy paths."*

Won't you trust Him today and allow Him to direct your ways?

BE RECONCILED

This particular spring afternoon, my husband and I set off in the pedal boat on the pond. We planned to spray the aquatic weeds and lily pads to deter any further growth. As we carried the little boat to the pond's edge, our cat, Goldie, trailed along behind us. Just like most cats, she was extremely curious about what was going on and just had to get close enough to check us out.

Once afloat, we proceeded to the first area to be sprayed and Goldie kept up with us along the bank. After a few minutes we heard the most mournful wailing. This sad and pitiful cry was coming from my cat. I suppose she thought we would be drifting further and further away, possibly never coming back to her. This was a strange and new behavior to us and we'd not had much experience with cats to make any comparisons.

For the entire time we were on the water, proceeding on our zigzagging course, she followed along the pond's bank continuing that sad sounding cry. When we came back to the shore, she actually came aboard without any coaxing! What was that I'd always heard about cats and water? Not so this day! She was so glad we came back to her she practically jumped in the boat.

Now, how might this relate as a devotion? Thinking back on the day, I was reminded how much God loves us and that often we as Christians drift away, just as Brooks and I did in the boat that day. I imagine that God circles about us, much like Goldie did, watching, waiting, and possibly in His spirit, wailing at our distance from Him.

There is joy for those that are in Christ Jesus if you find yourself having drifted far from God. We see this in 2 Corinthians 5:18: *"And all things are of God, who hath reconciled us to himself by Jesus Christ, and hath given to us the ministry of reconciliation."* God's Word also tells us that once sin is confessed, it is forgiven and forgotten. There are several places to find this promise. You can read it in 1 John 1:19, Hebrews 10:17, and Micah 7:19.

If you find that you have drifted, if you realize that you are far from God today take a few minutes to ponder this verse from Romans 5:11, *"And not only so, but we also joy in God through our Lord Jesus Christ, by whom we have now received the atonement."* The verse says that *now* we are reconciled, not in a few minutes, next week, or next year.

He is waiting and ready to hear your prayer. Reconcile yourself to God today and receive His grace *now*, new and fresh.

BE STILL

Today there is a gray crane standing in the pond shallows. His light-colored feathers are in stark contract against the dark green of the trees and bushes that line the pond's bank that he was easy to spot. What is so amazing about this bird is how perfectly still he is standing. He looks like a statue you might see in a garden, but ever so slowly he shifts himself by turning about one-quarter turn and once again is stark still.

The first thing that came into my head was a verse from Psalm 46:10 says, *"Be still and know that I am God."* Although a simple statement, it's so full of power. By just being quiet and still and opening our minds and hearts, we can be assured by God that He truly is the Great I Am. When we surrender to Him in the stillness of the day, we experience His peace, which passes all understanding, even in the midst of turmoil.

The following is an excerpt from an article in *Christian Courier* by Jason Jackson, and I think it clearly explains my thoughts in this devotion:

> So as your world crumbles around you, the call from Scripture is: don't flinch in faith in God. Stand still—not because of a self-made confidence, not because you are the most composed person in the face of disaster, not because *"you've seen it all."*

THE POND

Be still because of what you *know* about God.

It is "God's past" that provides calm for "our future." Know that he is God! Know it, not merely intellectually, but practically, spiritually, and emotionally. He is your God. He is the ruler of kingdoms of this earth and the all-powerful Creator of the Universe.

Has life's busyness overshadowed your stillness? Oh, step back and let God wrap His loving arms around you as you are still. Relish in the power and peace of your Heavenly Father in the serenity of His presence.

BE THANKFUL

I am sure you are familiar with the cliché "water off a duck's back." Well, today I am watching that in action. Once again we are experiencing wintery weather this time in the form of freezing rain. This has not hampered the pair of wood ducks that I have been watching out on the pond. They have been very near my observation spot—my chair parked in front of the glass patio doors. Most of the morning I have watched as they forged in the shallowest water seemingly unmindful of the rain coming down on them.

This made me think how often had I been oblivious to the blessings that God showers down on me? Was I like these ducks going through my daily life by rote, the same routines day in and day out and only giving a God a halfhearted (if that) nod in thanks? Have we come to just expect those blessings? Do we feel entitled because at one time we knelt and asked Jesus into our hearts? There are too many times that I miss acknowledging God's hand in my life.

Let's look back to the psalms for a reminder. Psalm 106:1: *"Praise ye the Lord. O give thanks unto the Lord; for he is good: for his mercy endureth forever."* God is good, and He has our best interests at heart. James 1:17 is our proof: *"Every good gift and every perfect gift is from above, and cometh down from the Father of lights with whom there is no variableness, neither shadow of turning."* Thank Him for His goodness.

Be thankful in whatever you do as seen in Colossians 3:17: *"And whatsoever ye do in word or deed, do all in the name of the Lord Jesus,*

THE POND

giving thanks to God and the Father by him." Here, Paul reminds us to give thanks, our perpetual duty when saved by grace and destined for streets of heaven.

And finally today, looking at Psalm 30:11–12, we see David's prayer of praise to God. *"Thou hast turned for me my mourning into dancing: thou hast put off my sackcloth, and girded me with gladness; To the end that my glory may sing praise to thee, and not be silent. O Lord my God, I will give thanks unto thee for ever."* Do you, like me, feel a bit shameful after reading this? I think about how often I carried a burden to the throne of Grace, sometimes I was sure I was kneeling in a rut carved out by my own knees. After God wonderfully, gracefully, and faithfully answered my prayer did I remember to go back to Him in thanks?

Has your mourning been turned into dancing and your sackcloth into gladness? Then pause a few moments and thank God for what He has done in your life.

After your meditation, I would encourage you to follow with speaking 1 Chronicles 29:13 out loud to God inserting yourself to make this a personal prayer. *"Now therefore, our [my] God, we [I] thank thee, and praise thy glorious name"* (additions mine).

CHARGING TO CHANGE

Have you ever witnessed to someone that once all was said, you felt that maybe, just maybe you were a little too aggressive? I know there are times that I'd like to "cut a hole in their head and pour it in," as my mother used to say. We want to get our point across and sometimes I wonder if the person on the receiving end feels that they were attacked by the Gospel.

This afternoon as I was coming down the driveway, or should I say as I was barreling down the driveway, I spied a large blue heron just in the edge of the water in the pond, standing so still it would make you wonder if he was real. I very quickly slowed down in hopes that I wouldn't startle him and set him to flight. I really wanted to get a picture of him standing there in the late-afternoon sun. The sun coming from the opposite side of the pond through the trees made several slanting rays of sunlight to glint off the water, twinkling like little diamonds there around him. But it wasn't to be. I came charging in too fast and loud and he was off in a flash. What a magnificent sight, that large, elegant heron swooping around the pond then off out of sight over the tall pines. Maybe another time, but…maybe not. As he flew off, my thought was how if we share the Gospel like I came into the driveway, then our audience is going to take flight just like my heron.

We must share our good news, the hope we as believers possess, in love and gentleness. In 1 Peter 3:15, we find these words: *"But sanctify the Lord God in your hearts: and be ready always to give an answer to every man that asketh of you a reason of the hope that is in you with meekness and fear."* Here, I am reminded of an old saying I'm sure you have heard: "You catch more flies with honey than with vinegar." People respond to love and kindness.

Lastly, in 2 Timothy 2:25, we find, *"Opponents must be gently instructed, in the hope that God will grant them repentance leading them to a knowledge of the truth."* I like this from the New International Version of the Bible because its meaning is so clear.

In both Romans chapter 12 and 1 Corinthians chapter 12, we find listed the gifts and fruits of the Spirit, and guess what! Nowhere do I find the gift of aggressiveness. We are called to spread the Gospel, but we must be careful to spread it in love, for like the heron, there may be another opportunity, but maybe not.

COMMITTED

This is the fifth Sunday of the month, and that means we have no evening service at church tonight. My husband and I have decided to relax around the pond. He's going to do a little fishing, and I'll be keeping an eye on our German shepherd, Silas. He has been known to slip away when nobody is looking, thus the need for a dog sitter.

Since we moved in about eight months ago, he's been slowly getting used to the water. In the beginning he would only get a drink of water and now he will venture out far enough to just get his belly wet. This particular evening I noticed he was inching out just a little farther, and farther still, until he got a bit deeper than he liked. He immediately started backing up, getting back to a spot where he felt safe. My thought was, "Just commit, Silas, and go for it." Oh, but don't we do the same thing? How often have I, have you, felt the Lord calling, only to respond, "Oh Lord, you know I can't do that!" Or like Silas, we stepped off a little too deep for comfort and began that backward motion to a more comfortable zone?

Paul reminds us in Philippians 4:13," *I can do* all *things through Christ which strengtheneth me."* May I point out that the little word *all* leaves out nothing! There is nothing which Christ can't strengthen us to do. I never expected to be able to write these stories or devotions, yet through Christ and Christ alone I am doing just that.

Don't think yourself weak, consider these words from 2 Corinthians 12:9, *"And he said unto me, My grace is sufficient for thee: for my strength is made perfect in weakness. Most gladly therefore will*

THE POND

I rather glory in my infirmities, that the power of Christ may rest upon me." Through our weaknesses, others can see the power of Christ in us, and for that, we are to give Him the glory.

So, I say to you today, "Commit, and just go for it." God will not send you without equipping you!

COTTON CANDY CLOUDS

Fall afternoons seem to have a golden shimmer that does not occur in any of the other seasons. Today, this was evident as I drove toward the pond when coming home from work. In addition to the late-afternoon gleam, the sky above was full of pink, fluffy, cotton candy clouds. I felt for a moment as if I was in a snow globe without the snow, but instead flakes of gold glitter floating about me. A picture perfect scene!

In a matter of a few minutes, this beauty had faded into twilight and then…darkness. This brought to my mind how God's Word warns us that our works will be tried. Let's look at 1 Corinthians 3:12–14: *"Now if any man build upon this foundation gold, silver, precious stones, wood, hay, stubble; Every man's work shall be made manifest: for the day shall declare it, because it shall be revealed by fire; and the fire shall try every man's work of what sort it is. If any man's work abide which he hath built thereupon, he shall receive a reward."* Paul goes on to tell us that just as those whose works are purified by the fire gain a reward, those people whose works are burned up will suffer loss. The person will be saved but without gaining the reward.

Second Corinthians 5:10: *"For we must appear before the judgment seat of Christ; that every one may receive the things done in his body, according to that he hath done, whether it be good or bad."* We as Christians, will have to account for what we did for the kingdom, even the missed opportunities. It is important to remember here, that it is not by our works that we gain salvation, but works are a result of our salvation.

There is a poem, "The Dash," by Linda Ellis, in which she talks about life between the dash. On either side of the dash is the date of birth and the date of death. I think about that when I consider my appearance at the judgment seat of Christ, only my dash is the time between my accepting Jesus as my Savior and by grace being saved and the date that I vacate my body and take up residence in heaven.

Take a moment and give this excerpt from the poem a chance to speak to you:

> For it matters not, how much we own,
> The cars…the house…the cash.
> What matters is how we live and love
> And how we spend our dash.

Will you fill your dash for the Lord?

CROWS EQUAL CARE

I can't recall a day that I did not see several crows in the yard and around the pond. Usually, I don't give them much thought. They seem to be more of a nuisance than anything else, hovering about pecking at anything and nothing on the ground. And the call of a crow, how annoying! More often than not, the lowly crow has a negative connotation. The Lord put in my mind to do a little query; crow references in the Bible! What I found was surprising....crows equal care.

The Bible speaks of the raven often, it is in the family Corvidae, and is probably where crows generated. For the sake of this devotion, I will take the stand that this thought is correct. In doing so, I would like to suggest as we look at the scripture references, that the crows are used by God in taking care of us, His children.

God used ravens to minister to Elijah as we see in 1 Kings 17:6: *"And the ravens brought him bread and flesh in the morning, and bread and flesh in the evening; and he drank of the brook."* God commanded the ravens to feed Elijah after his prediction of drought to Ahab.

In the New Testament, Jesus teaches using the parable of the rich fool in which is found reference to how God takes care of us. Look at Luke 12:24: *"Consider the ravens: for they neither sow or reap; which neither have storehouse or barn; and God feedeth them: how much more are ye better than the fowls?"*

These words were penned by Civilla D. Martin in 1905 for the hymn "His Eye is on the Sparrow" and is certainly biblical truth:

"Let not your heart be troubled," His tender word I hear, And resting on His goodness, I lose my doubts and fears; Though by the path He leadeth, but one step I may see; His eye is on the sparrow, and I know He watches me; His eye is on the sparrow, and I know He watches me.

If you have any doubt that God cares for you, watches over you and loves you; look at Luke 12:6–7, *"Are not five sparrows sold for two farthings, and not one of them is forgotten before God? But even the very hairs of your head are all numbered. Fear not therefore: ye are of more value than many sparrows."*

May I suggest that the next time you see crows take a minute and thank God for His care of you?

CRY OUT IN FAITH

Recently a high school friend asked if I would read and study Psalm 61:1, which is, *"Hear my cry O God; attend unto my prayer,"* in hopes that the Lord might give me a devotion relative to this verse. This is her go to verse, so I got my Bible and went out onto the back porch. It was already dark, and from the porch with the light on I couldn't even see the pond. Let me tell you, that out here in the country, away from street lights and the light from nearby homes, it is very dark!

I sat down and began to read the whole Psalm to myself, but in a moment I had an urge to reread it aloud. I was alone except for my son and daughter-in-law's dog, Ellie. Ellie accompanied me on the porch and paced back and forth a few minutes, but when I began reading aloud, she stopped and lay down quietly. As I read the words of the psalmist David, I thought how praying is much like this night looking on the pond and not being able to see it.

As I was contemplating the scripture, I thought that when I pray, even though I can't physically see God the Father, He is there. Tonight I can't see the pond, but it is there. I have enough evidence of its existence in the sounds around me. I hear the water running into the spill pipe; I hear the noises of the night everywhere. In the same manner, I have evidence God has provided of Himself, so that when I am in prayer I know He is there with me.

From Romans 1:20, we are told, *"Ever since the creation of the world, God's invisible qualities—God's eternal power and divine nature—have been clearly seen, because they are understood through the things God has made. So humans are without excuse."* I chose this verse from the Common English Bible for its clarity. As we look at the world, there is no excuse to not believe in the God of Creation.

What is so amazing and humbling to me is that this God, the One who made it all, attends unto my prayers. Again, turning to the Psalms, David really hits the nail on the head in Psalm 8:3–4, *"When I consider thy heavens, the work of thy fingers, the moon and the stars, which thou hast ordained: what is man, that thou art mindful of him? And the son of man that thou visitest him?"*

It is by faith that we know and believe that God is there beyond where eye can see. When our voice penetrates the throne room of heaven, God is delighted, and our faith assures us of an audience with Jehovah God.

In closing, be assured that if you are calling on Him in faith, He will surely hear your cry and attend unto your prayer.

DUCKS ON THE POND

The November morning began unseasonably warm, so I grabbed my cup of coffee and onto the porch I went. I know before long the mornings will be much too cold to actually sit outside. In the coming days I will have to set up my vantage point from the kitchen table looking out through the sliding glass doors.

My husband and my son were out hunting together, so I took advantage of a few quiet minutes. As I sat, I realized there was some movement off to my left, fairly close to the bank. I had to get a closer look, so I dug out the binoculars to help me out.

Two pair of wood ducks floated out on the pond, swimming silently on the surface of the water. Like ice skaters they glided effortlessly around. The males are the colorful ones, with green on their head that almost glitters in the sun. They pair up in winter and then arrive at the breeding ground in spring. What is amazing about the wood duck pair is that they house hunt together. When a prospective nesting site is found, the male stands guard outside while the female investigates the inside. This struck me as a bit humorous…it sounds like my husband and me; he takes care of the outside and I do the inside. At least for the most part, that is!

As I sat watching these two pair, knowing their habit mentioned above, I couldn't help but think of the scripture from 1 Corinthians 13 in which Paul talks about love. Particularly in verse 4, where we see, *"Love suffereth long, and is kind; love envieth not; love vaunteth not itself, is not puffed up."* While ducks don't experience love as we do,

I could not help but imagine that male patiently waiting as his mate checks out a possible new nest in which to lay her eggs.

This chapter of 1 Corinthians ends as verse 13 tells us, *"And now abideth faith, hope, love, these three; but the greatest of these is love."* How very true when we consider the greatest love has come from God our Father as He sent His only Son to the cross for you and me. God's love for us is so great, that there is nothing that can separate those that are in Christ Jesus from him. Romans 8:38–39 assures us by saying, *"For I am persuaded, that neither death, nor life, nor angels, nor principalities, nor powers, nor things present, nor things to come, nor height, nor depth, nor any other creature, shall be able to separate us from the love of God which is in Christ Jesus our Lord."*

Amen and amen!

I pray your assurance today is in the unchanging person of Jesus Christ.

FAITH IN THE FOG

As I watch the pond this evening, right before my eyes is it enveloped by a thick, heavy fog. Little by little my vision has been obscured and will continue to diminish until I can no longer see the pond or what lies beyond it. But I am very familiar with the pond and I know the area around it. I could describe it in detail if needed. In my mind I see the three blueberry bushes in the bend just before the dam begins; walking along the dam I hear the water as it comes out of the spillway into the creek bed below me. On the right the ground is soft, sometimes spongy nearest the water's edge. These are things I know because I know that pond. Just because I can't see it any longer doesn't mean it is not there.

That is the way it is with faith. Do you ever get wrapped in the fog of life? Sometimes it is so thick your eyes are blinded to the fact that Jesus is standing in that situation with you, going at it toe to toe. Faith is knowing, really knowing that He is there. Always, anywhere He is there. When Jesus gave the disciples the Great Commission he ended with *"And lo, I am with you always, even unto the end of the world."*

Joshua 1:9 assures us of this truth, *"Be strong and of good courage; be not afraid, neither be thou dismayed: for the LORD thy God is with thee whithersoever thou goest."* I would ask then, is there anywhere that He does not accompany us? I don't know about you, but I have been in places I shudder to think that He was there with me. That thought certainly woke me up!

We accept Jesus on faith. Since we have not been privileged to see Him in the flesh, we must believe by faith. Romans 10:17 tell us how: *"So then faith cometh by hearing, and hearing by the word of God."* We must hear the Word, then by faith believe what we've heard.

A perfect explanation of faith comes from Hebrews 11:1, *"Now faith is the substance of things hoped for, the evidence of things not seen."* This chapter of Hebrews goes on to list many heroes of faith. I would encourage you to take time to read it through.

So, just like tonight, when I can't see the pond, I know for certain it is there. Those times that we can't see Jesus through our personal fog, we have the truth of His word that He is always with us. We have heard the Word and we have the evidence of the Cross.

You may not be able see Jesus in your situation, but rest assured, He sees you!

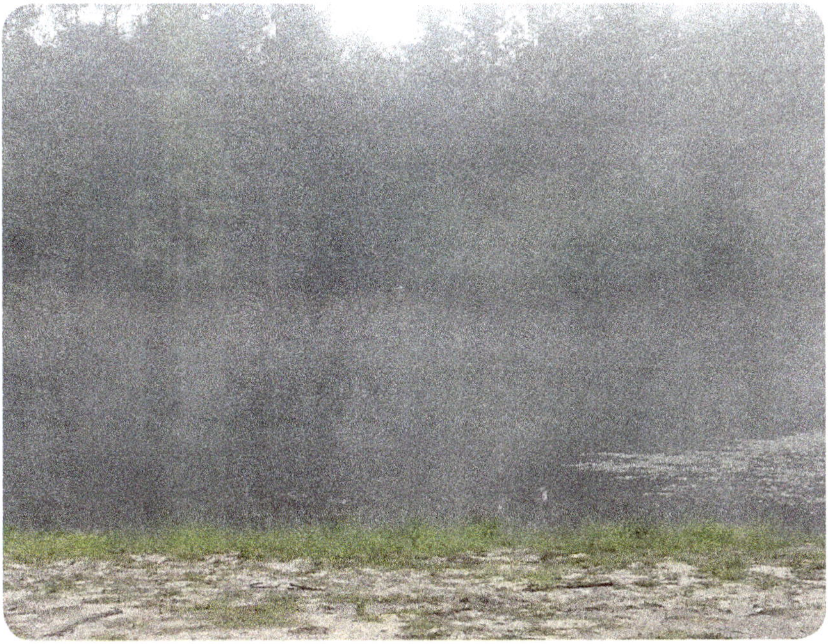

FAITH

I stopped by the new house this afternoon, as I often do just to check on things as work progresses and to sit and stare out at the pond…it's still a new thought to me, the fact that we have a pond.

Lately, I've had some things on my heart and it seemed a good time to sit in the quiet and talk to the Lord…as I'm sitting on the picnic table in the sun looking out at the peaceful still water, the wind begins to blow slightly. In my mind I hear, "This wind is like faith, you can hear it, feel it, and see the results of it." You don't actually see the wind and like it, faith can be heard, felt, and will produce results, but you can't see a piece of faith or touch it. Nevertheless, it's there…waiting to be used.

My faith says God will uphold His promises, and I'm looking for those results that shall be seen! From Hebrews 11:1, *"Now faith is the substance of things hoped for, the evidence of things not seen."*

Hebrews chapter 11 goes on to give numerous examples of faith and I would strongly encourage you to read on and discover, "by faith."

FALL COLORS

This evening as I sit looking out over the pond, I feel the coming of fall even though it's only late August. There is a particular way the sun looks during fall afternoons and I see that today. The sun of fall is a softer, more golden color, and as it shines through the leaves of the trees I notice there is already a bit of color change occurring. It's very subtle, but it is there nevertheless. There is something about every season that I love, but I do believe fall is my favorite.

These signs I'm seeing, feeling, and sometimes smelling, tell me that God is in control. Each season arrives in its designated time. Oh, we may have a few unseasonal days during each season, but in reality, God is controlling the days.

There is a lot of talk about unusual weather patterns, global warming, and the sort, but I fall back to God's Word and in it I find assurance that He who created the earth, the universe, and all components of each, holds time in His hands. Just look at Genesis 8:22, *"While the earth remaineth, seedtime and harvest, and cold and heat, and summer and winter, and day and night shall not cease."* What glorious assurance!

Psalm 104:19 says, *"He appointed the moon for seasons: the sun knoweth his going down."* The sun, moon, stars, and yes even the seasons, know their appointed times. These things we should not worry about. In fact, we read in Acts 1:7, *"It is not for you to know the times or the seasons, which the Father hath put in his own power."* We need not be concerned, for He arranged it all and controls it all! What an awesome God I serve!

The God that has set all this into place and controls and directs it all, also wants us not to worry for ourselves. As the Psalmist wrote, "What is man that thou art mindful of him?" This great God loves me, He loves each of us and desires that we love Him and wants a relationship with us. Only through salvation in Jesus can this accomplished, but if you will ask Jesus into your heart, then you have full access to this same God!

I think that a fitting last statement for this devotion is from Psalm 8:9, *"O Lord, our Lord, how excellent is thy name in all the earth!"* Whisper this as a simple prayer of praise today.

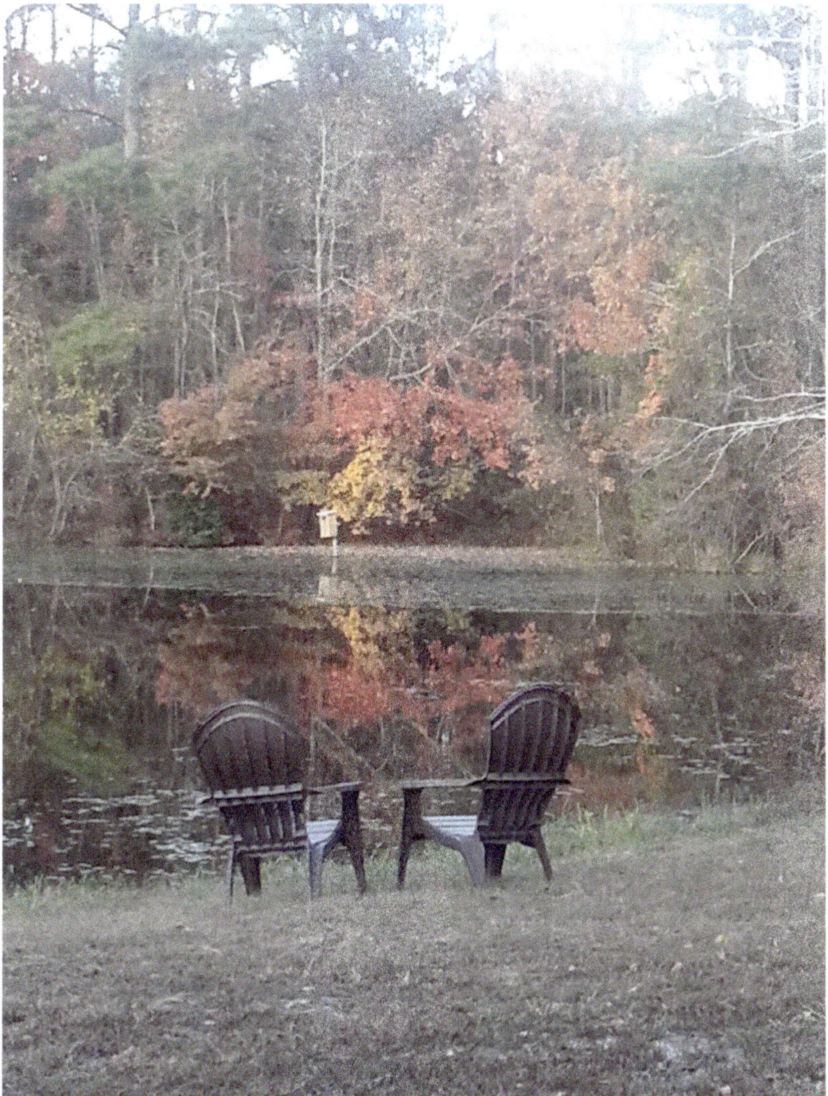

FAMILY BLESSINGS

Sitting out by the pond circled around the burning fire pit was my family, complete with our dogs. This gathering was in celebration of my upcoming birthday and my choice of where to dine, had been here at home. My desire was to spend a peaceful, unhurried evening with my children, their spouses and my husband. I couldn't think of a better place to be than sitting around the pond. As night drew close we lit a small fire in the fire pit and huddled close, sharing stories and laughter. Occasionally the sound of water gurgling into the spill pipe could be heard between giggles. From deep in the woods came the sound of an owl, a haunting melody to our ears. This was the perfect way to celebrate my birthday. My heart overflowed with thankfulness, and I knew this was a blessing from God. I find the truth of this is Deuteronomy 7:13, *"And he will love thee, and bless thee, and multiply thee: he will also bless the fruit of thy womb, and the fruit of thy land, thy corn, and thy wine, and thine oil, the increase of thy kine, and the flocks of thy sheep, in the land which he sware unto thy fathers to give thee."*

    God established the family first; therefore the family is of utmost importance. The father is to be the head of the house and spiritual leader. We see this from 1 Corinthians 11:3, *"But I would have you know, that the head of every man is Christ; and the head of the woman is the man; and the head of Christ is God."*

    I have been blessed with a husband who is a Christian, strong in his faith and has been a wonderful example to our children. Psalm

127:3 tells us, *"Behold, children are a heritage from the Lord, the fruit of the womb is a reward."* What a reward I have been given! Our children have been blessings from God. We also have a daughter-in-law and a son-in-law that I know God has placed in our family.

Both the parents and children have responsibilities in the family as we see in Ephesians 6:1–4, *"Children, obey your parents in the Lord, for this is right. "Honor your father and mother" (this is the first commandment with a promise), "that it may go well with you and that you may live long in the land. Fathers, do not provoke your children to anger, but bring them up in the discipline and instruction of the Lord."*

Psalm 127:1–5 tells us that first and foremost, the Lord must build the house. Allow God to build your house, making Christ the head of the family and blessings will follow. Would you make this statement from Joshua 24:15 your commitment? *"As for me and my house, we will serve the Lord."*

Serve and be blessed.

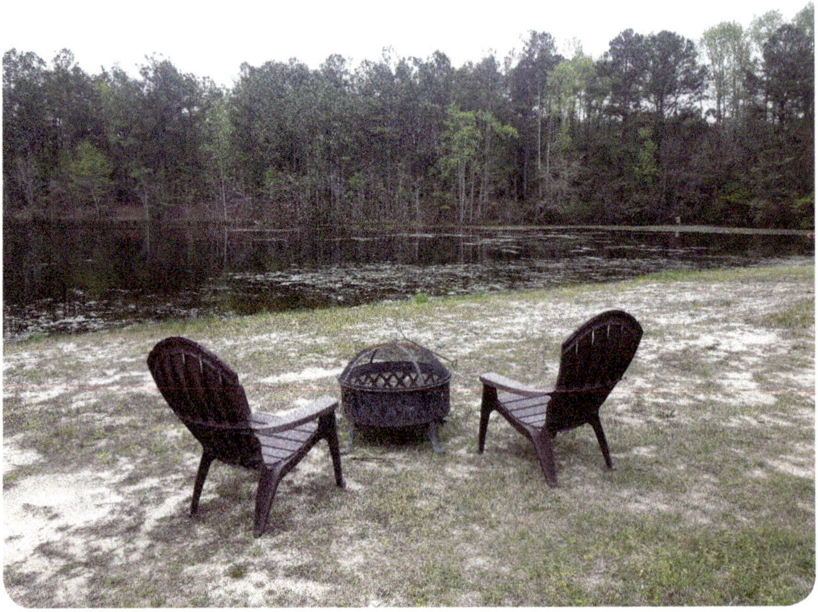

FEAR NO MORE

Last night when my husband went out to feed our dog, Silas, he thought he saw a critter across the pond! He came back to the door certain he had been watching a beaver near the bank. We looked like the Keystone Cops scrambling around finding the binoculars and flashlight! We ran outside and as I held the light aimed in what we thought was the right direction, he scoured the bank back and forth; he swept the field glasses in an attempt to catch this beaver in the act. When he could stand it no longer, he walked all the way around the pond to satisfy his curiosity. Yes, around the pond in the cold and dark night.

Before our conversion, when we invited Jesus into our hearts, we too walked around in the cold darkness of the unsaved. Is there fear when walking alone in the darkness? Certainly there is but with Christ all fear is gone! King David recognized this and wrote it in Psalm 27:1, *"The Lord is my light and my salvation; whom shall I fear? The Lord is the strength of my life; of whom shall I be afraid?"* And again in Psalm 56:3–4, *"What time I am afraid, I will trust in thee. In God I will praise his word, in God I have put my trust; I will not fear what flesh can do unto me."*

These verses speak to fear of something tangible, a physical fear. There is also the fear of the unknown to be overcome. How do we overcome? As a believer in Christ, we can confidently recite with Paul in his letter to the Romans these words from Romans 8:38–39, *"For I am persuaded that neither death, nor life, nor angels, nor principalities, nor powers, nor things present, nor things to come, Nor height, nor depth, nor any creature, shall be able to separate us from the love of God which is in Christ Jesus."* Once we have placed our lives in the nail-scarred hands of Jesus, there is nothing that can pluck us out. This truth you can read in John 10:29.

Friend, if you are walking in the dark today, take a look at this Jesus who brings light, casts out fear, and is always with His children. If you would but reach out to Him, you will find His hand already there, waiting for yours to grasp it.

No more darkness, no more fear, and you will find He is always near.

FISHING LINE OR LIFELINE

As I watched my husband fishing from the bank of the pond one afternoon, I considered all his equipment he had out with him. Particularly, for some reason, the fishing line; I felt as though that was what God had directed my focus toward. You see, line comes in different strengths, and depending on what you are fishing for, determines what size to use. That line has to be strong enough to allow the fisherman to reel his catch in without losing it. If your line breaks, that fish that you hooked is gone. That chance has been lost.

In both Matthew's and Mark's gospels, we find these words: *"And he saith unto them, Follow me, and I will make you fishers of men"* From Matthew 4:19, and from Mark 1:17, *"And Jesus said unto them, Come ye after me, and I will make you to become fishers of men."* Today, Jesus still calls us to be fishers of men. My prayer is that my line, which represents my relationship with Christ, be strong enough. Strong enough to make someone want to hang on and be "reeled in" to fellowship with Jesus.

We, as Christ's followers, are in the world daily and others should see Him in us; in me. How many "fish" do we encounter in a day's time, and how often do we cast our line? That line may be just what someone is holding on for—a lifeline.

The refrain from the hymn by Ernest S. Ufford says it best:

LUCY ALLEN

Throw out the lifeline! Throw out the lifeline!
Someone is drifting away;
Throw out the lifeline! Throw out the lifeline!
Someone is sinking today.

FROM DARKNESS TO LIGHT

There is a dark area at the far end of the pond. From where I sit, approximately a hundred yards across, the pond narrows a bit, and just beyond the wood duck box there is a small clearing before the woods merge in. I always find myself watching that area, expecting some type of wildlife to show itself. It's not dark as in opposition to the light, just dark as in little sunlight gets through the thick canopy of pine and hardwood trees.

Until we accept Jesus Christ, we have a dark area in our hearts. Ecclesiastes 3:11 says, *"He has made everything beautiful in its time. Also, he has put eternity into man's heart, yet so that he cannot find out what God has done from the beginning to the end. "Eternity* for the believer is life everlasting in the light of Christ. In John 14:6, Jesus tells us that He is the way, the truth and the life and the only way to the Father.

We learn in Jeremiah 17:9 that the heart is deceitful and desperately wicked. The only way one's heart is changed is by accepting Jesus as Savior. Then His light fills that dark and wicked heart the same way a candle, when lit, dispels darkness.

In closing, I'd like to leave you with the following quote by Blaise Pascal: *"There is a God-shaped vacuum in the heart of every man which cannot be filled by any created thing, but only by God, the Creator, made known through Jesus."*

Is your heart full of God today?

GOD IN NATURE

We have had extremely cold temperatures the last few days, below freezing on a couple of occasions. This morning as I looked out to the pond, I noticed that the water all along the edge had a skim of ice on top. The icy patterns reminded me of feathers. The ice had the appearance of being brushed out from the edge toward the pond's center looking almost as if someone had lain on the ground and blown each patch of ice away from the bank. Long icy fingers reaching out to meet the same icy fingers stretching out from the opposite side of the pond.

God controls every aspect of nature as we see in Job 37:10, *"By the breath of God ice is given, and the broad waters are frozen fast"* (ESV). I like this version because it is so plainly stated. We give little thought to such a trivial weather situation, but this just shows us that God, Creator of heaven and earth, is in control of even the smallest results of weather. If we read on to verse fourteen, we will see that Job is challenged to increase his knowledge of nature. Job 37:14: *"Hear this, O Job; stop and consider the wondrous works of God"* (ESV). Such excellent power surpasses our feeble comprehension.[2]

We too should stop and consider the wondrous works of God. As you read through this book, my prayer is that you will see, hear, and feel this nature He has placed all about us at the pond. Never forget who is in control. As our reminder take a look at Isaiah 45:6–7,

---

[2] Believer's Bible Commentary

THE POND

"That they may know from the rising of the sun, and from the west, that there is none beside me. I am the Lord, and there is none else. I form the light, and create darkness: I make peace, and create evil. I the Lord do all these things."

I would like to close with 1 Chronicles 29:11, as David offers a prayer of thanksgiving and worship. *"Thine, O Lord, is the greatness, and the power and the glory, and the victory, and the majesty: for all that is in the heaven and in the earth is thine; thine is the kingdom, O Lord, and thou art exalted as head above all."*

Whether a little ice or several inches of snow, a summer rain shower or days of rain, thunder storm, or tornado, God is in control.

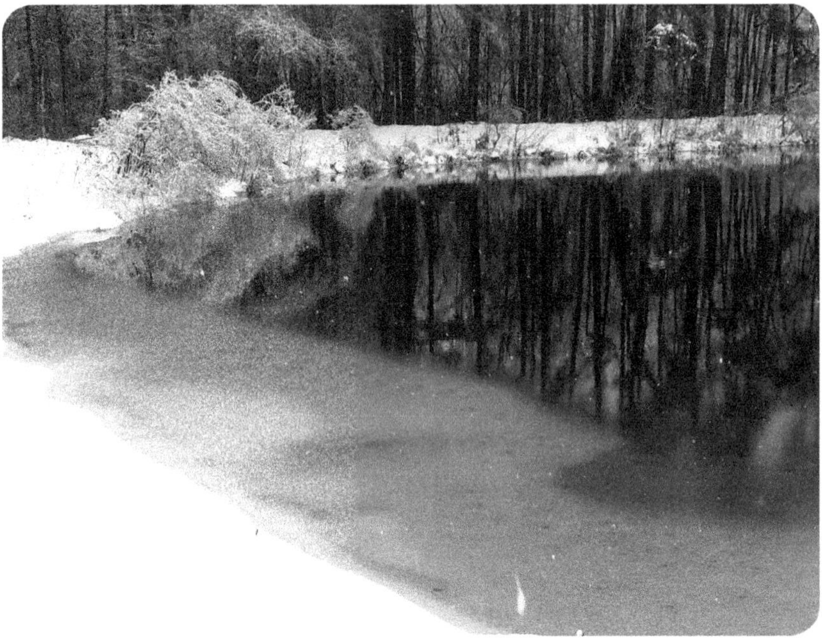

GOD'S GRACE

As we approach the midst of the fall season, the pond is showing color in the trees that form the wood line that just may best Joseph's coat of many colors! Daily I am amazed at the beauty that I am blessed to cast my eyes upon each morning. It's as if God reached down, paintbrush in hand, and created a masterpiece just for me.

In the Bible there are descriptions of the new heaven and new earth and the beauty that will be seen in them. I must say, as I look on the beauty of the pond, I wonder how anything could be lovelier. In a similar way, when we accept Jesus as our Savior and invite Him into our heart, God takes that same paintbrush and "paints" on us a white robe of righteousness. He then sees us through Christ's blood and although we have done nothing to warrant it, God the Father looks on us and sees us, perfect in His Son.

We can see this in Titus 3:5: *"Not by works of righteousness which we have done, but according to His mercy He saved us, by the washing of regeneration, and renewing of the Holy Ghost."* As this verse is contemplated, you may wonder about being saved, or how to be saved. Take a look at Ephesians 2:8–9: *"For by grace are ye saved through faith; and that not of yourselves: it is the gift of God: Not of works lest any man should boast."* In both verse selections we see that we can't do anything to obtain salvation aside from having faith in Jesus and acknowledging Him as the Son of God.

Do you know this grace today? God's grace brings salvation. Salvation from our Heavenly Father who can change hearts, forgive sins, and loves you when you can't imagine anyone would love you! May you know and experience this grace as you meditate on the chorus below:

> Grace, grace, God's grace
> Grace that will pardon and cleanse within;
> Grace, grace, God's grace,
> Grace that is greater than all our sin!

GOD'S VALENTINE

Valentine's Day, a day of love and showing love. There is no love greater than God's love for us. No Valentine can compete with His love. God's love for us sent His Son to the cross for me and for you. An example of this love is found in Romans 5:8, *"But God commendeth his love toward us, in that, while we were yet sinners, Christ died for us."* Did you catch that…*while we were yet sinners*! Jesus didn't say, "After you clean yourselves up, I'll go to the cross." No, in our sin, He accepted the Father's will and hung on that cross for all of mankind.

What, you might ask, does this thought have to do with "the pond"? I see love there, God's love is reflected in the pond in that He provided this place and the inspiration for this book. He loves you enough to use me and this pond as vessels to get His message to each one who reads "The Pond." I look around the pond and see the beauty in all seasons. Blooming blueberry bushes in the spring and summer, the fall brings brilliant colored leaves to the hardwood trees that surround the pond's banks. In winter, those leaves have fallen, leaving trees bare and as stark statues against the sky; then it snows; there is such quiet around the pond and woods as the snow settles to the ground. Against the whiteness of snow, the evergreens, pine and cedar, peek out and assure me that life goes on.

In the Old Testament, Jeremiah writes in 31:13, *"The Lord hath appeared of old unto me saying, Yea, I have loved thee with an everlasting love: therefore with loving-kindness have I drawn thee."* Actually, this is in reference to God's love of His people Israel but I think we can just as easily apply the same verse to ourselves individually. He loved us from the foundations of the world (Matt. 25:34) and we have been drawn by Him. Second Timothy 1:9: *"Who hath saved us, and called us with an holy calling, not according to our works, but according to his own purpose and grace, which was given us in Christ Jesus before the world began."*

Thinking also of the circle of life as I've mentioned above, we have that hope that once life on earth is done, we, who are saved by grace through faith, continue to live eternally in Heaven. Life, for the Christian indeed, goes on! There are many references to this truth, but I like John 5:24: *"Verily, verily I say unto you, He that heareth my word, and believeth on him that sent me, hath everlasting life, and shall not come into condemnation; but is passed from death unto life."* That's pretty straightforward. Hallelujah!

Spend a few quiet moments thanking God for His unspeakable gift, the greatest Valentine of all!

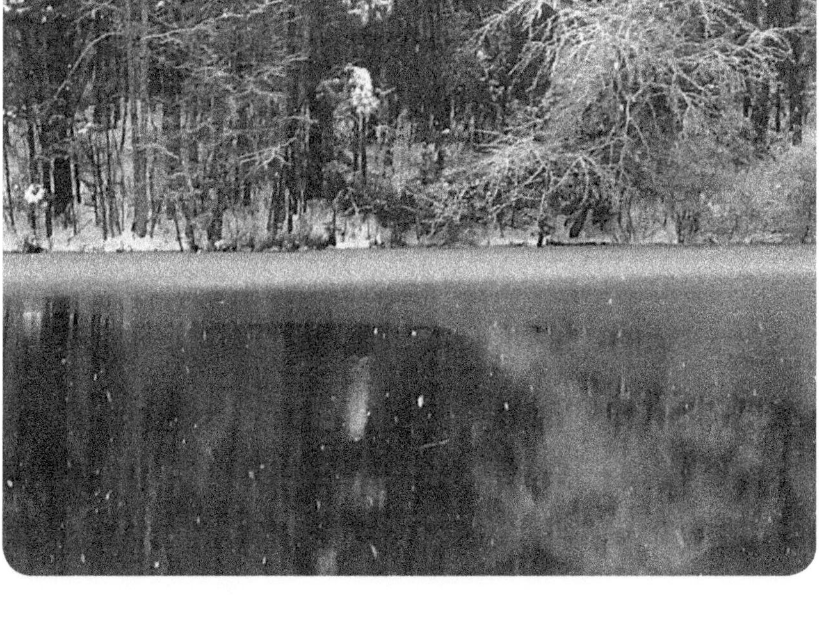

HE IS KNOCKING

As I was leaving for work one morning, I stopped before getting into my car and took a look around the pond checking for any wildlife that might have been out and about. Although I saw nothing, I did hear the rata-tat-tat of a woodpecker. I directed my gaze to the tallest trees and sure enough, I spied him sitting on a limb high up in a pine tree. I wondered how long he had been tapping and also how much longer would he continue knocking on that tree. I would guess the answer depended on whether the wood was a bit soft or really hard as to how soon he reached the innermost and desired area of the tree.

The scripture from Revelation 3:20 came to my mind. It says, *"Behold, I stand at the door and knock: if any man hear my voice and open the door, I will come in to him, and will sup with him, and he with me."* Have you ever read this verse and wondered, like I did about the woodpecker's patience in knocking? We find the answer in 2 Peter 3:9: *"The Lord is not slack concerning his promise, as some men count slackness; but is longsuffering to us-ward, not willing that any should perish, but that all should come to repentance."* Did you get that? He is longsuffering toward us and does not want anyone to go into eternity without knowing the Savior! From the Believer's Bible Commentary, I include this statement, *"He(God) purposely extends the time of grace so that men might have every opportunity to be saved."*

That is love and patience beyond my comprehension. The fact that we are still living in the time of grace is not happanstance, God purposed it! However, He has a plan and that plan involves the end of the age of grace, do not be caught unaware. We are warned in 2 Peter 3:10: *"But the day of the Lord will come as a thief in the night; in the which the heavens shall pass away with a great noise, and the elements shall melt with fervent heat, the earth also and the works that are therein shall be burned up."*

Oh, friend, do not stand unanswering as Christ is knocking upon the door of your heart. Open up to His saving grace and experience this love and patience firsthand.

Today is the day of salvation!

HEALING WATERS

Tonight, I began my "pond time" with a walk around the south side, the side closest to the house. As I walked I could see the Christmas tree shining through the glass door, each light twinkling its color. The air was brisk and had a bit of a chill, and as I walked, stopping ever so often to just close my eyes and listen I started to feel the stress of the day melt away. I was able to hear the birds, a squirrel barking, and what may have been the howl of a coyote.

God is using His creation to soothe and heal. And that healing has reached beyond me, a dear friend shared with me recently how being "at" the Pond has helped her to move past some hurt and find her path once again. Her story reminded me of the leper that was told to dip in the Jordan River seven times.

This story of Naaman is found in 2 Kings chapter 5, but I want to focus here on Naaman's faith. We read in verse 9 that he arrived at the door of Elisha the prophet, who sent out a servant with a message for Naaman to go and dip himself in the Jordan River seven times and that he would be cleaned and restored. Would this not seem too simple and unbelievable for any of us? I can imagine that you or I would expect a bit more to happen in order to create the miracle of cleansing a body of leprosy. Not right away, but Naaman did take himself down to the Jordan and bathed seven times just as he was told. In verse 14 we find these words: *"Then went he down, and dipped himself seven times in Jordan, according to the saying of the man of God: and his flesh came again like unto the flesh of a little child and he was clean."*

Naaman had faith that God would perform the cleansing. Did only the dip in the river do it? I don't think so, I believe that once Naaman waded in God reached down with His powerful, healing hand and swirled those waters about Naaman's body and by faith he was healed. In much the same way my friend has taken her own dip in the waters…the healing waters of the Pond and He has restored to her a new frame of mind.

We don't have to be literally dipped in the waters to receive healing. By crying out to God we can be healed, cleansed and restored to our loving Heavenly Father. Jeremiah 17:14 says this: *"Heal me, O Lord, and I shall be healed, save me, and I shall be saved: for thou art my praise."*

The scripture indicates that if the Lord heals and saves there is none that can change that. For that surety Jeremiah praises Him.

Do you need restoring and cleansing today? Come to Jesus with your "leprosy" for He is the way to healing. We find this in 1 Peter 2:24: *"Who his own self bare our sins in his own body on the tree that we being dead to sins, should live unto righteousness: by whose stripes ye were healed."*

Step now into the Living Water, Jesus our Savior.

HEAVENLY TREASURES

After quite a few days of rain and gloomy weather, I was thrilled to wake to the glorious sunshine over the pond this morning. The woodland creatures are thrilled as well if the actions of the squirrels are any indication! As I sit having my morning coffee, these comedic critters are seemingly having the time of their lives! They are chasing each other around the base of a large pine tree across the pond, and although I'm inside, I can almost hear the bark on the tree being crunched as their claws bite into it. From the tree they race off toward the corn pile my husband has there for the deer to feed on. It appears the deer have been forced to share with the squirrels. The morning has dawned much chillier than the last few weeks, so I think these little creatures with the plume like tails have been sent into panic mode. Suddenly, it's become winter and they haven't stored their treasure of nuts, and maybe corn, for the coming months.

We are to store up treasure too, not for things on earth but heavenly treasures. Matthew 6:19-21 tells us, *"Lay not up for yourselves treasures upon earth, where moth and rust doth corrupt, and where thieves break through and steal: But lay up for yourselves treasures in heaven, where neither moth nor rust doth corrupt, and where thieves do not break through nor steal: For where your treasure is, there will your heart be also."* Does this mean do not prepare for the future on planet earth? No, I think we are to make sound financial plans being good stewards of what God has given each of us. But we are not to put all our trust in the things that will rust and rot, but in Jesus Christ our

Savior. If our money, cars, boats, and other things are our treasures, then they will be the focus of our heart. If you are storing up heavenly treasures, then that is where your heart's focus will be. We've all heard the saying, "You can't take it with you" and that is true, the only thing that leaves this earth when we do is our soul.

God will supply all your needs from His riches in glory by Christ Jesus. This truth is from Philippians 4:19. Too often, we expect all of our wants to be supplied as well. Storing up riches in heaven is simply living your life for Christ by following His teachings, having pure motives and a desire for God's interests.

How full is your heavenly treasure chest today?

HOT OR COLD

As a result of recent cold weather that brought both snow and ice, we have created a very spoiled cat. During the days of nasty freezing temperatures and the accompanying precipitation we opened the back porch to our cat, Goldie. She now thinks that she belongs on the porch, sleeping on the chair's soft red cushions. That she has become too comfortable is an understatement! Most days she can be found exploring around the pond, and sometimes I believe she watches the small fish as they swim in the shallow water. When the sun is warm she likes to climb up onto the Adirondack chair and just spend a lazy afternoon by the pond.

What about us? Can we become too comfortable in our life of faith? The church at Laodicea certainly did and Christ rebuked them for it. Take a look at Revelation 3:14–16, *"And unto the angel of the church of Laodiceans write; These things saith the Amen, the faithful and true witness, the beginning of the creation of God; I know thy works, that thou art neither cold nor hot: I would thou wert cold or hot. So then because thou art lukewarm, and neither cold nor hot, I will spue thee out of my mouth."* Harsh words from our Lord. Laodicea was a wealthy city, the people surrounded by things that made them feel rich and successful, wanting for nothing. With an attitude like this, it can be easy to become comfortable making it so that we don't recognize that we are poor and wretched without Christ, the "Amen," living in our hearts without the indwelling Holy Spirit in our lives.

THE POND

These people were fence riders, being neither indifferent nor zealous in their faith. Comfortable, with their worldly influences deceiving them into thinking themselves "doing it right." This church at Laodicea was characterized by pride, ignorance, self-sufficiency, and complacency.[3] Do any of these descriptions sound familiar today?

The Lord would rather us be one or the other…hot or cold, rather than just lukewarm. So, if we find ourselves having become lukewarm, what is the remedy? Well, we serve a God of second chances, and in Revelation 3:19, we find this: *"As many as I love, I rebuke and chasten: be zealous therefore, and repent."* I can remember my mother telling me a number of times that she corrected me and disciplined me because she loved me. How much more does our Heavenly Father love us and would He not be about correcting us as His children? He will convict and chasten us and if we are repentant He will wipe clean our slate!

Ah, but prevention is worth an ounce of cure they say. Can we keep from becoming lukewarm Christians? Yes, and we find out how in 2 Corinthians 13:5: *"Examine yourselves, whether ye be in the faith; prove your own selves. Know ye not your own selves, how that Jesus Christ is in you, except ye be reprobates?"*

If this lesson today has brought conviction in your heart, I encourage you to whisper this prayer of repentance: *Father God, I confess that I have become lukewarm in my Christian life and I am truly sorry. Father, I thank you for being longsuffering and loving me. Forgive me and renew my life to Your glory. In the name of Jesus Christ I pray, Amen.*

---

[3] The Believer's Bible Commentary

ICE

We have had extremely cold temperatures the last few days, below freezing on a couple of occasions. This morning as I looked out onto the pond, I noticed that the water all along the edge had a skim of ice on top. The icy patterns reminded me of feathers. The ice had the appearance of being brushed out from the edge toward the pond's center looking almost as if someone had lain on the ground and blown each patch of ice away from the bank. Long icy fingers reaching out to meet the same icy fingers stretching out from the opposite side of the pond.

God controls every aspect of nature as we see in Job 37:10, "*By the breath of God ice is given, and the broad waters are frozen fast.*" *(ESV)* I like this version because it is so plainly stated. We give little thought to such a trivial weather situation, but this just shows us that God, Creator of heaven and earth, is in control of even the smallest results of weather. If we read on to verse fourteen, we will see that Job is challenged to increase his knowledge of nature. Job 37:14, "*Hear this, O Job; stop and consider the wondrous works of God.*" *(ESV)* Such excellent power surpasses our feeble comprehension.*

As you read through this work of God, my prayer is that you will see, hear, and feel this nature He has placed all about us at the pond. We take so much for granted, that when reading especially verse 10, I was truly amazed and

IN BLOOM

Our first year at the pond, I asked my husband to plant sunflowers in the empty field. Sunflowers are our daughter's favorite flower, so much so that for her wedding, the florist had them specially grown to enable her to have her favorite flower on her biggest day. My husband and our nephew worked the field over and the sowed the sunflowers. At the time they should have come up and bloomed, there was nothing! I was extremely disappointed.

A few weeks later as I drove down the driveway and around to the pond, I saw a most amazing sight! There, by the pond, where the ground was terribly dry and hard, was one tall, sunshine yellow sunflower! My husband explained that most likely the seed was dropped by a passing bird…I'll leave the rest to your imagination. There, where by all rights it shouldn't be growing, it was doing just that and thriving!

God has placed each of us as His children where we are to serve Him. In 1 Corinthians chapter 12 beginning in verse 27, Paul is teaching that we Christians corporately make up the body of Christ, but individually we each have our own part to play. Looking at verse 28 we see, *"And God hath set some in the church, first apostles, secondarily prophets, thirdly teachers, after that miracles, then gifts of healings, helps, governments, diversities of tongues."* Not everyone can be an apostle, or any of the other offices mentioned. Everyone is different and we all have different gifts and talents.

We can see a great example of being rightly placed by God in the book of Esther. Esther was a Jewish girl that God stationed in the palace of a king. He then used her to preserve the Israelites. If we could look in on that place today, we would probably view Esther as a nobody, just a girl. But God has a way of using nobodies! I trust your curiosity has the best of you, and I would direct you to read the account of Esther to get the whole picture.

Esther was truly a picture of "blooming where you are planted," as we see here in Esther 4:14. In a conversation between Mordecai and Esther we see, *"And who knoweth whether thou art come to the kingdom for such a time as this?"*

Each of us is here for such a time as this. Will you ask God to help you bloom wherever you are planted?

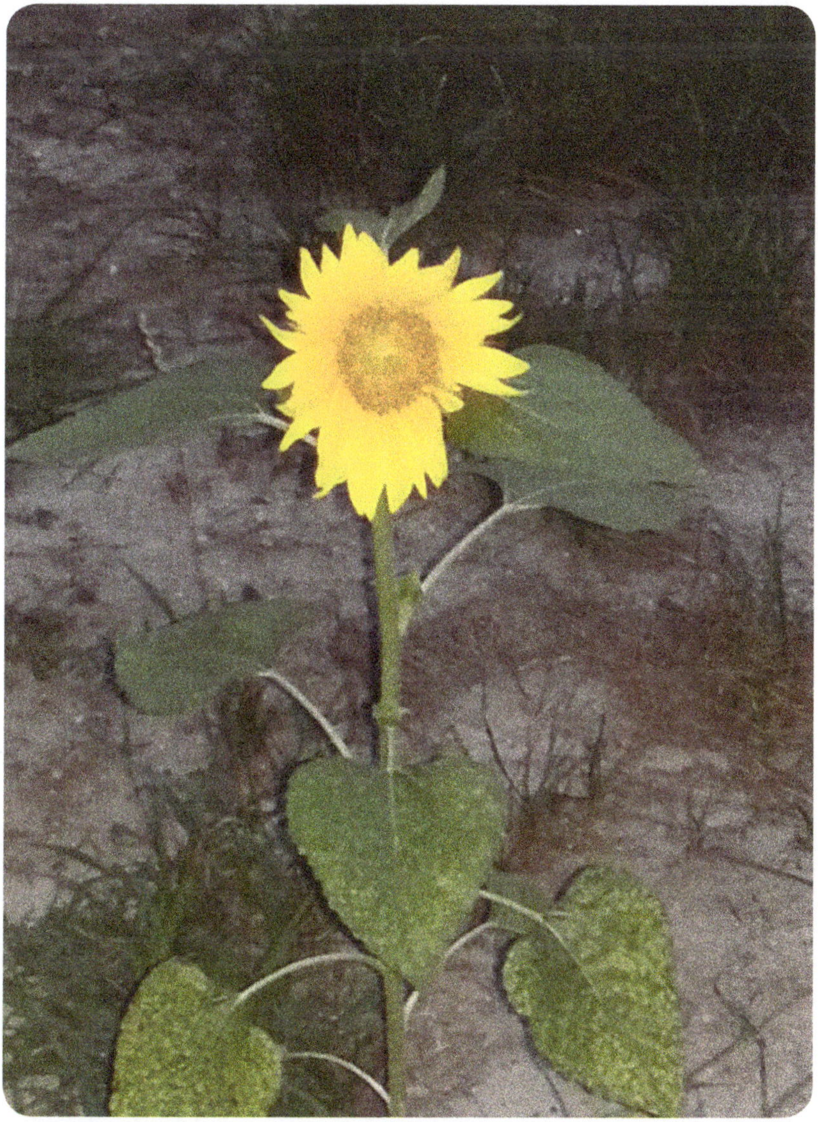

JOY!

Joy comes in the morning! This was my thought this afternoon as I looked skyward while out at the pond. Above me the sky looked layered; the top layer was just beginning to darken while the second layer was still bright underneath. It created a sensation of night and morning all at once. Were it summer this would be the time of day that all the night creatures begin to sound. However, we are well into winter so the bull frogs that will be found around the pond's edge are now quiet as are the crickets that hide in the grass on the bank of the pond.

There truly is joy in the morning. This truth is found in Psalm 30:5: *"For his anger endureth but a moment; in his favour is life: weeping may endure for a night, but joy cometh in the morning."* What promise, what hope, what JOY! How often do your worries and troubles seem magnified at night only to appear much less threatening in the morning? This is a physical analogy that I share with you, but if you have had this experience you know how exhilarating you feel when morning finally comes. As it pertains to spiritual things, I think the feeling is very much the same.

Consider that before our salvation we were enduring night, darkness, separation from God. Then along comes the morning, bright, beautiful and full of promise, full of hope. Morning here becomes a Who, no longer a "what." Who? Jesus Christ, the Morning Star! Look at another promise this one from 2 Peter 1:19: *"We have also a more sure word of prophecy; whereunto ye do well that ye take heed, as unto a light that shineth in a dark place, until the day dawn, and the day star arise in your hearts."* Take care to keep God's Word in your heart for it shines a light in this dark world until Jesus Christ comes again to take those belonging to Him to their heavenly home.

In closing, Jesus tells us Himself who He is. In the last half of the verse in Revelation 22:16, He says, *"I am the root and offspring of David, and the bright and morning star."* Remember that while the night is representative of separation from God the Father, Jesus is the light that dispels this darkness thereby giving us access to our Father and Creator.

Take a few moments to meditate on the words of the hymn, "Heaven Came Down." I pray this is your testimony!

> O what a wonderful, wonderful day, day I will never forget;
> After I'd wandered in darkness away, Jesus my Savior I met.
> O what a tender, compassionate friend,
> He met the need of my heart;
> Shadows dispelling, with joy I am telling, He made
> all the darkness depart. (John W. Peterson)

LEAVING A LEGACY

There among an accumulation of dried leaves I spied the rusted skeleton of an old, broken chair just up in the woods from the edge of the pond. As I have walked around the pond and in the woods since moving here I've often thought of those that walked here before me. This remnant of life I'd uncovered assured me of an earlier visitor to the pond. My hope is that they too enjoyed the peace of this place.

Looking at what was left of this chair, I knew that at one time it had been whole and worthy of use by its owner. The person that had sat in that chair depended on the strength of the chair's legs to support both its own weight and the added weight of the human body now sitting upon it. It seemed a sad old relic now left to fade away from sight. Soon, covered by layers upon layers of leaves and other brush, no one would ever know that someone had been there.

Well, this made me reflect on my life…my life lived for Christ. Have I been worthy of the calling Jesus has placed upon my life? Have I supported the Gospel by sharing it with others and when I am gone from this earth to my heavenly home, will my testimony be remembered as a vibrant life lived for Christ or will it be left rusty, old and broken like this chair? God's Word tells us in 2 Timothy 2:15, *"Study to shew thyself approved unto God, a workman that needeth not to be ashamed, rightly dividing the word of truth."* The focus of our efforts should be becoming a worker who does not need to be ashamed. According to the Believer's Bible Commentary, the latter portion of this verse as Henry Alford explains it means, to manage rightly to treat truth fully without falsifying.

So, then what does God require of His children? Look in Micah 6:8: *"He hath shewed thee, O man, what is good; and what doth the Lord require of thee, but to do justly, to love mercy, and to walk humbly with thy God."* These three, when followed as God requires along with being a workman not ashamed that manages the truth without falsifying it, leaves a life legacy that will not fade from sight. The memory of a life lived for God in Jesus Christ will always leave its mark upon those whose lives we touch with His light.

How do we accomplish this? In 2 Timothy 1:12, the Apostle Paul says, *"Nevertheless I am not ashamed: for I know whom I have believed, and am persuaded that he is able to keep that which I have committed unto him against that day."*

I know whom I have believed…do you?

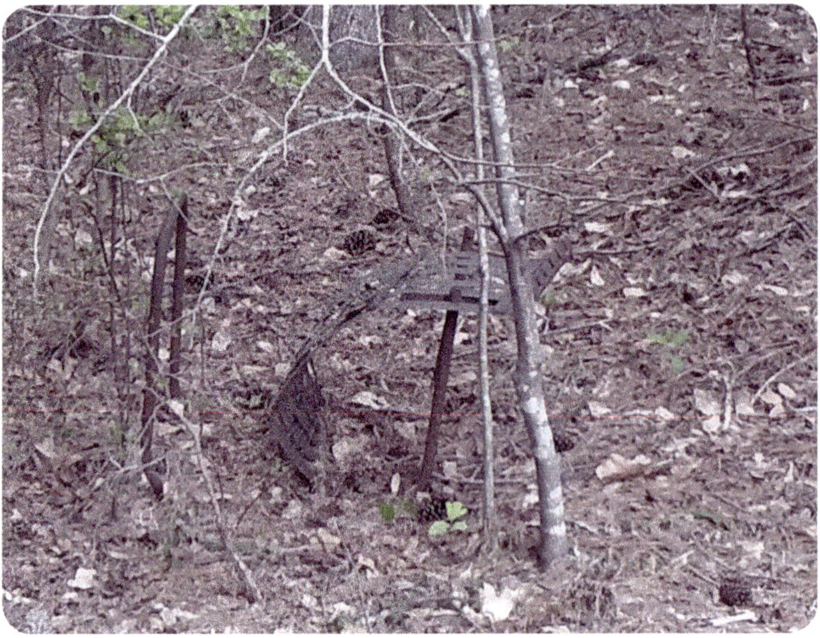

LET THE LIGHT IN

The darkness was complete as morning approached the pond. I sat by our bay window watching as the day dawned around me. The darkness slowly began to dissipate as the light started pushing its way into my line of sight. Before I knew it I was looking at the pond in full light. As I was admiring the scene, I realized the light was shining on sections of the wood line and appeared as light shining from a window. Ah, and so it was—the light of God and His Christ shining through the windows of heaven!

In our natural state our hearts are sinful and dark, as dark as the morning was when I first looked out. Take a look at Genesis 6:5, which says, *"And God saw that the wickedness of man was great in the earth and that every imagination of the thoughts of his heart was only evil continually."* As God works in our lives that darkness is pushed out by the Light of the World, Jesus. This truth is found in John 8:12, *"Then spake Jesus unto them, saying, I am the light of the world: he that followeth me shall not walk in darkness but shall have the light of life."*

The Bible teaches that the instant we ask Christ into our dark and sinful hearts a change occurs. This comes from Ephesians 2:5, *"Even when we were dead in sins, hath He quickened us together with Christ, (by grace are ye saved.)"* I am of the opinion that baptism by complete water immersion is a symbol of this change which indicates that the old man is gone and coming up from the water is a new creation. Again, a biblical truth from 2 Corinthians 5:17: *"Therefore if any man be in Christ, he is a new creature: old things are passed away; behold, all things are become new."*

You don't have to live another minute in darkness, right now, right where you are, ask Jesus to come into your heart and shed His light in your life.

Let these words of the hymn penned by Rufus H. McDaniel, "Since Jesus Came Into My Heart," speak to your own heart today.

> What a wonderful change in my life has been wrought
> Since Jesus came into my heart!
> I have light in my soul for which long I had sought,
> Since Jesus came into my heart!

LIFE IS A VAPOR

I am always amazed how quickly things around the pond can change. Depending on the angle of the sun shadows appear one way and within a few minutes the scene is totally different. Tonight as I came home from church, the moon was partially visible behind the clouds, creating a spot of pale luminous brightness in a velvety black sky. I couldn't wait to get inside so that I could get on the porch to view this beauty over the water. Alas, in the time it took me to unlock the back door, drop my purse on the kitchen counter, and get out on the back porch, the view was gone. The moon had slid completely behind the cloud cover and was practically invisible.

Our lives can change just as quickly. Surely, we all can think of people whose lives were changed in an instant either by the death of a friend or family member, illness, loss of a job or any number of similar traumatic turns. The Bible tells us this too. Look at James 4:14: *"Whereas ye know not what shall be on the morrow. For what is your life? It is even a vapor, that appeareth for a little time, and then vanisheth away."*

Does that sound frightening? We are not promised tomorrow, our lives are but vapors, mists on the annals of time. But there is no need for fear my friends, for if you are in Christ you have a hope—a hope of life eternal. Romans 15:13 affirms this promise: *"Now the God of hope fill you with all joy and peace in believing, that ye may abound in hope, through the power of the Holy Ghost."* Hallelujah!

Do you know the hope that is Jesus Christ or are you wondering how to obtain this hope today? It is by grace through faith as we read in Romans 3:23–24, *"For all have sinned and come short of the glory of God; Being justified freely by His grace through the redemption that is in Christ Jesus."* Redemption means to deliver by paying a price, and Jesus paid our debt through His death on the cross. All we have to do is believe in Him as we read in Romans 10:8–9, 13.

In closing, meditate on this last verse from the poem, "Only One Life, 'Twill Soon Be Past," by C. T. Studd:

> Give me Father, a purpose deep,
> In joy or sorrow Thy word to keep;
> Faithful and true what e'er the strife,
> Pleasing Thee in my daily life;
> Only one life, 'twill soon be past,
> Only what's done for Christ will last.

LILY PADS

For several weeks now, my husband and I have been trying to rid a small area of our pond of a growth of lily pads. The lily pads are winning the battle. Although they are pretty to look at, they can and do cause problems within the pond. If left alone, they spread quickly and would certainly affect the visual appeal of the pond as well as make it difficult to get around in the pedal boat. Thus we must control them, and that appears as if it will be a constant fight.

This makes me think about how, if left unchecked, sin can grow and spread. Romans 6:23 tells us, *"The wages of sin is death; but the gift of God is eternal life through Jesus Christ our Lord."* The sin may not immediately cause a physical death, but is certain to cause spiritual death; however, there is a hope...Jesus Christ. Over in the book of James this is addressed again in chapter 1 verses 15 and 21—and it says, *"Then when lust hath conceived, it bringeth forth sin: and sin, when it is finished, bringeth forth death."* But, as with our verse from Romans, James goes on to offer a hope in verse 21, *"Wherefore lay apart all filthiness and superfluity of naughtiness and receive with meekness the engrafted Word, which is able to save your souls."* Remember here, that we know from John's Gospel that the Word was with God in the beginning, and he goes on to say in verse 14 *"And the Word was made flesh and dwelt among us."* So, in looking back to our verse from James 1:21, we now know that the engrafted word is Jesus! We must receive Jesus, study the Bible, and pray daily.

Our best defense against Satan and his temptations is to take the words of the Psalmist as he says in chapter 119:11, *"Thy word have I hid in my heart that I might not sin against thee."* When Jesus was tempted by Satan, he quoted the Scriptures, and eventually, Satan left him.

Like our lily pads, temptations can be attractive and pretty to look at. Remember that Satan appears as an angel of light and will place before us those things that appeal to our eyes, minds, and flesh. Therefore, we must keep ourselves in check and under control... control of the Holy Spirit, that is.

This verse from by Samuel Longfellow brings a good close today:

>Holy Spirit, Right divine,
>King within my conscience reign;
>be my Lord, and I shall be
>firmly bound, forever free.

LOOKING BACK

On this chilly November morning, as I look over the pond, the wind is blowing a pile of leaves from the bank onto the surface of the water. On the water they look like a fleet of little boats setting off on their predestined courses. Some spin around and around not really going anywhere, others are moving ahead without deviating from the course ahead.

Aren't we like these leaf boats? Some of us seem to never really move ahead in our Christian walk, while others move boldly ahead without looking back. Remember Lot's wife? Looking back can be a big problem! But don't we all want to glance back over our shoulder at what we're leaving behind?

In Hebrews chapter 11, which I call the chapter of faith, we find that Abel, Enoch, Noah, Abraham, and Sara and many others are considered righteous because of their faith. Also in that same chapter, and in verse 15, after having made reference to Abraham's sojourn in the promised land, the writer goes on to say, *"And truly, if they had been mindful of that country from whence they came out, they might have had opportunity to have returned. (16) But now they desire a better country, that is, an heavenly: wherefore God is not ashamed to be called their God: for he hath prepared for them a city."*

We are to strive ever forward, not looking back at the past. Philippians 3:13–14 brings that point home when Paul says that he hasn't made it on his own. He goes on to say, *"But this one thing I do, forgetting those things which are behind, and reaching forth unto those things which are before I press toward the prize of the high calling of God in Christ Jesus."*

How do we avoid going around in circles and not advancing on our pre-plotted course? Trusting Jesus by faith, studying the Word of God, and prayer. Instruction can be found in 2 Peter 5:8: *"And beside this, giving all diligence, add to your faith virtue, and to virtue knowledge; and to knowledge temperance; and to temperance; patience; and to patience godliness; and to godliness brotherly kindness; and to brotherly kindness charity. For if these things be in you and abound, they make you that ye shall neither be barren or unfruitful in the knowledge of our Lord Jesus Christ."*

My prayer today is one of encouragement for any reader whose boat is not sailing boldly along on a direct path. Your boat's course can be adjusted but it must be done purposefully. How does one change the direction of a boat? By physically changing the direction of the rudder. In much the same way we change our spiritual direction by making the decision to do so.

Will you make the necessary changes to redirect your path today?

MILDNESS AND JUSTICE

Out by the pond the afternoon is chilly, and the sun bright on this day in mid-February. I can almost hear the low hum of the honeybees that will come in summer. The dance performed by the bees as they dip and sway is a mesmerizing act. They will hover over the plants around the pond that attract them and carry back to the hives the nectar that will be used to make honey. Thus another example of life's cycle provided by the pond.

I have been amazed at the way God has taught me the parallels between nature and Christ. Even the bees can be associated with the character of Jesus. A statement from *The Beekeepers Bible* caught my attention. It reads, "The bee is considered an emblem of Christ: His mildness and mercy on one side (honey) and His justice on the other (the sting)."

Speaking to the mildness and mercy of Christ we can look at Titus 3:4–5: *"But after that the kindness and love of God our Saviour toward man appeared, Not by works of righteousness which we have done, but according to his mercy he saved us, by the washing of regeneration and renewing of the Holy Spirit."* If we read onto verse seven we will find that we are justified by His grace and made heirs to the hope of eternal life!

We are justified! But this can only be appointed unto us by the Justifier, Jesus Christ himself. When we confess our sin we are forgiven as we see in 1 John 1:9, *"If we confess our sins, he is faithful and just to forgive us our sins, and to cleanse us from all unrighteousness."* In this example, just is equivalent to true, we could reword the verse as he is faithful and true and we would have the same meaning.

Jesus will also rule the nations with justice as we see in Isaiah 9:6–7, *"For unto us a child is born, unto us a child is given: and the government shall be upon his shoulder: and his name shall be called Wonderful, Counselor, The might God, The everlasting Father, The Prince of Peace. Of the increase of his government and peace there shall be no end, upon the throne of David and upon his kingdom, to order it, and to establish it with judgment and with justice from henceforth even for ever. The zeal of the Lord of Hosts will perform this."* When Christ returns and reins on earth, His government, carried forth from the throne of David, will be from pole to pole, peaceful and never ending. He will rule with judgment and justice.

For a closer look at the second coming of Christ, I would direct you to Revelation 19:11–16. To sum up this section of verses, the Believer's Bible Commentary simply says, "Our Jesus is the Supreme Ruler; all others must submit to His reign." Jesus, mild, merciful, and compassionate, now in righteousness judges the nations.

Oh, may we taste honey and not feel the sharp prick of the sting.

NEW AND BEAUTIFUL

Scuffing my feet as I walked on the bank of the pond, my shoes turned over piles of dry, dead leaves that had lain on the ground for an undetermined amount of time. Year after year, leaves drift onto the carpet of leaves from the previous fall creating many layers of time past. Today a beautifully decaying leaf peeked from under the newest layer, showing itself as a delicate piece of lace. It was paper thin and looked as if it had been created from a piece of parchment.

The amazing thing about this to me is that even in a state of decay as this leaf was, there is found beauty. If we can find beauty in this leaf, how much more does our Father God see us as beautiful in Christ?

Before we are saved we too are in a state of death and decay due to sin. When we come face-to-face with the Savior and ask Him into our hearts we become new and beautiful. This promise is from 2 Corinthians 5:17: *"Therefore if any man be in Christ, he is new creature; old things are passed away; behold all things are become new."* My leaf will eventually return to the earth and in doing so gives life to all manner of minute creatures that feed upon it or by being used to build a bird's nest. As Christians, we too hold the hope that promises life for others.

Ephesians 2:1 teaches us, *"And you hath he quickened, who were dead in trespasses and sins:"* I imagine that before I received by God's grace His salvation, my heart was as dry and brittle as our leaf. We however have a hope! We don't have to remain dead in our sin! John

20:31 give us assurance of this: *"But these are written, that ye might believe that Jesus is the Christ, the Son of God; and that believing ye might have life through His name."*

That is our hope, the hope we can share with a lost and dying world. Believe and be saved! What a beautiful picture of the love God has for us.

To close today, I have chosen to leave you with this chant by John Bell:

> Behold, behold, I make all things new,
> Beginning with you and starting today.
> Behold, behold, I make all things new,
> My promise is true, for I am Christ the way.

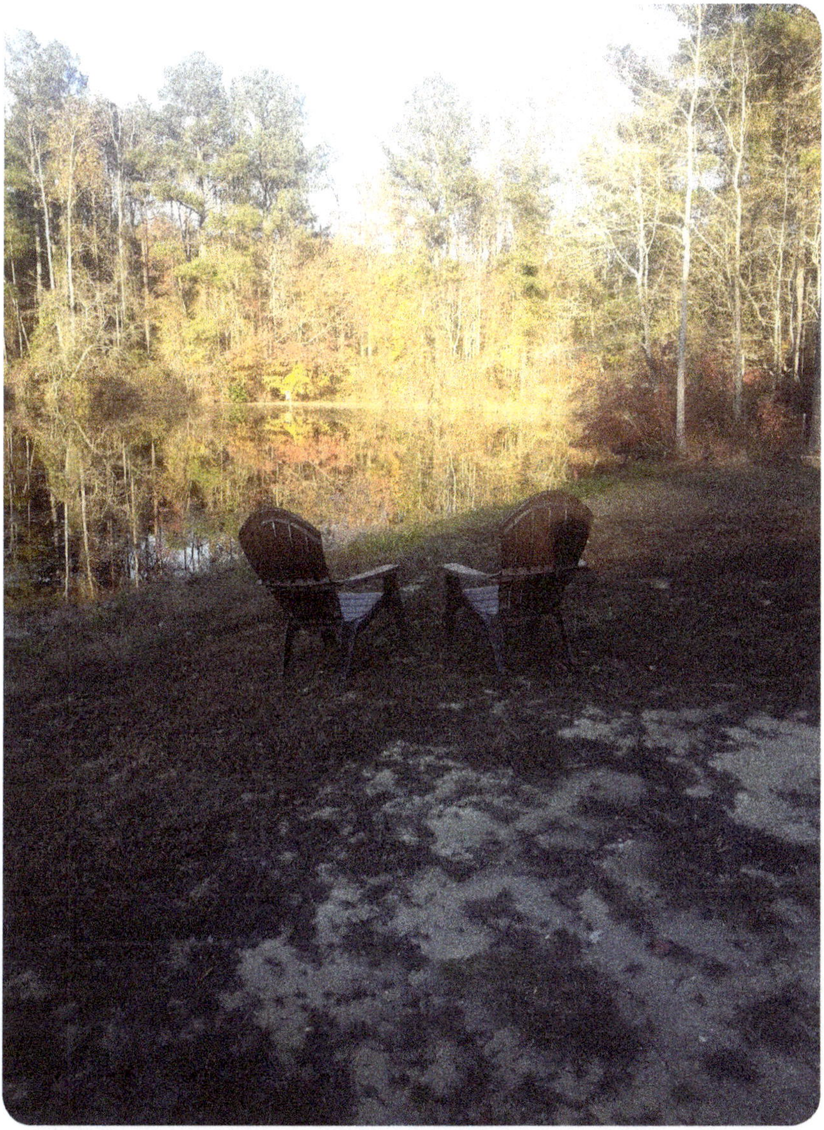

NEW LIFE

Renewal, that is what I saw this morning as I stood on the porch overlooking the pond. It is yet a few weeks away, but spring is in the air. The blueberry bushes that line one side of the pond are showing a little bit of red on the tips. As my eyes followed the circle of the pond all the way around I could see up through the woods spots of green here and there. From the distance I could not tell what type of plant I was looking at, but it was red as well. Color is popping up everywhere. In addition to these obvious signs of spring, the bull frogs were bellowing and birds were singing. New life—it is everywhere!

Have you ever considered the significance of the resurrection of Christ occurring during the spring of the year? The previous months consist of cold and dreary days; everything is brown and dead. I feel that is the way my life would be described before I came to know Christ…brown and dead. Oh, we think we're living, but until Christ is born in our hearts we don't know true, full and abundant life. In John 10:10 we find these words from Jesus: *"I am come that they might have life, and that they might have it more abundantly."* When we accept Jesus as our Lord and Savior, and He becomes the Lord of our life, we too, become new. Second Corinthians 5:17: *"Therefore if any man be in Christ, he is a new creature: old things are passed away; behold, all things become new."* We become a new creature by the washing away of our sins. The last of this verse states that all things become new, I take that as we will then see with spiritual eyes and everything will be new and shiny as we view it through the eyes that have been born again.

Just like the daffodils that have been planted as a bulb, brown and dead looking, begin to shoot out of the ground and up through the snow; we too, are *raised* to life. We see this truth in Romans 6:4: *"Therefore we are buried with him by baptism into death: that like as Christ was raised up from the dead by the glory of the Father, even so we also should walk in newness of life."*

As this Easter season dawns, I would ask that you consider that without the resurrection of Christ, there would be no new life for us. He was crucified, dead and buried only to rise on that glorious third day ensuring that we can say that we serve a living Savior!

For a few minutes of meditation, think on these words. This is the chorus from the hymn, "He Lives" by Alfred Henry Ackley.

He lives, He lives, Christ Jesus lives today!
He walks with me and talks with me along life's narrow way.
He lives, He lives, salvation to impart!
You ask me how I know He lives?
He lives within my heart.

OUR PROTECTOR

Much to the delight of the men in my family, deer season is upon us! They are all hunters, I on the other hand watch from my porch as the deer move about the woods surrounding the pond. I've been blessed to see deer on several occasions as they gathered across the pond and munched on the corn that my husband had put out for them.

On this particular afternoon God showed me a true jaw-dropping scene! As I walked through the house something caught my eye, I took a step backward and looked out the bay window and there in the shallow water was a fawn! This fawn, complete with spots, wasn't just standing in the water…Oh no, he was running, jumping and kicking up his heels! I believe he was having the time of his life, but just in the edge of the woods was his mama. She was staying hidden but definitely had her protective eye peeled on her baby.

As I stood, spellbound by this sight, it was as if God spoke and said, "Take a good look, for I do the same with my children." Oh, and how He does protect us. We have several references to His protection and watch care. Look at Psalm 91; it's all about God's care of us. Particularly, verse 4 says, *"He shall cover thee with his feathers and under his wings shalt thou trust."* Psalm 17:7: *"Shew they loving-kindness, O thou that savest by thy right hand them which put their trust in thee from those that rise up against them."*

Do you, like David in 2 Samuel 3, say, *"God is my rock, in him shall I trust; he is my shield and the horn of my salvation, my high tower and my refuge, my savior; thou savest me from violence."*? He wants us

THE POND

to look to Him for our every need and desires that we trust in His protection.

Will you trust in His promise of protection? Trust and believe that He who has promised it is more than able to perform it!

PEACE

The summer night was warm and the darkness fell around us like velvet. The night creatures were humming and in the distant woods could be heard the hoot-hoot of an owl. Above, the stars twinkled like diamonds, and the half moon was luminous. My husband and I sat in our chairs out by the pond and experienced the night. What peace! We were doing nothing more, just sitting and enjoying God's handiwork.

Peace that's a nice thought, you may say, but just a thought. Oh, not so, for if you are in Christ you have His peace. As long as the world stands, humans will desire peace, peace between nations, peace between races, peace within families—but peace will not come.

However, as Christians, we can have peace even in these days. Isaiah records these comforting words in chapter 26:3: *"Thou wilt keep him in perfect peace whose mind is stayed on thee."* Even the disciples needed encouraging after the last Passover, and we find in John 16:33 the words of Jesus as he tells them, *"These things I have spoken unto you, that in me ye might have peace. In the world you shall have tribulation: but be of good cheer for I have overcome the world."* I can think of no better assurance. If I'm in Christ, I shall have peace amidst all the turmoil in the world. Peace is available to me!

If you don't know this peace I speak of, I would encourage you to read and think on these verses: Matthew 11:28–30, John 14:27, and Romans 5:1.

THE POND

In closing, I will leave with you the words Paul uses as he begins his letter to Philemon: *"Grace to you and peace from God our Father and the Lord Jesus Christ."*

PLANTING THE SEED

As I stood watching, a large blue heron swooped in low over the pond and landed on a tree that has fallen partially into the water. The wind was buffeting him about, causing the big bird to make a bit of a wobbly landing. Once he touched down on the log he shook his head as if to say, "Whew, I made it." It was a rather comical sight! In just a few minutes, he took flight once again moving on to the next stop in hopes to nab a few more fish for his dinner. There are many unsuccessful attempts at fishing for the great blue heron, and just as with an frustrated fisherman, eventually, the great blue will move on to another spot. Hopefully his next landing will be a bit smoother.

This makes me think about the fishermen Jesus chose as his disciples. How often were they frustrated because their nets were not filled with fish? How many times did they pull in empty nets and pull up the anchor to sail toward another location in hopes of finding an abundance of fish? How many times do we get frustrated as we Christians fish for new believers? Jesus told his disciples, *"And he saith unto them, Follow me, and I will make you fishers of men."* Matthew 4:19. If Jesus told them that he would make them fishers of men, then He will provide the power to draw the crowds in. We must trust that He is still doing the same today.

We have been given a great commandment as we see in Matthew 28:19: *"Go ye therefore and teach all nations, baptizing them in the name of the Father, and of the Son, and of the Holy Ghost."* Jesus teaches that no man can come unto Him except that the Father draws him.

This means that humans, in and of themselves are not able to come to Jesus on their own. Unless the Father works in someone's heart and life they will never realize their need for a Savior. We, Christians, are to tell the story, but God changes the heart.

We plant the seed, the seed of the Gospel. In Luke chapter 8 we find the parable of the sower. In verse 11 we find, *"Now the parable is this: The seed is the Word of God."* A seed doesn't just grow; it needs soil, sun, and water to grow. Each of us has a part in the growing of a seed; you may be the soil, the sun or the water. We all work together to grow the Kingdom. If you have shared the Gospel with someone who doesn't accept Christ right then, do not be disheartened but trust that another worker will come along after you and water that seed.

Like the heron, don't just stay in an unproductive spot. Share the Word and move on to where God directs you.

Remember, the planted seed is not harvested the same day! Do your part, God will do the rest.

POWERED BY THE *SON*

Driving into the garage one night, I was aware of just how dark the sky was above the pond. This particular night I saw no stars, only a little sliver of moon was showing. A slice of light in an otherwise dark sky. Although it was a small amount of moonlight, it was being reflected in the pond. The water was still; there was no breeze to send ruffles across the surface. The pond was as dark as the sky, and there was that moon, looking back at me from the mirror of water.

The moon is referred to in Psalm 89:37 as a faithful witness in heaven and was placed in the sky by Creator God as we see in Genesis 1:16, *"And God made two great lights; the greater light to rule the day, and the lesser light to rule the night: he made the stars also."* In our solar system, the moon borrows its light from the sun. Should the sunlight be blocked, the moon would be dark. It reflects the light of the Sun. Does this sound familiar?

As Christians, we are to reflect the *Son* and His light. Here is what the Bible says in 1 Peter 2:9, *"But ye are a chosen generation, a royal priesthood, an holy nation, a peculiar people; that ye should shew forth the praises of him who hath called you out of darkness into his marvelous light."* We have been called…into light. We do not possess this light within ourselves, but can only reflect the light of Jesus, our Savior.

Ephesians 5:8 tells us, *"For ye were sometimes darkness, but now are ye light in the Lord: walk as children of light."* If we profess to be children of the light, our walk should then correspond with our standing.

There is coming a day in which we will have no need of sun or moon, we will have the glory of God as our light. Take a look at Revelation 21:23, *"and the city had no need of the sun, neither of the moon, to shine in it: for the glory of God did lighten it, and the Lamb is the light (lamp) thereof."* This is portion of the Scripture is John's description of the New Jerusalem. For further study, read chapter 21 in its entirety.

The *light* of Jesus is available to all (John 3:16) so that anyone that believes on Him shall reside with Him in the glorious light of God's glory in this city to come.

In closing here are words from the hymn, "The New Jerusalem" by Matt Gilman:

> Every tear will be wiped away, there'll be no sorrow, hurt, or pain
> There'll be no more night
> All things will be made new, it will be a brand new day
> And in righteousness He'll reign and the Lamb will be the light

PRAISE IN THE RAIN

Not again, I thought as I heard the rain begin to pour. What was just a drizzle minutes earlier had now become a gulley washer! I stepped outside onto the back porch to listen to the rain. Different sounds occur, depending on where the drop hits. A myriad of musical raindrops were playing, a flat thud as drops hit the ground, a brassy ringing where the drops landed on the metal awning above the screen door, and then the plink-plink of drops on water. All at the same time, I thought of it as a raindrop symphony.

Even the rain drops make music for God, obeying the Word of God from Psalm 98:4, 7–8, which is, *"Make a joyful noise unto the Lord, all the earth...Let the sea roar, and the fullness thereof; the world, and they that dwell therein. Let the floods clap their hands: let the hills be joyful together."* Boy, there is divine power in the shower!

Again in Revelation 5:13, we read John's description of adoration from creation for Christ. *"And every creature which is in heaven, and on the earth, and under the earth, and such as are in the sea, and all that are in them, heard I saying, Blessing, and honor, and glory and power, be unto Him that sitteth upon the throne, and unto the Lamb for ever and ever."* What a vision this brings to my mind! To think that every creature imaginable, on earth and in the seas along with all of God's children will be worshipping and praising God the Father and our Savior, Jesus Christ. My mind is so finite I can't grasp what it will be like. My faith tells me it is truth and in His time it will come to pass, but for now I will praise Him in the rain!

THE POND

Are you able to praise His name today? Are you brokenhearted or downtrodden? Read Psalm 147 and see that God is worthy to be praised and that He heals, He is understanding, and He cares for you and me. Verse 11 says that He takes pleasure in those that fear Him. This does not mean He wants us to be frightened, but that in awe and reverence we hope in His mercy.

The next time you experience a storm or see the seas rolling, recall the verses above from Psalm 98 and know that even as creation praises Him, we, His children are to do the same.

REDEEMING BLOOD

Due to a bit of inclement weather today, I am sitting in my kitchen watching the wintery mix swirling around depositing a white carpet on the ground around the pond and creating an icy coating on the tree limbs. The birds are plentiful today as they are scouring the back yard for food. Looking out the glass door toward the pond I saw a brilliant red bird. His red color was in distinct contrast to the white snow on the ground. My first thought was how much it looked like a drop of blood. This thought drove me to do a little inquiry on the cardinal.

I learned that the cardinal's name is taken from the high-ranking officials of the Catholic Church who wear rich red robes. The term *cardinal* is used to denote something with primary or essential qualities. The word comes from the Latin *cardo*, meaning hinge. Something that has cardinal qualities is so important that it functions as a keystone or axle; other things hinge around it.[4] Aha! The blood of Christ for Christians is that thing that other things hinge around; it's the keystone of our faith, is it not?

Let's explore the thought, shall we? As Christians, we believe that our salvation has been purchased by the death of Christ upon the cross of Calvary. On that cross, His blood was shed for our sins, and through that blood we are redeemed. From Matthew 26:27, 28, *"And He took the cup, and gave thanks, and gave it to them, saying,*

---

[4] Beliefnet.com

Drink ye all of it. For this is my blood of the new testament, which is shed for many for the remission of sins." These are Jesus's words to the disciples at the Last Supper shortly before His crucifixion.

In Ephesians 1:7, we find, *"In whom we have redemption through his blood, the forgiveness of sins, according to the riches of his grace."* His blood paid our ransom; nothing else would do.

Blood is vitally important to the body, in the same way the blood of Christ is vitally important to us spiritually. Without the blood, we remain lost in our sin and eternally separated from God the Father. I like the last verse of the poem, "Only the Blood of Jesus," by Connie Campbell Bratcher, for it says it all.

> Praise God for that precious blood,
> Flowing from heaven to earth,
> A stream of cleansing power…
> That redeems and gives new birth

Have you found redemption, forgiveness, and salvation in the blood of Christ?

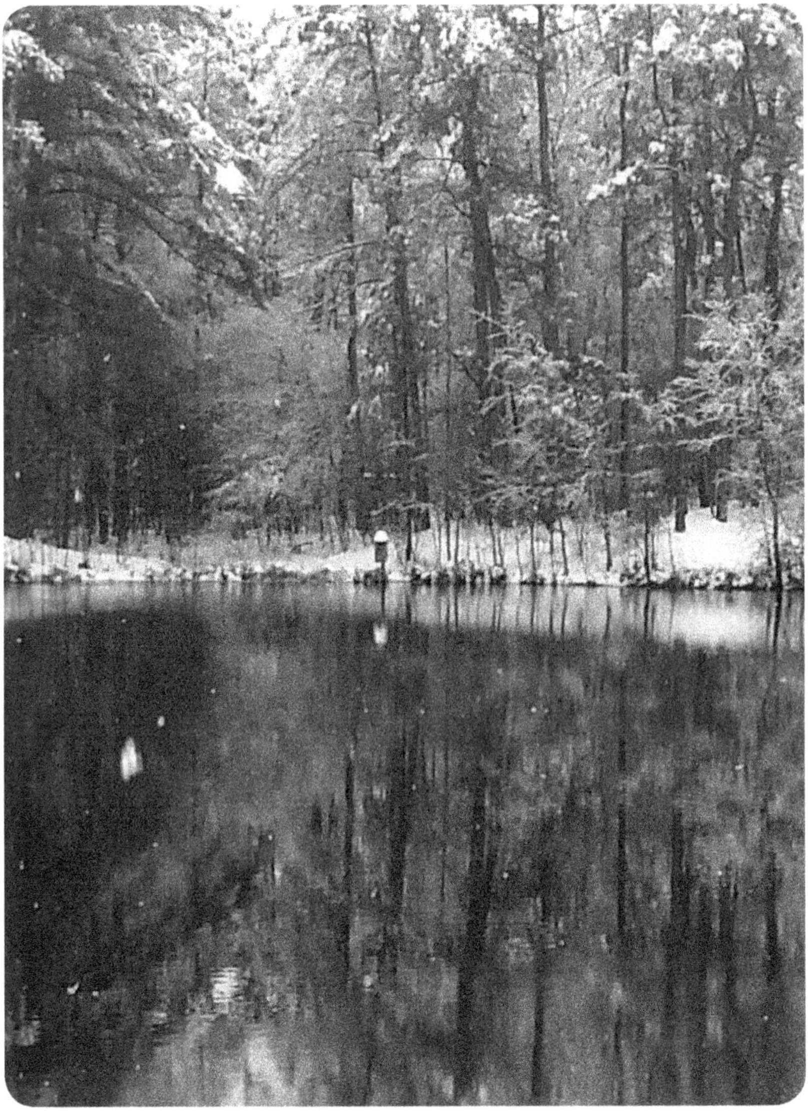

REVIVING RAIN

A soft rain was falling as I stepped out onto the screened porch for a few minutes of quiet reflection on the day. There was not a visible sunset for the day had been cloudy and gray. The pond was still and the only sound I heard were the spring peepers, even though spring is still a few weeks away. I watched as the raindrops hit the surface of the water and made little circlets that grew ever wider until they dissipated. Most often rain brings groans of disappointment, we would rather have sunshine! We enjoy the sun, but we must also have rain.

God knows what we need and when we need it as we see in Leviticus 26:4: *"Then I will give you rain in due season, and the land shall yield her increase, and the trees of the field shall yield their fruit."* Even though He knows and is in control of the rain, we show obedience when we go to God in prayer for rain when the earth is dry. Zechariah 10:1 says, *"Ask ye of the Lord rain in the time of the latter rain; so the Lord shall make bright clouds, and give them showers of rain, to every one grass in the field."*

Rain replenishes, restores and rejuvenates the earth. When we come to Christ, He rains on our hearts in much the same way to restore us, to replenish hope within us and to rejuvenate our spirits. Without Christ, we are not unlike the dry, cracked earth before the rain.

A perfect example of restoration, rejuvenation and replenishing is found in Psalms 23:1–3, *"The Lord is my shepherd; I shall not want. He maketh me to lie down in green pastures: he leadeth me beside the still waters. He restoreth my soul: he leadeth me in the paths of righteousness for his name's sake."*

How might we find restoration? There is a word on this that comes from Acts 3:19, *"Repent ye therefore, and be converted, that your sins may be blotted out, when the times of refreshing shall come from the presence of the Lord."* This verse addresses the people of Israel but we can make a personal application just as easily.

Christ is waiting and is ready to bring the replenishing rains of restoration and rejuvenation to your heart.

Will you let the Shepherd of Psalm 23 become the Shepherd of your life?

SEEING THE LIGHT

As I'm sitting out by the pond, darkness falls. A velvety, black night envelopes me as the stars appear in the sky. Just to look up at the star studded heaven inspires awe! But then I begin to see what looks like mini stars floating through the night…on my level. The tiny lightening bugs are out in the summer night. These twinkling little creatures bring back many childhood memories of summers past. Tonight, however, God's Word comes to mind.

We are told in Romans 1:20 (I'll paraphrase) that all of creation bears witness to God, so we are without excuse to believe in Him. So, I say the lightening bug with his light is bearing his witness for us. Matthew 5:16 says, *"Let your light so shine before men, that they may see your good works, and glorify you Father which is in heaven."* I would venture to say this little summertime torch bearer is doing just that.

In Luke's gospel, we can read of the parable of the lighted candle and make application to ourselves: *"No man, when he hath lighted a candle, putteth it in a secret place, neither under a bushel, but on a candlestick, that they which come in may see the light"* (Luke 11:33). We too are not to hide our light, the light of Christ that lives within us when we have been saved.

What a lesson we can learn from the lowly little lightening bug!

Place your light high on a candlestick for the world to see. Share Jesus, the light of the world, with someone today.

SHADOW TO LIGHT

It was a pleasant Saturday morning in August and I was having my coffee on the porch facing the pond. The sun was back over my shoulder in the eastern sky, a cool breeze was blowing, and it felt like a gentle caress as it came around me. As I watched the far side of the pond, the woods began to grow bright. As the light moved around the wooded edge of the pond, it was as if a stage curtain was being pulled back and the light pushed the shadow further and further away…until the whole area was lightened by the sun. I immediately thought how once we accept Christ and repent of our sins, he rolls the darkness of our former lives away, replacing it with His light.

We find in John 8:12, Jesus saying, *"I am the light of the world: he that followeth me shall not walk in darkness, but shall have the light of life."* I find it interesting that Jesus refers to himself as the light, and we know as Christians, that in Christ we have eternal life. So in having the light of life, we have Jesus! Look also at John 14:6, where Jesus tells us, *"I am the way, the truth and the life; no man cometh unto the Father but by me."* Here He confirms that He alone is light and life for those who will come to Him for salvation.

As a result of receiving Jesus as Savior, we become light to a dark world. In Matthew's gospel chapter 5, verses 14–16, we find instructions on what to do with our light: *"Ye are the light of the world. A city that is set on a hill cannot be hid. Neither do men light a candle and put it under a bushel, but on a candlestick; and it giveth light unto all that are in the house. Let your light so shine before men, that they may see your good works and glorify your Father which is in heaven."* I find these words very clear, and although we aren't saved by our works, it is those works that is an outward expression of our hearts. For clarification, Ephesians 2:8–9 tells us, *"For by grace are ye saved through faith, and that not of yourselves: it is the gift of God: not of works lest any man should boast."*

It is my prayer that you have this light in your life today. If you are not sure of your standing with Christ, I would direct you to read the gospel of John to begin your journey. As you read John 3:16, realize that this verse states that Jesus was sent so that *whosoever* believes will not perish. That leaves out no one!

SHOWERS OF BLESSINGS

On waking this morning the view that greeted me was not a most desirous one. The beginning of the day was, well it was just gray. That is the only way to describe it…gray. Crooked little lines of rain covered the glass of the bay window that looks out over the pond. I must admit, it was a bit depressing as I observed the heavy downpour. It was raining hard enough that we could hear the drops as they pounded against the glass as well as the "ting-ting" of drops hitting the attic fan above.

I began to think about the heavy rains that come into our lives in the form of death, illness, loss of income or any number of other hardships that we all will face in time. John 16:33 says, *"These things have I spoken unto you that in me ye might have peace. In the world you shall have tribulation, but be of good cheer; I have overcome the world."* Does this verse bring comfort and peace in light of a difficult situation? Oh yes! And assurance that even in tribulation we can have joy because of Jesus.

Tribulations may come to us as a result of our own actions, the way we respond to a temptation, but even in this God has provided an escape route. Look at 1 Corinthians 10:13 and the words of Paul as he tells us, *"There hath no temptation taken you but such as is common to man: but God is faithful, who will not suffer you to be tempted above that which ye are able; but will with the temptation also make a way to escape, that ye may be able to bear it."*

Sometimes rains come in life, clouds are gray and just as the dirt is washed by the rain into the pond and the water becomes muddy, our lives can become muddied. If you will notice in both verses the three letter word **but**. By way of simple definition it is used to introduce a statement that adds something to a previous statement and usually contrasts with it in some way. And how do the ending of those verses contrast with the beginning! The Believer's Bible Commentary adds a little something more in reference to 1 Corinthians 10:13 that I'd like to include here. It states, *"God does not promise to deliver us from temptation or testing, but He does promise to limit its intensity. He further promises to provide the way of escape, that we may be able to bear it."* Friend, that is how much God loves you and me!

After studying on these verses and reading the commentary, I want to offer the thought that these "downpours" we sometimes experience may actually turn out to be "showers of blessings!"

As I close with the last verse of the hymn "Showers of Blessing," think about how God may have used rain showers in your life as blessings and refreshings.

> There shall be showers of blessing,
> If we but trust and obey;
> There shall be seasons refreshing,
> If we let God have His way.
>
> —Daniel Webster Whittle

SITTIN' OR GETTIN'

The morning dawned bright and beautiful, so by the time I sat down with my cup of coffee, I had already decided that after lunch on this Lord's day, I would accompany my husband and our dog, Silas on their Sunday afternoon jaunt around our property. As soon as we finished lunch, we loaded up the golf cart, and away we went. The day, though bright and sunny had a bit of chill in the air, but otherwise was a perfect afternoon for exploring all the way around the pond.

Not looking for anything specific, I just opened my eyes to the things around me. God never ceases to amaze and delight me with everything He has placed before me! I saw the unabashed happiness of Silas as he ran free, with a grin on his lips and a light in his eyes; and yes, dogs do grin! The beauty of the evergreens, both pine and cedar trees. As we crossed the dam I looked over and saw the water coming from the spill pipe in a rush creating a little bit of froth as it hit the creek on the opposite side. These are things I don't see if I sit in my chair on the porch!

Neither can we accomplish our Lord's command if we do not "get up and get out." Mark 16:15 speaks to this as we see: *"And He said unto them, Go ye into all the world, and preach the gospel to every creature."* We as Christians are not to just "sit on the porch," but we have to be in the world telling the *good news* of salvation through Jesus. This very thought can be frightening. Often, we are uncomfortable approaching friends or family for a variety of reasons. There are two scriptures that come to mind as we wonder how we can follow this command. From Ephesians 4:11–12: *"And he gave some apostles; and some prophets; and some evangelists; and some pastors and teachers; For the perfecting of the saints, for the work of the ministry, for the edifying of the body of Christ."* We cannot do the task in and of ourselves, but only through the supernatural gifts of the Spirit. These gifts enable us to do what would be humanly impossible. The second reference is from Philippians 4:13: *"I can do all things through Christ which strengtheneth me."*

One thought I always shared with the young girls in my GA's class was to remember that each of us is required only to "plant the seed," there may be someone else to "water" and yet someone else to see that soul "harvested." Keep Philippians 4:13 in your mind and trust Him to always give you the words that are exactly what the person you are to share the Gospel with needs to hear.

It is a lot easier to just sit on the porch, but be assured you will be blessed by getting up and getting out! Do not miss what God has in store when you trust Him and venture out.

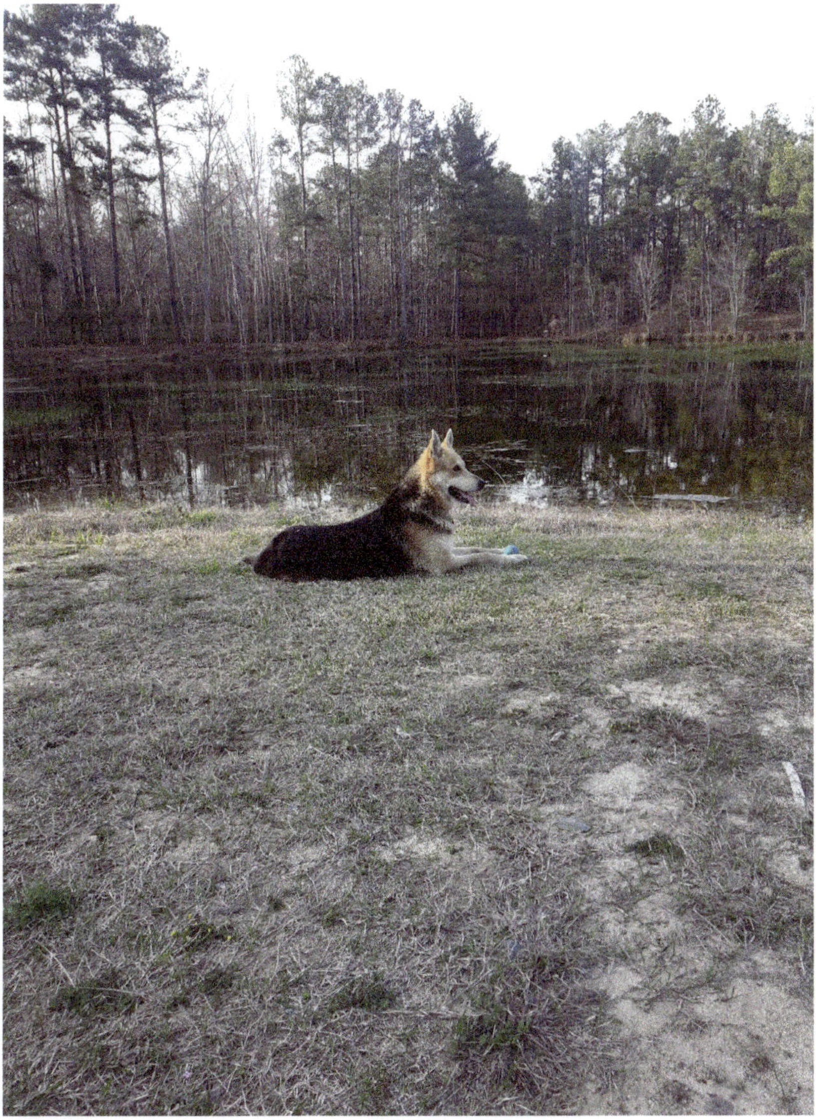

STILLNESS

Once again, this afternoon finds me at the kitchen table gazing out over the pond. For the last several days there has been no unusual wildlife, or sights or sounds to inspire a new devotional piece. After a time of study, prayer, and a plea that God would show me something to write about, it occurred to me that maybe I should just "be still and know that He is God." This passage comes from Psalm 46:10, and really hit home with me. I constantly watch the pond hoping to see something God will use to give me a fresh Word to pass along. Maybe I need days like this to be still and rest in Him.

The afternoon sun is glorious as it so often is, the surface of the water is moving slightly in the breeze and the occasional leaf turns loose of its branch and floats ever so gently on that breeze until it lands on the pond. With the movement of the water, the leaf is pushed to and fro, moving so easily that it reminds me of the grace and ease of an ice skater on a frozen winter lake. How calming it is as I rest my gaze upon that leaf, but how much more can God calm me if I will rest and trust in Him?

If you know my Savior Jesus today, you too can find the calming peace that I write about. Isaiah 32:17 says, *"And the work of righteousness shall be peace; and the effect of righteousness quietness and assurance for ever."* There will be other days that God shows me things from the pond, but today is a day to revel in quietness and the assurance of His loving presence and enjoy a peaceful day of sunlight and the breeze of the Spirit in this place.

THE POND

The hymn writer McAfee, in "Near to the Heart of God," speaks about a place of quiet rest, a place of comfort sweet, a place where we our Savior meet, near to the heart of God. That's how I think of the pond, for 'tis where God shows me His heart and quiets mine.

STORMS AND RAINBOWS

As I sit in my chair on the porch I know that the wind is picking up. I see the silvery underside of leaves waving on the hardwood trees, feel the coolness of the breeze, and hear a tree that is out of my line of sight creak and groan as it bends with the wind. A few scattered raindrops hit the pond, making little dimples on the surface.

There are so many aspects of a storm that are exhibitions of God's power. Lightening, with its brilliant light and sharp crackle of noise is like the Father is saying, "Okay, pay attention now." Thunder follows momentarily as if He is clearing his throat, getting ready to speak. And of what does He speak? Conviction, reproof, correction? A God of love that corrects or reproves? Oh yes, because He loves us, and do we not do the same with our children? Then how much more does a righteous and just God handle us, His children, in the same manner?

Take a look at Proverbs 3:12, *"For whom the Lord loveth he correcteth; even as a father the son in whom he delighteth."* Also in Hebrews 12:6, *"For whom the Lord loveth he chasteneth, and scourgeth every son whom he receiveth."* When my children were young and not happy with me over something I would not let them do, I would tell them that the reason I said no was because I loved them and wanted to keep them safe. Our Heavenly Father only wants the same for us. In Revelation 3:19, He goes a bit farther and says we must be zeal-

THE POND

ous and repent. Remember repentance follows confession; therefore when you feel that God is working in your heart by way of reproof, confess it and repent, knowing that He will be faithful to forgive and cleanse you from all unrighteousness.

Always remember that the rainbow comes after the storm! I like this verse from a poem by Joyce Guy:

> I see the brilliant rainbow,
> Reflection of His tender care;
> And know that throughout the storm
> He was standing, guarding there.

SWEET FREEDOM

When I first saw the pair of ducks they were already airborne, flying quickly from the pond. I had frightened them off the water as I pulled into the yard in the late afternoon. Such a majestic sight, these two, strongly winging it up higher and higher. Pure freedom is what I was reminded of as they flew. No bonds held them on earth, no tethers kept them trapped. No, they were free, flying completely unfettered and effortlessly away from me.

Jesus offers freedom from the things that bind us. From John 8:36, *"If the Son therefore shall make you free, ye shall be free indeed."* From what do we need to be freed? That is different for each of us, it could be an addiction, an abusive relationship, a financial burden or one of a multitude of "prisons" we may find ourselves bound by. Where do we find this freedom? For the answer, look at John 8:32, *"And ye shall know the truth and the truth shall make you free."* I do not think it a coincidence that Jesus refers to Himself as "the Way, the *truth*, and the Life" in John 14:6.

So simple is this thought: Jesus is the Truth, the Truth shall make you free, therefore Jesus sets us free! This freedom also requires we serve one another and this we find in Galatians 5:13, *"For, brethren, ye have been called unto liberty; only use not liberty for an occasion to the flesh, but by love serve one another."* Farther down in verses 19–21, the Apostle Paul goes on to explain the works of the flesh.

Today, if you are a Christian and find yourself in shackles, get alone with God and confess the sin that has you imprisoned. Because of the shed blood of Jesus, He is at the right hand of the Father interceding for you. God's Word tells us that if we will confess our sin, He will be faithful to forgive. If, however, you do not have a relationship with Christ, you can change that in the blink of an eye.

Romans 10:9–10 tell us how to be saved: *"That if thou shalt confess with thy mouth the Lord Jesus, and shalt believe in thine heart that God has raised him from the dead, thou shalt be saved. For with the heart man believeth unto righteousness; and with the mouth confession is made unto salvation."*

The lyrics in Bill Gaither's hymn "He Touched Me," speak the truth of this devotion today. As is said in the following verse, just the touch of Jesus can change circumstances and bring sweet freedom.

> Shackled by a heavy burden
> 'Neath a load of guilt and shame
> Then the hand of Jesus touched me
> Now I am no longer the same.

THE BIRD FEEDER LESSON

Having received a new cedar bird feeder for Mother's Day, I was anxious to get it hung in the large Bradford pear tree out front. There are three other feeders in its branches, with a bird bath close by and a pretty red outdoor bench that completes this area. I think of as my own "secret garden."

My husband agreed to fix the hanger for me and I proceeded to drag out the birdseed to fill up the feeder when I noticed that the manufacturer's tag said this was an easy to clean feeder. Well, apparently that message didn't apply to the "2 EASY CLEAN FEEDER" stickers that had been pasted to each side of the Plexiglas seed holder compartment! When they didn't easily remove by peeling, I brought them inside to the sink. After a while, with lots of soap and water, I was headed back out to finish this project, but with a bit of sticker remaining on one side. I suppose eventually it will wear away, but it will probably take some time. Maybe with the tree branches as camouflage nobody will notice it anyway.

As Christians, we can be thankful that with God's washing, we don't carry any residue of our "stickers" out into the world. The Psalmist said in Psalm 51:2, *"Wash me thoroughly from mine iniquity, cleanse me from my sin."* While in Acts 22:16 we find, *"And now why tarriest thou? Arise, and be baptized, and wash away thy sin, calling on the name of the Lord."* We can be certain that when we find salvation

THE POND

in Christ Jesus, our sins are washed away by the spilling of His blood on Calvary. We are clean, and our sins though scarlet, will be white as wool.

Do you have that confidence today? Ponder these words of an old hymn, "Nothing but the Blood":

> What can wash away my sin?
> Nothing but the blood of Jesus;
> What can make me whole again?
> Nothing but the blood of Jesus.
>
> —Robert Lowry

THE BRIDGE TO RECONCILIATION

All was quiet as I walked along the pond's edge. Every now and again I would hear the crow's cawing in the distance and a ways off a dog barked. Not any sounds of vehicles along the road or planes in the sky. Just me and God's creation, which made me think about the creation story.

There has been a lot of rain in our area recently and that in turn has brought a good bit of dirt from our yard into the pond. Those two thoughts slowly began to circle in my mind. God formed us in His image from the dust (dirt) of the earth. This comes from Genesis 1:26–27, *"And God said, Let us make man in our image, after our likeness: and let them have dominion over the fish of the sea, and over the fowl of the air, and over the cattle, and over all the earth, and over every creeping thing that creepeth upon the earth. So God created man in his own image, in the image of God created he him; male and female created he them."*

With this story in mind, I imagined how it was on that day, I think it was much like today. God at this time had created everything. Putting a simple and humanistic view on the scene, I see that our Creator Father rocked back on His heels, took a deep breath, and looked around. He was next to a pond with crystal clear water, the surface like glass. Around Him just the animals and birds trying out their voices for the first time. A gentle breeze swept through the trees making a raspy sound as the leaves moved against one another. "Ah," He said, "this is good." But He was not through, this Creator of the earth and everything in it wanted a creature that He could have a relationship with! So this Great God, knelt down and begin to sculpt the dirt into the image of Himself. Carefully and lovingly His hands moved as he formed each part of Man, until finally He leaned over him and into his nostrils blew the breath of life!

Man became a living soul! God still wants a relationship with us today. The way to commune with God is through Jesus Christ, the Son of the Living God. Because of man's disobedience in the Garden of Eden we have been separated from God. Jesus is our bridge back to our Heavenly Father. It is through His shed blood on the Cross of Calvary that God sees us, not in our sinful state but as standing before Him in the righteousness of Christ. Hallelujah and hallelujah!

Which side of that bridge are you on today? Have you made it across and become reconciled with the God that gave you life? In Psalm 139:13–14, we find, *"For thou has possessed my reins: thou hast covered me in my mother's womb. I will praise thee; for I am fearfully and wonderfully made: marvelous are thy works; and that my soul knoweth right well."*

He is waiting to meet you across the bridge; you have only to take the first step.

THE DANCE OF THE HUMMINGBIRDS

This morning I was privileged to witness a wonderfully choreographed ballet at the hummingbird feeder. I had stepped out into the carport and heard the familiar squeak of the tiniest of creatures; the beautiful and joyful little jewels of the air; hummingbirds! I stood stock still while two of them swirled and twirled around the feeder, darting in and out to get a sip of the sweet liquid. I gazed in wonder as this scene played out right before me, wondering how they managed to do all that dancing without colliding into each other. But God is in control, and the scriptures tell us in Matthew 6:26, 28–29, *"Behold the fowls of the air; for they sow not, neither do they reap, or gather into barns; yet your heavenly Father feeds them. Consider the lilies of the field, how they grow; they toil not, neither do they spin. And yet I say unto you that even Solomon in all his glory was not arrayed like one of these."*

    I marveled at this display of God's handiwork this morning and felt that it was created just for me! I was reminded, as I watched my little hummies, that all of creation is His. You can find this in Psalm 24:1, *"The earth is the Lord's, and the fullness thereof; the world, and they that dwell therein."*

    There is such beauty here that I can't fully imagine how glorious the new heaven and new earth will be! Until that day, I am thankful for what I see every day and that in His creation, I can see His hand.

THE POND

    The last stanza of the hymn "For the Beauty of the Earth" completes my thoughts today:
> For each perfect gift of thine to our race so freely given, Graces human and divine, Flow'rs of earth and buds of heav'n: Lord of all to thee we raise this our joyful hymn of praise.

—John Rutter

THE DETERMINED DANDELION

After many long weeks the afternoon is finally pleasant enough for me to do a little porch sitting and pond looking! We are definitely gaining ground toward spring. Already around the pond I see a few little yellow "flowers" beginning to poke up their heads. These "flowers" will soon fade and what replaces them is a puff of white seeds that most all of us have picked and then blown away. If you have guessed this "flower" is a dandelion you are correct! If you have children, most likely you have been presented a bouquet of these little yellow "flowers" by a precious chubby little hand.

The dandelion is a hardy little plant. It can withstand temperatures to negative forty degrees and will grow in any type soil. They will bloom from spring to the start of winter—hardy and determined, as we should be as Christians. If you have ever attempted to rid your lawn of them, it becomes quickly apparent just how determined they are with their bright yellow faces. You just can't get rid of them! We should strive to be so strong in our Christian witness.

Romans 12:2 gives us an example of how to be strong: *"And be not conformed to this world: but be ye transformed by the renewing of your mind, that ye may prove what is that good, and acceptable, and perfect will of God."* We have to withstand hatred in the world just as Jesus did. Isaiah 53:3, foretold of this: *"He is despised and rejected of men; a man of sorrows, and acquainted with grief: and we hid as it were our faces from him; he was despised, and we esteemed him not."* If we are followers of Christ, we too will experience rejection. John 15:18, *"If the world hates you, ye know that it hated me before it hated you."*

Be strong in the Lord. Be like that dandelion that just can't be destroyed. Be stubborn for Christ, and remember the lowly dandelion…if it can't grow where it is, it will just grow somewhere else!

In closing, I would direct you to read Psalm 34:17–22 to assure yourself of God's care and protection as we "dig in" for Him. Verse 22 says it all: *"The LORD redeemeth the soul of his servants: and none of them that trust in him shall be desolate."*

The dandelion by appearance is just a delicate flower, but it has the heart of a stubborn weed. Think on this as you begin to see them popping up this spring.

THE EYES OF GOD

Right before my eyes this morning as I stood at the bay window looking out to the pond a large, red-tailed hawk dipped down over the pond before sailing up to light on a limb on a nearby pine tree. He was so majestic sitting there, ever on the lookout for a meal. The red-tailed hawk is a permanent resident of the Piedmont of North Carolina, so it is not uncommon for them to be seen in the wild. It was, however, the first one I had seen at the pond. The hawk is always looking, always watching.

Thinking along this line brought to mind the fact that our Father always has His eye upon His children. Psalm 121:3–4 we find the promise of His watchful eye. *"He will not suffer thy foot to be moved: he that keepeth thee will not slumber. Behold, he that keepeth Israel shall neither slumber or sleep."* What comfort knowing that nothing will escape the eye of God. His face is always turned toward His people as we see in 1 Peter 3:12, *"For the eyes of the Lord are over the righteous, and his ears are open unto their prayers: but the face of the Lord is against them that do evil."*

To consider that God, the Author of Creation, Sustainer of all life, and Controller of the universe watches over me (and you) so intently is beyond comprehension. But, I am sure glad to know that He does! I have just recently undergone some medical tests, one being a heart cauterization quite to my surprise! My Heavenly Father, however, had His loving eyes on me and I came through without any problem. During my time of need, shock and anxiety He never

THE POND

slept, His eyes were upon me and His ear bent to my prayers and the prayers of my family and friends. I like the ESV version of Proverbs 2:8: *"Guarding the paths of justice and watching over the way of his saints."*

We know that God watches over His own, but He sees not only good but evil as well. From Proverbs 15:3 we see, *"the eyes of the Lord are in every place, beholding the evil and the good."* I shudder to think of the things He saw of me before I was saved. I am thankful that having been saved, my sins are washed away!

Johnny Diaz has penned these lyrics to "God Is Watching," and I think they are a fitting closing to today's devotion. Thank God that He is ever vigilant.

> There is nowhere, nowhere, we escape from Your side
> No valleys too low, no mountains too high
> There is nowhere, nowhere, we escape from your side
> God is here
> God is watching.

THE FIVE *DS* OF SATAN

We were sitting around the outdoor fire pit near the pond's edge, the moon bathing our area in a pale silvery light. In the moonlight the trees closest to the pond could be seen in shadows and the deeper I looked into the woods the darker it became. As we sat quietly the occasional bullfrog sounded in the far recesses of the pond. Suddenly, in the distance I heard what sounded like a cacophony of sirens wailing. As I turned toward my husband, my eyes big as saucers to question him, he began to nod his head and cast a knowing look toward our son. Coyotes! I thought there must have been hundreds of them! That sound was not sirens, but their howls. Sinister, frightening sounds closer than I wanted to know. I've been told the coyotes are plentiful in our area, but I had never seen one. But, they are here, lurking about in the dark distance....prowling and waiting on their prey.

How like the coyotes Satan is! Why, isn't that what he does? In the lives of Christians, he paces and prowls, lurking about in the shadows to catch one unaware and take our eyes off of Jesus. We see these words in 1 Peter 5:8: *"Be sober, be vigilant; because your adversary the devil, as a roaring lion, walketh about, seeking whom he may devour."* Lions lurk, they creep up on their victim and pounce. Christian, take note, Satan's done his best work when he causes one of God's children to stray.

Satan likes to cause us to doubt as he did Eve in the garden of Eden as we see in Genesis 3:1: *"Now the serpent was more subtle*

THE POND

than any beast of the field which the Lord God had made. And he said unto the woman, Yea, hath God said, Ye shall not eat of every tree of the garden?" Eve then confirms what the Lord God had instructed them that they were not to touch it or eat of it. Then I imagine that Satan might have responded like "What! Are you nuts? You won't die." Eve begins to question herself, and we know the rest of the story.

He is a deceiver as we see in 2 Corinthians 4:4 from the Common English Bible: *"The god of this age has blinded the minds of those who don't have faith so they couldn't see the light of the gospel that reveals Christ's glory."*

In Numbers 13:28, after Moses had sent the spies into Canaan they came back to the camp with this report, *"Nevertheless the people be strong that dwell in the land, and the cities are walled, and very great: and moreover, we saw the sons of Anak (giants) there."* After all the things the Israelites saw God do, these findings by the spies were discouraging. Exactly what Satan desired.

Satan causes division. Look at Romans 16:17–18, *"Now I beseech you, brethren, mark them which cause divisions and offences contrary to the doctrine which ye have learned; and avoid them. For they that are such serve not our Lord Jesus Christ, but their own belly; and by good words and fair speeches deceive the hearts of the simple."*

The devil can delay us. Even the apostle Paul knew of this as we see in 1 Thessalonians 2:18, *"Wherefore we would have come unto you, even I Paul, once and again; but Satan hindered us."*

He also wants to defeat us—John 10:10: *"The thief cometh not, but for to steal, and to kill, and to destroy: I am come that they might have life, and that they might have it more abundantly."* Hallelujah! The last of this verse is the answer to each of Satan's ploys. When Jesus gave His life for you and me on the cross, it was Satan that was defeated!

Every day we must put on the full armor of God so that we can continue to defeat our adversary, the devil. Read about the armor in Ephesians chapter 6 and follow it up with James 4:7, *"Submit yourselves to God. Resist the devil, and he will flee from you."*

THE FRUITED VINE

Today, I stopped and studied our grapevine. It is not a pretty sight! It was left to its own devices by the previous owner and over time has gotten out of hand. My husband and I want to prune it back and give it a fresh, new start; we just have not had the time since moving in. That project is a little further down on our "to do" list. As I was discussing this with a friend, she made this statement, "you know you will have fruit only on new growth." Wow! This conversation occurred after a friend at church presented me with Andrew Murray's "The True Vine"—wow again! Are you thinking what I thought? God is leading me to the grapevine, so this afternoon I followed His lead.

The vine coming out of the earth is thick and sturdy and it supports the rest of the vine. When tended, this grapevine would have been beautiful and loaded with fruit. Presently, from this strong supporting base flows a chaos of vines, growing and reaching in every direction, but no fruit is produced.

Let me take you to John's Gospel, chapter 15 in which we find the lesson on the vine and its branches. In the fifth verse, Jesus says, *"I am the Vine, ye are the branches: He that abideth in me, and I in him, the same bringeth forth much fruit: for without me ye can do nothing."* Jesus is the Vine, the sturdy, strong, never-failing support of us, the branches. When we were new Christians, I daresay we were excited and on fire for Christ, most likely producing fruit. Looking back to verse 2, we find out those branches that do not bear fruit are taken away, and those that are bearing fruit are purged in order to bring them into a greater production of fruit. If something is purged, it is removed, and this brings to mind the act of pruning the vine—removal of the dead branches. Are we in need of pruning?

If we are dead in our spirit, no longer producing fruit what happens? John 15:6 says this: *"If a man abide not in me, he is cast forth as a branch, and is withered; and men gather them, and cast them into the fire, and they are burned."* As you contemplate this verse realize that it does not say that God or Jesus cast out these branches, but people do. A Christian that through carelessness has allowed this to happen has affected his testimony negatively.

In closing, verses 7 and 8 tell us how simple it is to avoid being a withered and defunct branch. *"If ye abide in me and my words abide in you, ye shall ask what ye will and it shall be done unto you. Herein is my Father glorified, that ye bear much fruit; so shall ye be my disciples."*

Abide in Him, the True Vine, and be a fruit producer!

THE GEESE'S EXAMPLE

Geese—they add beauty to the pond as they float across the surface. Graceful and regal, they glide together as a group. They move across the water silently aside from an occasional "honk." As I step outside toward the pond they rise as one, flying off in formation in the group. While in flight, the leader is often relieved by another goose when he tires. If one is sick or injured, one or two geese may drop out of formation to help and protect him. They will fly with him till either he dies or is able to fly once again. They honk while flying to encourage the others. While reading these facts, something I have heard over the years came back to mind. How many times have you heard someone say they believed in God, but did not need to be in church to be a Christian? Even saying they could worship in the forest, on the lake, at the beach, or even just sitting in their own living room. This is not a completely false statement, but…to grow in faith, to be encouraged, to be helped by others of like faith, we must be in church with people of like precious faith!

Our Heavenly Father, in His Omniscience, knew that we would struggle with this idea. He knew there would be problems within churches as we are a society of fallen men. There are many people who find it easier not to belong to a church than to try to understand that it is Satan's lie. In Hebrews 10:25, we find this: *"Not forsaking the assembling of ourselves together, as the manner of some is; but exhorting one another: and so much the more as ye see the day approaching."*

Only by God opening our eyes and hearts will we understand the Scriptures. He alone can give that wisdom. James 1:5: *"If any of you lack wisdom, let him ask of God, that giveth to all men liberally, and upbraideth not; and it shall be given him."* And 2 Timothy 3:16–17 reminds us, *"All scripture is given by inspiration of God, and is profitable for doctrine, for reproof, for correction, for instruction in righteousness: That the man of God may be perfect, thoroughly furnished unto all good works."*

On the ground, the group of geese is called a gaggle, in flight they are referred to as a skein, but whether in flight or on the ground we Christians can take a lesson from them. They do not attempt life alone, they are only animals but know the importance and benefits of staying within their group.

If you are a Christian but are not currently a member of a church, I would encourage you to pray for God to lead you to a church that preaches and teaches the Bible as the inspired Word of God. The benefits of belonging will far outweigh trying to live a Christian life on your own.

We begin our walk of faith within a gaggle (on the ground), but will complete it as a skein when we take flight to our eternal home when the Lord Jesus comes back with trumpet sound. I Thessalonians 4:16–17, *"For the Lord Himself shall descend from heaven with a shout, with the voice of the archangel, and with the trump of God; and the dead in Christ shall rise first: Then we which are alive and remain shall be caught up together with them in the clouds, to meet the Lord in the air: and so we shall ever be with the Lord."*

Don't miss the flight!

THE KINGFISHER AND THE FISHER OF MEN

The late afternoon had turned off cool and windy. We were experiencing the ending of weather conditions associated with a category 4 hurricane. My husband and I were standing at the glass door watching the wind, and we noticed a bird atop one of the citronella torches along the pond's edge. After discussing what kind of bird he was, I thought blue jay, but my husband felt that he wasn't blue enough and was pretty certain our visitor was a kingfisher. As we watched, he took flight low over the pond across to the opposite side and landed on top of the duck box. From that vantage point, he proceeded to study the water below just waiting for the right time to strike, and strike he did! Time after time, he dived and came up with a fish. As I stood watching this bird with his amazing speed and accuracy, I thought that this is so like our Heavenly Father.

Jesus is the Fisher of Men. He is just waiting…waiting for that exact moment, the perfect opportunity to strike out and save us from the devil and eternal separation from God. He is always ready and waiting for us to invite Him into our hearts. I imagine Jesus watching each one of us, walking with us daily, and as soon as we utter the words, we are snatched up and set apart as Christians.

In Matthew 4:19, we find these words as Jesus spoke to Simon Peter and Andrew, as He called them to be disciples: *"And He saith unto them, Follow me, and I will make you fishers of men."* Now Jesus couldn't make them fishers of men unless He was *the* fisher of men. Our Lord doesn't stop there. In Matthew 28:19–20, He says, *"Go ye therefore, and teach all nations, baptizing them in the name of the Father, and of the Son, and of the Holy Ghost: Teaching them to observe all things whatsoever I have commanded you; and lo, I am with you always, even unto the end of the world."*

I think there is a twofold lesson here. Not only are we called to teach and baptize, bringing more and more people into the family of God, but Jesus promises that He is always with us, encouraging and renewing our spirits as we as followers of Christ fish for men.

In closing, I leave you with this verse from the hymn "Fishers of Men":

> Cast your nets aside
> and join the battle tide
> He will be your guide
> To make you fishers of men

THE LITTLE DIPPER

The Lord has once again used the tiny hummingbird as inspiration for me. I have to admit that I am mesmerized by them, the way they zoom in to the feeder and flutter all around it. They can be very protective of their space as well, boldly chasing off intruders.

It was a Sunday afternoon, and I was standing fairly close to the feeder, as still as I could be and they were literally zooming around me. One particularly nervous acting little fellow flew up to the feeder and his wings didn't stop beating as he went from spout to spout. I noticed as he drank from each spot he seemed to hover in one place and just dip his long, slender beak in time after time. Dip, dip, dip went his little head and as I was watching, the thought that that is how we must be as Christians with God's word came to mind. Constantly dipping in; that's how we stay nourished.

There are many scriptural references to the need to be in the Word, to study it and recall it. In Deuteronomy 11:18–19, we find, *"Therefore shall ye lay up these my words in your heart and in your soul, and bind them for a sign upon your hand .... and ye shall teach them your children, speaking of them when thou sittest in thine house, and when thou walkest by the way, when thou liest down and when thou riseth up."* Think about that, no time of the day is left unmentioned. We are to keep our minds focused on His Word.

I love this explanation from my Bible commentary: "The Word of God was to be the subject of household conversation. It was to be loved and lived." What an eye-opener and what truth! Christ calls us

THE POND

to love and live our faith. We see this truth in 1 Timothy 4:6: *"If thou put the brethren in remembrance of these things, thou shalt be a good minister of Jesus Christ, nourished up in the words of faith and of good doctrine, whereunto thou hast attained."* Oh, how I desire to be a good minister of Christ, to do so I must continue to dip into His Word.

These dips refresh, recharge and remind me of Him and of who I am…His child!

Finally, I would direct you to Psalm 1:2 as we read, *"But his delight is in the law of the Lord; and in his law doeth he meditate both day and night."* Will you make this your focus today to get deeper into God's Word and see what He has in store for you?

THE MOVING SPIRIT OF GOD

"And the Spirit of God moved upon the face of the waters." This was my thought this cool fall morning as I stepped outside and saw a low lying mist hovering just above the pond. The sun was not quite up, yet there was light enough to see well. No noise could be heard, just this swirling mist that made me wonder if this is what Moses envisioned as he penned day one of the Creation story.

Let's go back to the beginning of Genesis 1:2, where we find this description: *"And the earth was without form and void; and darkness was upon the face of the deep."* In my imagination I see a dark, undefined mass of chaos and nothingness. *Webster's Dictionary* defines *void* as containing nothing.

God's Spirit moved and the chaos and nothingness became the earth and was called good! Along with this change from nothing to something came order. God's order that nothing can change! Think of the sea, how does the tide know just where to stop? The sun and moon know their times, and our earth continues to spin on its axis without our assistance. Our God is an awesome God!

God can do this same thing in a life! Your life or mine—no matter how chaotic, empty and dark we may find ourselves that same Spirit can move upon lives and bring order out of confusion.

THE POND

Will you allow God's Spirit to move in your life and let chaos become good? Would you make these lyrics from Jordan & Kristin Rippy your prayer today?

> Spirit of God
> Move in our hearts
> Change how we think
> And who we are.
> Spirit of God
> Make us like You
> In all we say
> In all we do.

THE ROBE

Over the pond, the day began wet and cold with a strong wind. One of those mornings you just want to stay in bed all snuggled down in the toasty warmth of the quilt or comforter with just the tip of your nose and top of your head to be seen. But not this morning, this was Sunday morning and we needed to be up and about getting ready for church. As my husband and I were standing before the glass doors looking out at the rain as it hit the water, it started to snow! I must admit, I am like a child when it snows. I can hear my mother's words when she used to wake me if it had snowed overnight, "Lucy, have you looked out the window?" In fact, that habit continued into my adulthood and I asked the same question of my children when they were small.

    The flakes were big and fat and as they fell seemed heavy with moisture. As the flakes fell onto the pond, they were absorbed by the water immediately. Although the snow was not sticking it was still a bit of excitement for me. I grabbed my phone and sent a text message to my cousin whose reply was "It covers up the ugliness." Yes! Yes, it does, and I had a thought come into my mind that in much the same way Jesus covers up our ugliness with His shed blood and then we are clothed in a robe of righteousness—a white robe just like the snow. This truth comes from Isaiah 61:10, *"I will greatly rejoice in the Lord, my soul shall be joyful in my God; for he hath clothed me with the garments of salvation, he hath covered me with the robe of righteousness, as a bridegroom decketh himself with ornaments, and as a bride adorneth herself with her jewels."* Only dressed in this robe of righteousness will we be seen by God as clean and pure.

Let's look at another robe reference from Luke 15:22, *"But the father said to his servants, Bring forth the best robe, and put it on him;"* This is from the story of the prodigal son, who as he returns to his father is presented with the best robe, and reading on we find also jewelry, shoes and the fatted calf. Are we not represented by the prodigal son in our coming to Christ?

And lastly, in Revelation 7:9, *"After this I beheld, and lo, a great multitude, which no man could number, of all nations, and kindreds, and people and tongues, stood before the throne, and before the Lamb, clothed with white robes, and palms in their hands."*

There are many more lessons we could draw from the study of robes, but just imagine if you will, a row of white robes hanging, each one on its own hook, awaiting being plucked from the hook and placed about a body. We have a robe waiting for us…if you have accepted Christ as your Savior, then you have been clothed with the first robe, the robe of righteousness. Many of us in our Christian walk, have found ourselves far from God at some time. Upon realizing it and making our way back to God, we are then wrapped in the second robe…the best robe by our Father. The final robe awaits us in heaven as we stand before the Lamb (Jesus) as His redeemed!

Have you claimed your robe from the hanger?

THE SNEAKY SNAKE OF SIN

I knew it was bound to happen, with the pond so near. You may be thinking, *What, what it could be?* Or you may already know.

One Sunday afternoon, I walked out of my back door headed to the car. By the steps next to the screened porch something caught my eye. It was a dreaded snake! I did what any wife would do when her husband isn't at home…I called my neighbor. Thank goodness he was ready and willing to come over and help a damsel in distress!

God has used this experience to show me how that snake represents sin, and how that sin can quickly and quietly invade a calm and serene being. A mere two hours before, I was standing in that same spot watching my hummingbirds…happy and secure in my surroundings.

As Christians, we must be ever on our toes. We must not get complacent in our faith, but as 1 Peter 5:8 tells us, *"Be sober, be vigilant; because your adversary the devil, as a roaring lion, walketh about seeking whom he may devour."*

Every day, I look toward that area checking for another slithery visitor, but what are the odds that another one would come to that same place? Satan can be the same way. Don't expect him to show himself the same way, in the same place every time. He is sneaky and deceptive. Don't let him catch you unaware.

THE POND

The following prayer really speaks to this lesson. Won't you make it your prayer today?

> *Sovereign God and Heavenly Father, give me an alert and discerning mind so no sinful or deceitful thought can take root. I need Your Spirit to be the gatekeeper of my mind and Your Word to be my shield. Please show me any sinful habit that is growing in my life; I want to serve You, and You alone.*

THE TEMPTATION

One Friday afternoon my husband was off from work and he decided to get out early that morning to cut grass. After working for a couple of hours, he took a break, parking the mower under the shade of the Bradford pear in the front yard. This particular tree has all my birdfeeders hanging in it and as he was heading toward the house, he heard a noise that caused him to stop and investigate. What he found was a small bird trapped inside one of the feeders. The glass had slipped out of position and she just wriggled herself right inside. What a better place to be than right there with all that tasty birdseed!

Of course, he took the feeder down right away and released her to go on her merry way. I'm thankful he was home and noticed her in the feeder. God used this to bring to my mind the way Satan traps us. The Bible tells us that Satan is an angel of light in 2 Corinthians 11:14. And in John's Gospel, we find that Satan, the thief, comes to steal, and kill and destroy. I immediately associated things in my life to this trapped bird. That birdseed was almost her undoing. It was what tempted her, and in the end, could have meant her life. There are things that tempt us, things that are attractive to us and Satan will use those things to try and draw us in and away from Jesus. Satan does his best work when he can lure a Christian from his walk with the Lord.

What things have been to you like the birdseed was to this little bird? Money, cars, antiaging products? Anything Satan can use to entice us he will, but if we belong to the King, we have assurance that we can't be plucked from His hand. This promise is found in John 10:28, 29.

In closing, be reminded: *"For Christ also hath **once** suffered for sins, the just for the unjust that he might bring us to God, being put to death in the flesh, but quickened by the Spirit"* (1 Pet. 3:18).

THE UNSEEN SEES

From my vantage point—be it the kitchen, screened porch or the bay window—each time I look out across the pond I can see my husband's hunting blind. This structure is camouflaged so that it blends right in with the surrounding woods. He becomes invisible as he sits inside and the animals are not even aware of his presence. He sees everything that goes on in his little spot in the woods!

Just as he sees everything but is unseen, God sees and knows all things. Hebrews 4:13 says, *"Neither is there any creature that is not manifest in His sight; but all things are naked and opened unto the eyes of him with whom we have to do."* Unlike Brooks, God does not hide Himself for the purpose of entrapment or capture but for our protection. According to the Scriptures, we cannot gaze upon God and live. This is from Exodus 33:20 after Moses had asked God to show him His glory, God says, *"Thou canst not see my face: for there shall no man see me, and live."* The next few verses go on to explain that God placed Moses in the cleft of the rock and covered him with His hand as He passed by. Moses was able to only see God's back for His glory is too great for us to see with human, mortal eyes.

Is there anywhere God is not? Is there anywhere God does not see? No! This truth comes from Jeremiah 23:24, *"Can any hide himself in secret places that I shall not see him saith the Lord? Do not I fill heaven and earth saith the Lord?"* In the story of Jonah, he tells us that from the belly of Sheol, he cried and the Lord heard him (Jonah 2:2).

THE POND

What a comfort to know God is with us everywhere, in the best of circumstances or the worst of situations. What love He has for us! A beautiful picture comes from Psalm 139:8: *"If I ascend up into heaven, thou art there: if I make my bed in hell, behold, thou art there."*

No situation is too bad for God's presence to abide with you. As you study these verses, allow His spirit to minister to you, no matter where you are today.

THE WONDER OF WATER

I am drawn to the water. The water of the pond, a lake, the ocean. I stand at the pond now in the quietness of early evening, as the darkness closes in and the chill increases. The pond is silent, the water still and yet I stand and watch.

Water, what is its pull on us? Physically, we cannot do without it; spiritually it is necessary to us as well. I would like you to consider with me Jesus and water. Beginning this train of thought with the following quote by Jenny Phillips will hopefully get us into the mindset for today's lesson. *"We drink water to nourish our bodies. We drink the wine of communion to nourish our spirits, and we are baptized with water as a symbol of transformation and redemption. Just as Christ transformed water into wine, through the cross He transformed His lifeblood into cleansing, redemptive, living water."*

I believe there are five points on which we can compare Jesus and water. First, water is a carrier; Jesus carries us. Galatians 2:20: *"I am crucified with Christ: nevertheless I live; yet not I but Christ liveth in me:"* If Christ is in me, then He must be carrying me! Second, water removes waste; Jesus removes our waste when we invite Him into our hearts. First John 1:7: *"But if we walk in the light, as He is in the light, we have fellowship with one another, and the blood of Jesus Christ his Son cleanseth us from all sin."* Third, water transports; Jesus is our transport. Ecclesiastes 12:7: *"Then shall the dust return to the earth as it was: and the spirit shall return unto God who gave it."* Fourth, water is a regulator. Jesus is our regulator, the rule maker, and the One by which we can follow the rules. James 2:8, *"If ye fulfill the royal law according to the scripture, Thou shalt love thy neighbor as thyself, ye do well."* The fifth and final point is that water is a lubricant and lessens friction. Doesn't knowing Jesus lessen friction in our lives? Colossians 3:12–13: *"Put on therefore, as the elect of God, holy and beloved, bowels of mercies, kindness, humbleness of mind, meekness, longsuffering; Forebearing one another, and forgiving one another, if any man have a quarrel against any: even as Christ forgave you, so also do ye."*

Only Jesus can provide this endlessly flowing stream of Living Water. In the Gospel of John, chapter 4, is the account of Him meeting the Samaritan woman at the well. It is there that she received the wellspring of Jesus! Read the account of this encounter, concentrating on verses 13–14, which say, *"Jesus answered and said unto her, Whosoever drinketh of this water shall thirst again: But whosoever drinketh of the water that I shall give him shall never thirst; but the water that I shall give him shall be in him a well of water springing up into everlasting life."*

Are you thirsty today? Take a drink from the fountain that will never run dry—Jesus!

THREE IS THE NUMBER

Gazing out at the pond in the golden morning light I thought about the fact that the majority of the devotions I have written for "the pond" are about life *around* the pond. Today I was struck with the notion that while yes indeed life abounds in, on and around the pond; the pond itself represents life.

The number of components of the pond is three; the bottom, the water and the air. The pond is circular in shape and these features together present a picture of God to me. Now I am certain you are wondering about this comparison. A pond…God…?

We recognize that God is a triune God, meaning there are three persons represented—God the Father, God the Son, and God the Holy Spirit. In the Old Testament, we see a number of examples of men who were counted righteous because they believed and obeyed God. You can read about this in Hebrews chapter 11. Because of sin, we are separated from God. Jesus's death on the cross has provided a way back to God and once we accept Jesus into our hearts and believe on Him, He sends the Holy Spirit to live within us.

Looking now at the pond, I see the bottom as the foundation (God), and the air represents the Holy Spirit. Just as the Spirit lives within us, we live within this air God has provided. What now, bridges the gap, the distance between the two? That water! Water equals Jesus, and without going through the water, we can't get to the bottom and from the bottom we must go through the water to get air. And what do you know, Jesus calls Himself the Living Water!

THE POND

John 4:14: *"But whosoever drinketh of the water that I shall give him shall never thirst; but the water that I shall give him shall be in him a well of water springing up into everlasting life."*

I also made mention of the shape of the pond, round, circular, and never-ending. God's love is a never-ending love, and we see this in Psalm 36:5: *"Your steadfast love, O Lord, extends to the heavens, your faithfulness to the clouds"* (ESV). A. W. Pink says concerning this verse, "Far above all finite comprehension is the unchanging faithfulness of God. He never forgets, never fails, never falters, and never forfeits His Word. To every declaration of promise or prophecy the Lord has exactly adhered."

I was awestruck by this revelation from God today! I pray that you know this fount of Living Water that stands in the gap for those who are saved by His grace and mercy.

One of my favorite hymns is "Holy, Holy, Holy" written by Reginald Heber, and I close with the first verse for your meditation.

> Holy, holy, holy! Lord God Almighty!
> Early in the morning our song shall rise to Thee;
> Holy, holy, holy, merciful and mighty!
> God in three Persons, blessed Trinity!

TURTLES IN THE SUN

It was a brilliant sunshiny afternoon. One of those early spring days that tease you with a hint of summer to come. I could hear the bullfrogs' loud droning, birds calling and just a whisper of a breeze through the pine boughs. On the eastern side of the pond, I noticed a couple of turtles out on a log, sunning themselves. Perfect components to create a lazy afternoon! On really warm days they will spend hours just parked on a log or the side of the bank soaking up the sun's rays. I was curious as to why turtles bask in the sun. A little research told me that basking actually strengthens the turtle's shell and helps to reduce the amount of algae that might grow on the shell, keeping the shell clean and the turtle healthier.

My mind immediately began to whirl. What happens when we Christians bask in the glow of the Son? Oh yes! We are strengthened and cleaned, just like my turtles. Jesus does strengthen us as we see in Philippians 4:13: *"I can do all things through Christ which strengtheneth me."* Let's also look at Ephesians 6:10 for another word of this truth: *"Finally, my brethren, be strong in the Lord, and in the power of His might."* God will and does use people and situations to make us strong, but be mindful that ultimately the strength comes from Him. Not only does our Father strengthen us emotionally and spiritually, but physically as well. I find this in Philippians 4:19: *"But my God shall supply all your needs according to his riches in glory by Christ Jesus."*

How are we cleaned as we bask in Jesus? Take a look at 1 John 1:7: *"But if we walk in the light as he is in the light, we have fellowship one with another, and the blood of Jesus Christ his Son cleanseth us from all sin."* Jesus is the light as we see here; walking with him enables us to fellowship with the Son and the Father. By the shed blood of Jesus we are cleansed! In the Old Testament, Ezekiel 36:25, also speaks of cleansing: *"Then will I sprinkle clean water upon you, and ye shall be clean: from all your filthiness, and from all your idols, will I cleanse you."* Remember that Jesus refers to himself as the Living Water, and think of Him as the water being used here to cleanse.

We have been bought with a price; we are to glorify God in our body and in our spirit (1 Cor. 6:20). We must acknowledge that our strength comes from the Lord, and that we are refined only by the precious blood of Jesus that was shed on the cross for our sins.

As you bask in the glory and joy of Jesus your Savior, remember to be still and know that He is God (Ps. 46:10).

UNCHANGED AND IN CONTROL

This evening as I was coming home from running a few errands, the driveway straightened to allow me to get the pond in full sight and I was once again amazed at the power and might of God. Still high enough in the sky to be seen above the tree tops was the biggest, brightest, and most perfect circle of sun in an otherwise empty predusk sky. Just hanging there, no wires or duct tape, steadily in place as if held there by God's invisible hand. And my thought was, control. He is in control! God set the stars, moon, and sun in place in the heavens as we read in Genesis 1:16–17.

Isaiah 45:6 says, *"That they may know from the rising of the sun, and from the west, that there is none beside me. I am the Lord, and there is none else."* This God, who created the lights in the heavens, the majestic mountains and seas, then knelt down and formed man and oh so gently breathed into man the breath of life, was and is in control. Notice in the scripture above; He says, "I am the Lord." That, my friend, is in the present tense! Look also at Job 12:10: *"In whose hand is the soul of every living thing, and the breath of all mankind."*

We all have times that we feel out of control and when those times come, remember that God is the same yesterday, today, and tomorrow. Whatever comes your way, never doubt that He is aware of what is going on, for He isn't tied to time as we are, but He has looked down through time until that day of your trials, and He is not caught off guard!

My go-to verse in many situations is Romans 8:28: *"And we know that all things work together for good to them that love God, to them that are called according to His purpose."*

I pray this assurance is yours today. If you aren't certain, or you know that you do not have this surety of salvation, your circumstance can be quickly and easily changed. Study Romans 10:9–10 and you too can be a child of the King!

UNCHANGING PROMISES

Even though the afternoon was cold and gray, I took advantage of an afternoon off early from work and grabbed an afghan, threw it around my shoulders and headed out onto the porch. The weather had changed rapidly, earlier in the day the sun was shining brightly and the temperature was comfortable just in a long sleeve tee shirt. The pond was calling. The wind was blowing, gusting fairly strong at times, and it seemed to come from all around me. I watched as the surface of the pond went from still to rough in a matter of moments. The movement of the water changed directions constantly. As I sat wrapped up in my blanket, God spoke into my mind this thought, "I am unchanging."

What a comforting thought when all we see is change. Families change; there are changes in jobs, finances, and health. Changes in people as we have all seen our society's morals and ethics take a downhill turn. There are even changes in the church. What or who does not change? Only God does not change, further, He will not change. He tells us as much in Malachi 3:6, *"For I am the Lord, I change not."*

God has always been and will always be as we see in Hebrews 1:10–11: *"And Thou, Lord in the beginning hast laid the foundation of the earth; and the heavens are the works of thine hands: They shall perish; but thou remainest."*

But what happens when those winds of change hit us, God's children? Do we then have doubt, anger, and questions? Might we even be found unfaithful at times? God is faithful even when we are not. He is faithful and will not go back on His promise to forgive us when we confess and repent. This truth can be found in many places in scripture, but I like what is said in 1 John 1:9: *"If we confess our sins, he is faithful and just to forgive us our sins, and to cleanse us from all unrighteousness."* Thanks be to God!

In life, winds may blow us off course; but if we know the Navigator, we also know what it takes to get back on track.

In closing, I leave you with these words from the hymn by R. Kelso Carter, "Standing on the Promises":

> Standing on the promises that cannot fail,
> When the howling storms of doubt and fear assail,
> By the living Word of God I shall prevail,
> Standing on the promises of God.

UNCOMFORTABLE BUT STRENGTHENED

My husband was buzzing around the pond in our golf cart with Silas dancing and prancing just ahead of him. Silas, our German shepherd, loves the afternoons that his "Dad" takes him along when he goes out to check the wild game camera has mounted on a tree on the far side of the pond. It's not unusual for Silas to take a dip in the pond during the hot days of summer, but this particular afternoon was anything but hot. As I watched, Silas waded into the pond! Oh, how cold that water must have been, but even so, he did not exit the pond quickly. Of course, I quickly inhaled as if I had stepped into that cold water myself. How uncomfortable stepping into the water would have been for me. I would have chosen not to take that step.

Wow, that thought hits home! How often I have not taken a step because it would make me uncomfortable? As Christians, we will be uncomfortable in this world. The world does not want Jesus; therefore if we are following His example and doing what He asks of us, we can expect to have to step out of our comfort zone.

First we are asked to deny ourselves as we see in Matthew 16:24: *"Then said Jesus unto his disciples, If any man will come after me, let him deny himself, and take up his cross, and follow me."* Take up my cross? This means the willingness to endure shame, suffering and perhaps martyrdom for His sake. To follow Him means to live as He lived; in humility, poverty, with compassion, love and grace.[5] That is way beyond my comfort zone!

He also asks those who follow Him to not be concerned with the future. Look at Luke 12:22: *"And he said unto his disciples, Therefore, I say unto you, Take no thought for your life, what ye shall eat; neither for the body, what ye shall put on."* How often do we hear that we must prepare for the future?

There are many ways we may be called into an uncomfortable situation as a Christian. It could be helping feed the homeless at a soup kitchen or participating in a prison ministry. Maybe it's associating with people that society looks down on such as working in a halfway house or with unwed and pregnant teens. Some are called as missionaries to a foreign land, and lastly, just the act of sharing Christ with an unsaved friend or family member can find us most uncomfortable.

None of these can we do on our own, but only with Christ in our hearts. Before we can love others, we must realize His love for us and harbor the love of Christ within ourselves. Philippians 4:13 attests to this as it says, *"I can do all things through Christ which strengtheneth me."*

We have a challenge, be we also have a strength at our disposal that is like none other! Will you step into the uncomfortable with Christ?

---

[5] Believers Bible Commentary

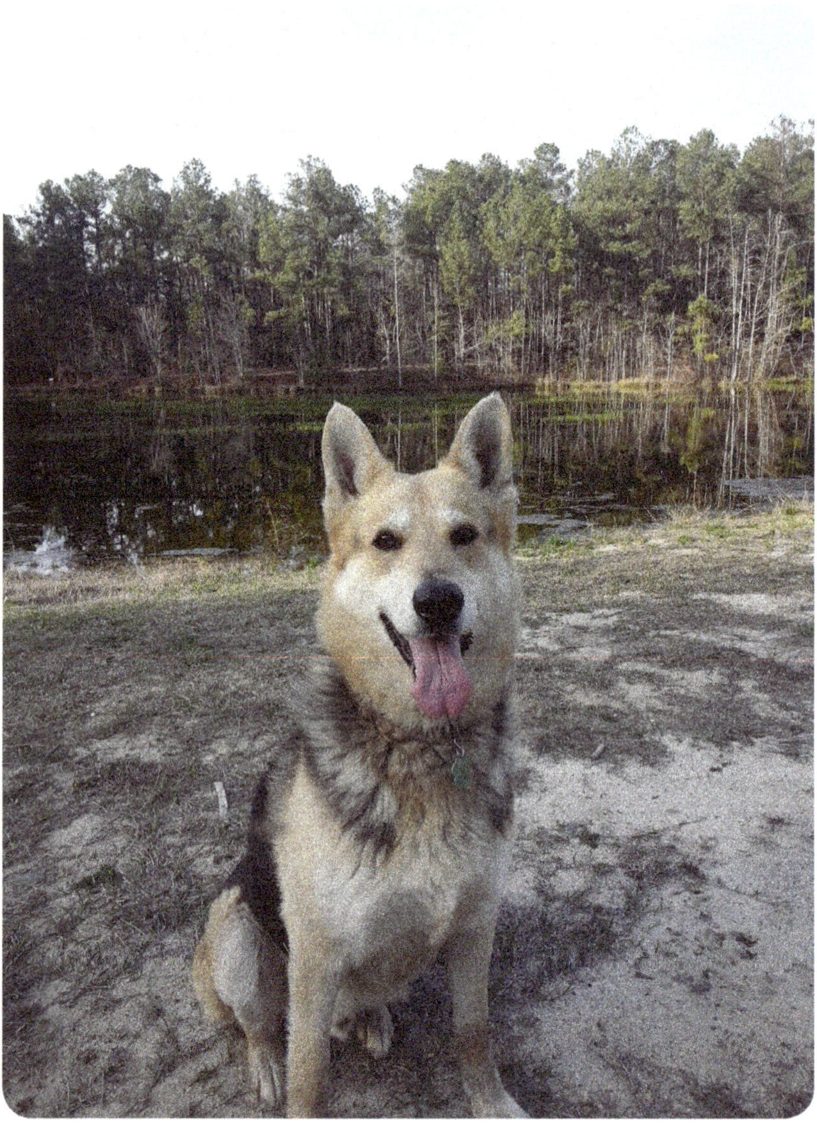

VICTORY

Something disturbs the water in the pond ever so slightly. Just enough to notice movement. What is stirring just beneath the surface? Taking a casual glance, one may not even be aware of this slight motion of an otherwise still pond.

I think about what manner of aquatic creature might be lurking about, far enough under the surface that I can't see. The story of Jonah comes to mind. Although the waters were turbulent on the day that Jonah was on the ship to Tarshish, I can only wonder what was going through his mind as he told the sailors to toss him overboard to calm the seas. I imagine he too wondered what was just under the surface of the water that was waiting to receive him.

Even though Jonah was running from the mission the Lord had given him, God protected him in his disobedience. Rather than allowing Jonah to perish in that raging sea, He sent a great fish to swallow Jonah and he spent three days and three nights in the belly of that fish. In Jonah 2:2–9, read Jonah's prayer to Jehovah God. In verse 9 he says, *"But I will sacrifice unto thee with the voice of thanksgiving; I will pay that that I have vowed. Salvation is of the Lord."* Considering all that Jonah experienced from the time he boarded the ship until the Lord caused the fish to vomit him out onto dry land, Jonah expresses thanksgiving! And he realized that his salvation came from the Lord.

Do we, when we have trials and tribulations, still give thanks? My reminder comes from 2 Corinthians 15:57: *"But* thanks be to *God, which giveth us the victory through our Lord Jesus Christ."*

WE HAVE A MANSION

It was an unseasonably warm December day, so after lunch my husband, Brooks, decided he should take advantage of it and fish a while. He brought out all of his fishing equipment and let Silas, our German shepherd, out to roam about. As I sat on the back porch watching and doing a little writing, I recalled something my friend Kathy said to me. In a conversation about my working on *The Pond*, she mentioned it would be a good idea for me to walk around the pond, noting differences in locations and scenery. What a better time to take a walk than right then, so I began my trek along to the far side of the pond.

How right she was! I took notice of the direction of the ripples across the surface, they were moving east to west. Normally, what I see is the north to south movement. From the back porch I can see several white "things"…On closer examination, I found they were old stumps quite covered in mushrooms. Even though we're into December, there are several bunches of still red leafed growths, along with numerous tiny and very delicate ferns. A whole other world than what I see daily.

I continued on to the opposite side and turned to look back across the pond toward our house. What a welcoming sight that was! Home! Waiting for me whenever I got back. As the afternoon turned to dusk the lights inside glowed warm and inviting through the windows. Similar to a Thomas Kincaid painting, you know the ones… golden lights shining bright from every window.

As I gazed upon the sight, the old hymn "I've Got a Mansion" came into my mind. The chorus goes this way:

> I've got a mansion just over the hilltop
> In that bright land where we'll never grow old
> And some day yonder we will never more wander
> But walk on streets that are purest gold.

This is not just in the songwriter's imagination. God has prepared a place for those called by His name. His children, followers of Jesus Christ. We see this in John 14:2, *"In my Father's house are many mansions: if it were not so I would have told you. I go to prepare a place for you."* This is spoken by Jesus to the disciples at the Last Supper. In later verses He goes on to say that He will come back for us, so that we may reside with Him for eternity. What a beautiful picture!

The home I saw today across the expanse of the pond, is not my permanent home. No, I have a place already prepared for me in Heaven with God the Father and Jesus Christ. Someday, as I step from this life into life eternal I will see that mansion waiting for me.

Is your home in heaven? I pray that it is, but if you are not certain today, know that in an instant that assurance can be yours. Study John 14:23: *"Jesus answered and said unto him, If a man love me, he will keep my words and my Father will love him, and we will come and make our abode with him."* Love the Lord Jesus Christ and believe in Him and you will be saved. Your mansion will be ready for you!

WEB OF LIES

There hanging between two trees was the most perfect spider web I think I've ever seen. It was early morning, the sun at just the right angle to light it up enough to get a glance of the sparkle of dew drops that still clung to the silky, delicate creation. I will have to admit the thought did cross my mind how thankful I was to have seen it there before walking face-first into it! But how often does that happen, that we unknowingly walk face-first in Satan's web?

Spider's webs can be so perfect and beautiful that they fool us into thinking that they are a work of art. Satan's webs are that and much more. Remember what we see in scripture, Satan is a thief. John 10:10 speaks to this: *"The thief cometh not, but to steal, and to kill and to destroy."* We must be diligent to stay in the Word and prayer so as to not fall for the lies of Satan. First Peter 5:8 tells us, *"Be sober, be vigilant; because your adversary the devil, as a roaring lion, walketh about seeking whom he may devour."*

In chapter 6 of Ephesians, we find Paul's teaching of the armor of God and the necessity of putting in on daily, because of what is stated in verse 12, *"For we wrestle not against flesh and blood, but against principalities, against powers, against the rulers of the darkness of this world, against spiritual wickedness in high places."*

In closing, I have chosen an excerpt from Maureen Lefanue's poem, "Put on the Full Armor of God."

Put on the Full Armor of God,

LUCY ALLEN

So you can stand against the Devil's schemes.
Our struggle's not against flesh and blood,
That on the surface seems.
It's against the powers of darkness
And spiritual forces of evil,
So put on the full armor of God
To protect you from the Devil.

WHO I AM

The night sky took my breath away. The moon was nearly full and the stars seemed bright and close enough to touch. These orbs of light hanging in a velvety black sky illuminated the pond. The light from the moon bouncing off the water's surface made the night seem magical. Just warm enough for the crickets to hum a little I was tempted to take a seat and take in the night. The water moved in ripples and made the moonlight appear to dance across the pond. I could have been easily fooled into believing this was an early spring night. The slight breeze that caressed my arms had a chill that caused me to recall that it was after all, still winter.

I realized looking up into that great expanse of nighttime sky, just how small and insignificant I seemed. Am I too small for God to know me, to know about me? Absolutely not! Look at Psalm 8:3–6: *"When I consider thy heavens, the work of thy fingers, the moon and the stars, which thou hast ordained; What is man that thou art mindful of him? And the son of man that thou visitest him? For thou hast made him a little lower than the angels, and hast crowned him with glory and honour. Thou madest him to have dominion over the works of thy hands; thou has put all things under his feet."* Wow! We are just a little lower than angels, crowned with honor and glory and have dominion over *all* things.

From Jeremiah, we know that our Father has plans for us. Here in Jeremiah 29:11, we find, *"For I know the thoughts that I think toward you, saith the Lord, thoughts of peace, and not of evil to give you an expected end."* Let's look on to verse 12: *"Then shall ye call upon me, and ye shall go and pray unto me, and I will hearken unto you."* He will hearken unto us, He who hung the moon and the stars in the night sky and holds them there with His hand, promises to incline His ear to us when we call upon Him. Suddenly, I don't feel quite so insignificant any longer. God knows me, has a plan for me, and has thoughts of peace for me.

God also knows you; He has a plan for your life and desires peace for you. There is, however, a great divide between God and man until one invites Jesus Christ into the heart as Savior and Lord. This invitation serves as a bridge and closes that distance. There is no one else by which we can gain salvation. Acts 4:12: *"Neither is there salvation in any other: for there is none other name under heaven given men, whereby we must be saved."*

Call on that name, that wonderful name, the name of Jesus, close the distance between you and God and allow Him to fulfill His plan in your life.

WINDSWEPT

Midmorning on this cold and windy day, I dared not take a step out to the pond but chose rather to watch through the glass doors in the breakfast area. There were three ducks on the pond, and I must admit, I am amazed that they managed not to freeze off their tail feathers! Those ducks were moving very swiftly across the pond pushed along by the wind. If I could see below the water's surface, I wonder if I would see their feet paddling like mad trying to stay in control?

Do you ever feel that you are being pushed along, having little control in today's world? It can be easy to get swept up in the goings on in life. And remember that Satan's lie is to make you think those things that have your attention are good things. Maybe an activity that the family does together, allowing that precious family time, but perhaps that activity is in opposition to attending worship service or another church activity where God's Word is taught. What seems a good thing has us right where Satan wants us...away from God!

What if you find yourself in the tide of the world? We know that it can be hard to go against the tide, and once swept out, well, it requires some effort to work our way back to shore. First, be reminded that whatever the temptation, there is a way out. Look at 1 Corinthians 10:13: *"There hath no temptation taken you but such as is common to man: but God is faithful, who will not suffer you to be tempted above that ye are able; but will with the temptation also make a way to escape, that ye may be able to bear it."* What a promise!

Temptation is common to man. God knows all about it, and even in the temptation He will provide a way out.

There are trials and temptations in the world, if we are not careful, things that we go through can consume our time, our minds. We can become obsessed with finding a solution, a cure, an answer. But, for those in Christ, there is peace amidst the trial. This truth is from John 16:33 as Jesus is talking to his disciples: *"These things I have spoken unto you, that in me ye might have peace. In the world ye shall have tribulation: but be of good cheer;* I have overcome the world*"*(emphasis mine). I know of no one else that can make that claim. Only Jesus can give us peace in an out of control situation.

If you have realized that you are being swept along out of control, by whatever is represented by strong winds in your life, you need only call for Jesus in faith. See in James 1:6: *"But let him ask in faith, nothing wavering. For he that wavereth is like a wave of the sea driven with the wind and tossed."*

We don't have to go through life windswept and tossed about. Call out in faith.

A DETERMINED WOODPECKER

As I was leaving for work one morning, I stopped before getting into my car and took a look around the pond checking for any wildlife that might have been out and about. Although I saw nothing, I did hear the rata-tat-tat of a woodpecker. I directed my gaze to the tallest trees and sure enough, I spied him sitting on a limb high up in a pine tree. I wondered how long he had already been tapping and also how much longer would he continue knocking on that tree. I would guess the answer depended on whether the wood was a bit soft or really hard as to how soon he reached the innermost and desired area of the tree.

The scripture from Revelation 3:20 came to my mind. It says, *"Behold, I stand at the door and knock: if any man hear my voice and open the door, I will come in to him, and will sup with him, and he with me."* Have you ever read this verse and wondered, like I did about the woodpecker's patience in knocking? We find the answer in 2 Peter 3:9: *"The Lord is not slack concerning his promise, as some men count slackness; but is longsuffering to us-ward, not willing that any should perish, but that all should come to repentance."* Did you get that? He is longsuffering toward us and does not want anyone to go into eternity without knowing the Savior! From the Believer's Bible Commentary I pulled this statement, *"He(God) purposely extends the time of grace so that men might have every opportunity to be saved."*

That is love and patience beyond my comprehension.

WORDS OF LIFE

As I got out of my car at home this afternoon, I was treated to the tinkling sounds of my wind chimes that hang from the carport just a short distance from the pond. The temperatures had cooled off as the day ebbed into evening and now there was enough wind to tickle the chimes. It was much too chilly to stand outside and enjoy the musical notes sing off into the air, so I hurried inside and threw open the blinds that impeded my view of the pond. I could stand in the warmth of the kitchen and still hear the chimes as I studied the pond. The sun was now in the western sky, and as the rays reached the opposite side of the pond, where it shone on a few trees that had patches of missing bark on their trunks, it looked like shimmering flames of liquid gold.

I considered my thought from above about the notes singing off into the air. I imagine those notes, tiny cleft notes, sharps and flats, floating around the wind chimes farther and farther out until no longer seen, but forever circling about in the air. Maybe I have a strange imagination! This thought led me to think about the scripture from John 6:63: *"It is the spirit that quickeneth; the flesh profiteth nothing: the words that I speak unto you, they are spirit, and they are life."* Words can live on and on in our minds. Has someone said something hurtful to you that you just can't seem to forget? What about those of us that call ourselves Christian? Have we ever uttered hurtful words that not only keep repeating themselves in the receiver's ear but also continue to haunt the one that spoke them? It is so important to utter words of life instead of words of hurt and discouragement.

God's Word teaches that we are to encourage and build each other up. This truth is found in 1 Thessalonians 5:11: *"Wherefore comfort yourselves together, and edify one another, even as also ye do."* It is important that we fellowship with people of like faith as well as we see in Hebrews 10:25: *"Not forsaking the assembling of ourselves together, as the manner of some is; but exhorting one another: and so much the more, as ye see the day approaching."* We find strength, comfort, encouragement and joy in corporate worship. Do not fall into the temptation to isolate yourselves to avoid reproach or suffering making oneself a secret disciple. We all need words of life and encouragement.

I would challenge us all to recall the words of the old hymn "Wonderful Words of Life"[6] to help keep this thought in our minds. The chorus is, "Beautiful words, wonderful words, wonderful words of life." As we are involved with others may we speak "wonderful words of life."

---

[6] Hymn by Phillip P. Bliss

AS A BUTTERFLY

As I sat enjoying another gorgeous afternoon on the back porch, I caught sight of a butterfly out over the pond. Probably too early for butterflies but perhaps this one was a bit confused since we have had such warm temperatures recently. I'd walked around the edge of the pond before I decided to sit down and just absorb some late-afternoon sun and while I walked I noticed the fish were active, popping the surface and leaving ever widening ringlets as they broke the water's surface. Just about the time I got settled in my chair, I heard the whistle of the wood duck and looked up just in time to see him as he shot out of the duck box up above the treetops on what I supposed was a mission to find dinner. Creatures are stirring as the sun sets on the pond.

    My mind goes back to the butterfly, the first one of the season, and as I consider how the butterfly is formed, I am amazed that God would bring this to me at Easter. To make the science of the butterfly's transformation simple, I will just remind you that a caterpillar spins a cocoon and it is within that cocoon that the metamorphosis takes place. What exits the cocoon is a completely new creature! This is what happens when we are saved by grace and accept Jesus Christ as our Lord. Look at 2 Corinthians 5:17: *"Therefore if any man be in Christ, he is a new creature; old things are passed away; behold, all things are become new."* We will be seen as new in appearance and action.

    Easter is the season of new birth, the season of transformation. Jesus was put to death on the cross, dead and buried, even having a stone rolled against the opening of the tomb to prevent the theft of His body. During the miracle of miracles Jesus was transformed from His human body to a body incorruptible and not bound by this earth. Luke 24:34, 36–37: *"Saying, The Lord is risen indeed, and hath appeared to Simon. (36) And as they thus spake, Jesus himself stood in the midst of them and saith unto them, Peace be unto you. But they were terrified and affrighted, and supposed that they had seen a spirit."*

As believers, if we are still living when Christ returns we too shall be changed. See 1 Corinthians 15:52 for this scriptural truth: *"In a moment, in the twinkling of an eye, at the last trump: for the trumpet shall sound, and the dead shall be raised incorruptible, and we shall be changed."* From the worm of sinful man to the beauty of a new creature; the butterfly.

Revelation 1:7 concludes today's devotion and depending on our stance with Christ, we will either be looking forward to this time or looking at it with dread. *"Behold, he cometh with clouds; and every eye shall see him: and all kindreds of the earth shall wail because of him. Even so, Amen."*

CLOSING THOUGHTS

These reflections are truly gifts from God, as is the pond itself. It brings peace and tranquility to me, and my prayer is also to whomever reads this collection of writings. May you experience the calmness, hear the wind and pond noises and feel the storms as you read.

Much appreciation and love goes to my husband, who has been my biggest supporter and cheerleader, to my children who've been subjected to read them again and again. To the friends who knew I was working on this project, thank you for not laughing at me.

Finally, a huge thank you to my friend, prayer partner, encourager, and sister in Christ, Kathy Crouch. Thanks for the help and guidance and for reading each and every devotion. For the help in preparing the first seventy-five paperback copies of *The Pond* for the ladies of Crestview Baptist Church. Her poem "The Pond" is included in this collection and she has captured exactly my feelings and thoughts as I worked on this project.

In everything, you'll find God's hand if only you are willing to be still and know that He is God. (Psalm 46:10) In several of the devotions, there are scripture references for those that may not know Jesus as Savior and Lord. If that is you, I would encourage you to take the time to reread them and let Jesus speak to your heart. Salvation is simple, just believe on Him as the one who bore your sin, died in your place, was buried, and whom God resurrected. His resurrection powerfully assures that the believer can claim everlasting life when Jesus is received as Savior.

THE POND

You may want to follow with a simple prayer of salvation:

Heavenly Father,

I know that I am a sinner and my sins have separated me from you. I am truly sorry, and now I want to turn away from my past sinful life toward you. Please forgive me, and help me avoid sinning again. I believe that your son, Jesus Christ, died for my sins, was resurrected from the dead, is alive, and hears my prayer. I invite Jesus to become the Lord of my life, to rule and reign in my heart from this day forward. Please send your Holy Spirit to help me obey You, and to do Your will for the rest of my life.

In Jesus's name I pray. Amen.

If you have made a decision for Christ or would just like to share your thoughts about *The Pond* with me, I would love to hear from you. Let me know how God is working in your life by emailing me at:

lucybythepond@yahoo.com

ABOUT THE AUTHOR

The Pond is the first book for Lucy. She has always felt it easier to write her thoughts and feelings than to vocalize them. Having been in church since childhood, Lucy became a Christian at thirteen years of age. For nearly forty years, Lucy has been a member of Crestview Baptist Church in Rockingham, North Carolina, where she has served in several positions. Most recently, cofacilitating a study of Francis Chan's *Crazy Love*. It was during this study that she realized God was urging her to write things she was encountering at the pond on the family's property. It seemed watching the wildlife and family activities around the pond could teach a spiritual lesson. Thus the devotions began. Lucy's career has always been centered on customer service because of her love for people. It wasn't always so, in the early years Lucy was very shy, a fact she enjoys sharing, and most find it hard to believe. Her desire is to reach people for Christ and she is prayerful that *The Pond* will do just that. Lucy and her husband, Brooks, have been married since 1976 and are the parents of two grown children, both of whom are married. "We have been blessed with two wonderful children and then God saw fit to add to our family a wonderful son-in-law and daughter-in-law," says Lucy. Living in North Carolina allows Lucy to enjoy both the beach and mountains, but she also enjoys traveling outside of her home state when given the opportunity. The family also enjoys boating and fishing when they are not gathered at the Allen home enjoying just being at the pond.

Stafford Library
Columbia College
1001 Rogers Street
Columbia, MO 65216

HISTORY OF THE
MISSOURI METHODIST CHURCH
OF COLUMBIA, MISSOURI
AND ITS COLUMBIA PREDECESSORS

History of the
MISSOURI METHODIST CHURCH
OF COLUMBIA, MISSOURI,
and Its Columbia Predecessors

FRANK F. STEPHENS

Stafford Library
Columbia College
1001 Rogers Street
Columbia, MO 65216

THE PARTHENON PRESS—NASHVILLE, TENNESSEE

Copyright 1965 by
THE MISSOURI METHODIST CHURCH
Library of Congress Catalogue
Card Number 65-63217

Printed and bound in the United States of America

To the ministers who have been my pastors in the Columbia Methodist Church since my arrival in Columbia in 1907, this history is respectfully and affectionately dedicated.

FRANK F. STEPHENS

FRANK F. STEPHENS

Foreword

BISHOP A. FRANK SMITH in his Baccalaureate sermon to the graduates of Southern Methodist University in 1961 said, "A man with little interest in where he has been will have little appreciation for where he is and little sense of direction as to where he is going."

Any member of Missouri Methodist Church in Columbia who appreciatively reads this *"History of The Missouri Methodist Church of Columbia, Missouri, and Its Columbia Predecessors"* by Dean Frank F. Stephens will love his Church more. The reading of this book by our people will make us more useable to God as He would guide and empower us to be a genuine Christian community making its witness for the Gospel in our day and culture.

Frank F. Stephens brings a rare combination of qualities to fruition in this History. He is a competent professional historian, having received his Ph.D. in History from the University of Pennsylvania and having taught, researched and written history at the University of Missouri for 58 years. Then, he has been at the center of the life of this congregation for fifty-eight years —since 1907. Again, he has maintained a close understanding of Methodism as a denomination through all these years, being elected as a delegate to the General Conferences of 1930, 1934, 1938, 1940, and the Uniting Conference of 1939. Lastly, he has spent almost his full time for some three years in doing research for this project and in writing. All this adds up to an extraordinary volume for the History of a local church. If it has any inaccuracy this will be because his modesty prevents the author from giving adequate place to his own life and that of his family in the development of this Church.

It is at my urging and the insistence of the Committee that Dean Stephens has consented to the use of his picture here in the opening pages of this book.

This volume is one of several efforts we of Missouri Methodist Church are making to express our grateful indebtedness to those who have gone before. The *Book of Remembrance,* given by The Reverend Gid J. Bryan as a memorial to his wife, Era Bryan, provides for an impressive and permanent record of all special gifts. A permanent selection has been established in the

Church Library where such items as annually bound copies of our Sunday Bulletins, our weekly mailed *Messengers,* our annual *Directories* of Church Membership and officials, Annual Conference *Journals* and other materials will be carefully preserved. Efforts are extensive not only to keep current Membership Records in proper form but also to keep the best of care of earlier Membership Records and Quarterly Conference Minutes. We are seeking to have paintings made of the five buildings that have housed our congregations. And we are collecting information and pictures so as to make a handsome board with bronze plaques of the names and dates of all our Ministers since the beginnings in the early 1820's. We shall also make a permanent placement of all the pictures of the Ministers that can be secured.

It is my hope that all our people will read this *History of the Missouri Methodist Church of Columbia, Missouri, and Its Columbia Predecessors* and that it will become a cherished volume in all our homes. Joyfully I commend it to you.

MONK BRYAN

Acknowledgments

IN WRITING THIS HISTORY, the author wishes to express his appreciation of the aid given to him by the staff of the Library of the State Historical Society of Missouri. Indeed, many portions of the history could not have been written without material made available from the files of the Library, and the author can never forget the patience and helpfulness of these good friends. Through them he has also been able to receive books and records from the Library of the Central Methodist College at Fayette.

He wishes also to acknowledge his indebtedness for much information from different members of the Missouri Methodist Church. He appreciates the aid given by the secretaries in the office of the church. The present minister, Monk Bryan, read the entire manuscript and gave valuable suggestions. He wishes also to express his appreciation to Jerry Statler, Associate Minister, and to Mrs. G. Ray Ridings, Co-Chairman of the Public Relations Committee, who have worked many hours on securing pictures, reading proof, indexing, and considering layout. The author is also indebted to James W. Schwabe who gave his artistic work for the dust jacket.

Finally, to his wife, Louise I. Stephens, he is grateful for an infinite number of helpful changes.

F.F.S.

Table of Contents

Foreword 7
Acknowledgments 9
I. Origin and Organization of the Methodist Episcopal Church 19
II. Western Expansion of the Church and the Establishment of the Missouri Conference in 1816 .. 23
III. The Missouri Compromise and its Effect upon the Church 27
IV. Building of the Union Church and Organization of Columbia Circuit 29
V. Slavery Questions Divide the Church in 1844. Columbia "goes South" 35
VI. First Methodist Church Building in Columbia 43
VII. The Uneasy Fifties 47
VIII. "Martyrdom in Missouri" 55
IX. Back to Normalcy 63
X. The Columbia Methodist Congregation Outgrows its First Church and Builds its Second 75
XI. Growth of the Church Through the last Third of the 19th Century 85
XII. Building of the Broadway Church 103
XIII. The Broadway Church Moves Forward with Methodism 113
XIV. Growth Circumscribed by Lack of Space 131
XV. The State Assumes Partial Responsibility for Expansion 145
XVI. Construction of the Missouri Methodist Church.. 153
XVII. The Church Through the Great Depression 167
XVIII. Methodism becomes a United Church 179
XIX. Final Settlement of the Building Debts, and Dedication of the Missouri Methodist Church 183
XX. The Church Looks to the Future 193
Appendices:
   I. Church Statistics. Continuation of Table on page 106 207
   II. Broadway Church Pastors and Officers, 1904-1930 209
   III. Some Church Officials, 1930-1965, Missouri Methodist Church 210

IV. Sessions of Missouri Conference
   1. From Its Formation to 1845 212
   2. From formation of M.E. Church,
      South, 1845-1880 213
   3. From 1881 to 1916 215
   4. From 1917 to Uniting Conference of 1939 .. 217
   5. From United Methodism to Reorganization of
      the Missouri Area, 1961 218
   6. From Organization of the Missouri East
      Conference, 1961-1964 218
V. General Conferences, M. E. Church, South 219
VI. Declaration of Union, 1939 220
Index 223

Illustrations

Page

18. John Wesley, founder of Methodism.
20. Francis Asbury, one of the first Bishops.
22. Shiloh Meeting House, where Missouri Conference was organized in 1816.
    McKendree Chapel, where Missouri Conference met in Missouri for the first time, 1819.
30. Top half, Moses U. Payne and William Jewell, co-builders of the Union Church of Columbia in 1837.
    Bottom half, W. W. Redman and Andrew Monroe, early Methodist preachers in Columbia.
42. Top half, first Methodist church building in Columbia, 1852-1870, Sixth and Broadway.
    Bottom half, Berry Hill Spencer, pastor 1852-1854, and J. P. Nolan, pastor, 1866-1867.
81. Second Methodist church building in Columbia, Broadway opposite Hitt Street, 1870-1904.
82. Top half, Bishop Enoch M. Marvin, who dedicated second church in June, 1875.
    Bottom half, J. D. Vincil, pastor, 1870-1873, and secretary of Missouri Conference, 1863-1904, and Thomas J. Gooch, pastor, 1868-1869.
93. Some Nineteenth Century Pastors:
    E. K. Miller, 1882-1884; C. Grimes, 1884-1885; J. R. Jackson, 1888-1892; T. E. Sharp, 1892-1895; and W. F. Packard, 1895-1897.
94. Some leading lay members.
    B. McAlester, 1847-1902, J. P. Horner, Mrs. James D. Bowling, W. T. Maupin, Dr. A. W. McAlester.
114. Broadway Methodist Episcopal Church, South, Broadway and Short Street.
127. Presiding Bishops, Missouri Conference, 1901-1956. W. A. Candler, 1901, 1909; A. W. Wilson, 1902; C. B. Galloway, 1903; E. R. Hendrix, 1904, 1905, 1914-1917.
128. J. S. Key, 1906, 1907; H. C. Morrison, 1908; Collins Denny, 1910, 1911; E. D. Mouzon, 1912.

Page
129. E. E. Hoss, 1913; W. B. Murrah, 1918-1921; W. F. McMurry, 1922-1929 and General Chairman of the Building Committee of the Missouri Methodist Church; A. F. Smith, 1930-1933.
130. John M. Moore, 1934-1937; W. T. Watkins, 1938; Ivan Lee Holt, 1939, 1944-1956; J. G. Broomfield, 1940-1943.
132. Columbia Methodist Pastors, 1898-1913. Pastors: M. H. Moore, 1898-1902; S. P. Cresap, 1902-1905; Charles M. Bishop, 1905-1909; C. M. Aker, 1909-1912; Charles W. Tadlock, 1912-1913.
146. Congregational Leaders Through This Period. J. M. Baker, Judge J. A. Stewart, Mrs. Blanche H. Stephens, George H. Beasley, and J. W. Schwabe.
152. Columbia Methodist Pastors, 1913-1930. Charles C. Grimes, 1913-1917; S. W. Hayne, 1917-1919; Joseph D. Randolph, 1919-1923; Mavin T. Haw, 1923-1927; M. W. Waldrip, 1927-1930.
155. Building Committee, Missouri Methodist Church.
159. Cornerstone laying, October 20, 1925.
166. The Missouri Methodist Church (with John Epple, builder, inset).
168. Congregational Leaders Through This Period. Manuel Drumm, J. E. Hawkins, Mrs. Laura Evans, Cecil Coffman.
176. Columbia Methodist Pastors, 1930-1957. Frank C. Tucker, 1930-1934; R. C. Holliday, 1934-1942; J. Wilson Crichlow, 1942-1947; A. G. Williamson, 1947-1951; Hugh O. Isbell, 1951-1957.
187. Locust Street Entrance.
188. Interior of Sanctuary.
189. John and Charles Wesley
    From the center panels of The Methodist window.
190. Pulpit and Lectern.
191. Altar and Sanctuary Cross.
192. Contemporary Ministerial Leadership:
    Eugene M. Frank, Bishop, 1956-
    Monk Bryan, Pastor, 1957-
196. Interior of McMurry Chapel.

Page
201. Official Board, 1961.
203. Some recent Church leaders:
    Dale Summers, Donald Bird, L. D. Johnston
    Leeon Smith, H. R. Mueller
204. Rev. H. A. Lehwald, Supt. of Jefferson City District.
    Jerry Statler, Associate Pastor, 1962-
    Walter A. Hearn, Methodist Professor in Missouri School of Religion, 1928-1965.
    Jyles Whittler, Custodian, 1933-

HISTORY OF THE
MISSOURI METHODIST CHURCH
OF COLUMBIA, MISSOURI
AND ITS COLUMBIA PREDECESSORS

John Wesley

HISTORY OF THE MISSOURI METHODIST CHURCH OF COLUMBIA, MISSOURI AND ITS COLUMBIA PREDECESSORS

"The world is my parish."—John Wesley

Section I
Origin and Organization of the Methodist Episcopal Church

The origin of the Missouri Methodist Church in Columbia, Missouri, goes far back of even the first settlers in Columbia. Like all things Methodist, the beginning goes back to that little band of students in Oxford University who dared to set themselves apart from their fellow students, and to live a more devout life than was practiced commonly in their day. They set up rigid rules to be followed in their daily lives, and adopted "methods" for the daily study of the Scriptures and for daily devotions. Hence, in derision, they were called "Method-ists" by their fellow students. But they persisted, and went out from the University to be missionaries to the working classes of England who had been neglected by the Established Church of England, and who had seldom heard the "news of salvation" now brought to them by these devoted followers of Jesus Christ. The Wesleys were not content to stop at the borders of the "tight little islands," but followed the English settlers across the wide waters of the Atlantic. When the American Revolution separated the colonists from their mother country politically, the Wesleyans already had thousands of adherents in the fringe of states along the Atlantic coast.

A year after the Treaty of Peace of 1783, the Methodist circuit riders met at Baltimore; and, in what has been called the Christmas Conference and with the approval of John Wesley, organized the Methodist Episcopal Church of America, and chose and consecrated two of their number, Thomas Coke and Francis Asbury, to be their overseers or "Superintendents." This again was with the approval of John Wesley. The itinerants went out from that Conference to their assigned areas, and before many years had elapsed converts of these early circuit riders appeared across the mountains in Kentucky and Tennessee, and in the southwestern and northwestern territories of that day. After the Louisiana Purchase Treaty of 1803, the circuit riders were free to follow the settlers across the Mississippi River

Francis Asbury

ORIGIN AND ORGANIZATION

and up the fertile valleys westward, preaching and baptizing wherever they went. The fields were ripe for the harvest! Thus, it was that Methodist "classes" were formed, the initial phase for beginning a local Methodist organization, followed by the erection of a "Methodist meeting house."

In the meantime the general Methodist organization was developing. The Christmas Conference had not been a delegated conference, nor did it provide for follow-up meetings every four years. It was not until 1792, eight years later, that another such all-inclusive meeting, called a "General Conference," was held. This was followed in 1796 by a second General Conference which for the first time divided the whole country into Annual Conferences, a term which was both geographical and ecclesiastical. As first organized in 1796, there were six Annual Conferences; namely, New England, Philadelphia, Baltimore, Virginia, South Carolina and Western. The latter included nearly all the territory west of the Allegheny Mountains. The number of Annual Conferences was gradually increased thereafter in subsequent meetings of the General Conference.

These early sessions of the General Conference, all held until 1812 at Baltimore, were undelegated; any recognized Methodist preacher could attend and take part, but in the General Conference of 1800 it was decided that thereafter only ministers in full connection with the Methodist Church, who had been ordained as "Elders," [1] could attend and participate. At this same Conference of 1800, Richard Whatcoat was elected a Bishop. Coke had withdrawn to England, and Asbury was nearly worn out by his incessant labors.

---

[1] The term "Elder" came to have a special meaning in the Methodist Church and represents the highest order in the rank of the ministry. One of the Elders would be appointed as leader in a district and hence came to be called Presiding Elder. This term lasted until 1939 when the term "District Superintendent" was substituted in the entire reunited church.

Shiloh Meeting House near Belleville, Illinois
Where the Missouri Conference was organized in 1816

McKENDREE CHAPEL.

McKendree Chapel near Jackson, Missouri
First meeting of the Missouri Conference in Missouri in 1819

Section II
Western Expansion of the Church and the Establishment of the Missouri Conference in 1816

In the West, William McKendree [2] was coming to the front rapidly as one of the great Methodist leaders of that region. Following his advice, Bishop Asbury, in the Western Annual Conference of September, 1806, appointed John Travis to "Missourie." There had been other itinerant Methodist preachers west of the Mississippi River before that time, but Travis was the first regular appointee to that region. He and his presiding elder, McKendree, held the first Methodist camp meeting in Missouri the following summer near Cape Girardeau. They had about forty conversions, and the influence of that camp meeting extended over several counties. This was symbolic of the rapid growth of the church throughout the entire West. In the General Conference of 1812, which was held in New York City, the first delegated General Conference, the Western Annual Conference was divided into the Ohio Annual Conference and the Tennessee Annual Conference, the latter including roughly the territory of Illinois, southwestern Indiana, Kentucky, Tennessee, Missouri and all the country west and north of those regions. The Illinois District of the Tennessee Annual Conference included the circuits being formed in Missouri. By 1814 there were enough circuits in Missouri to form the Missouri District, with Samuel H. Thompson as the first Presiding Elder.

One of the circuits of this Missouri District was at first called the Missouri Circuit, and included in general that region north of the Missouri River and west of the Mississippi River and extending westward to the land occupied by various tribes of Indians. But as immigrants pushed westward up the Missouri River, a new circuit was organized in 1815, and was given the

---

[2] William McKendree was elected and consecrated a Bishop in the General Conference of 1808, the first native American chosen for that position. His picture appears in the great west window of the Missouri Methodist Church along with those of John and Charles Wesley and Francis Asbury. Richard Whatcoat had been elected a Bishop in the General Conference of 1800, but died July 5, 1806. Coke had withdrawn to England by consent of the General Conference, so that with the election of McKendree in 1808, that still left only two bishops. McKendree died March 5, 1835.

name of the Boonslick Circuit.[3] For the first circuit rider appointed to this region in that year, Bishop McKendree chose Joseph Piggott, and he may be thought of as the first regularly appointed minister to the region which afterwards included Boone County, though this was before there was any Columbia or any Boone County. Piggott was a new member of the Conference, having just been admitted "on trial."

The General Conference of 1816 held in Baltimore again, established the Missouri Annual Conference.[4] Its territory was taken from the Tennessee Conference and at first included the region which later became the states of Illinois, Missouri, Arkansas and the southwestern part of the state of Indiana, as well as the territory north and west occupied by Indian tribes to which the Conference sent missionaries annually. The formation of the Missouri Conference made it much easier each year for the "travelling preachers" in Missouri to attend the annual conference sessions, for instead of having to ride horseback to some distant point in Kentucky or Tennessee, the trip was to some point in Missouri or Illinois.

The first session of the Missouri Conference was held in Illinois, near the site of the present town of Belleville, and commenced September 23, 1816. It had for its presiding officer Bishop McKendree. There were nine members present from the Missouri part of the Conference, and a little less than one thousand persons were reported as being members of the church in Missouri, a small part of them being colored.[5] It is difficult to understand the changes in the statistics of membership from year to year unless one remembers that camp meetings were held every summer at various points, and that there might be from fifty to a hundred or more conversions added to the roll of the local membership, but that on the other hand population was changing rapidly on the frontier with immigrants moving on to

---

[3] See H. N. McTyeire, *A History of Methodism*, for additional information about the spread of Methodism westward.

[4] It was while on his way to attend this General Conference that Bishop Francis Asbury died on March 31. Asbury was never married and left no blood children, but he left thousands of spiritual children; it became rather common for Methodist parents all over America to name one of their sons for Francis Asbury, so that the name became widespread throughout America. This Conference elected Enoch George and Robert R. Roberts as Bishops, so with the death of Asbury, three Bishops were left, McKendree, George and Roberts.

[5] Members of the church who owned slaves would take them to the church for baptism and to become members.

lands further west. The membership reported one year might all be gone before another year had passed. They were leaven in the new regions, but it was confusing as to statistics. At this first session Jesse Walker was appointed presiding elder of the Missouri District, and Joseph Piggott was returned to Boonslick.

The fourth session of the Missouri Annual Conference was the first to be held within the boundaries of what later became the state of Missouri. It convened at McKendree Chapel, Cape Girardeau circuit,[6] September 14, 1819, and its presiding officer was Bishop Enoch George. Two persons were appointed to the Boonslick circuit, reflecting the growing population of central Missouri. But this was still before the County of Boone had been organized and before there was a town of Columbia, though Franklin a few miles away was a prosperous river port.

For its fifth session, beginning September 13, 1820, the Conference went back to Illinois. The business of this fifth session was fairly typical of all those early Conferences, and indeed of all Methodist Annual Conferences. The names of all members (there were no lay members at that time) were called and their "character passed" (that is, it had to be seen that they were free from any charges of misdoing or wrongful conduct); three preachers were admitted "on trial," four after examination remained on trial, seven were ordained as deacons, three deacons were ordained elders, and one preacher was expelled from the Conference (with no explanation in the minutes as to what his fault had been). The appointments for work during the coming year were read as the concluding business. Jesse Haile was made Presiding Elder of the Missouri District, and John Scripps and John Harris were appointed as the circuit-riders for the circuit of Boonslick and Lamine (soon to be divided into two circuits).

---

[6] This chapel, pictured also in the Methodist window of the Missouri Methodist Church, was built for this first Conference in Missouri, and is still preserved as a Methodist memorial.

SECTION III
The Missouri Compromise and Its Effect Upon the Church

By this time a grave question in the economic and political growth of the United States had suddenly burst on the country and caused great excitement in Missouri. This was the question as to whether Missouri would be admitted into the Union as a slave state or a free state. The holding of slaves by members of the church had been a controversial question almost from the beginning of the Methodist societies in America. Since this question of slavery played such a large part in the later history of the church, locally and nationally, a brief review of the subject as far as the church was concerned, is not out of place.

Even before the Christmas Conference of 1784, meetings of the itinerants of Methodist societies had adopted regulations requiring the circuit riders to free their slaves, and in the Conference of 1784 the most rigid rules on this subject ever adopted by the Church were promulgated. These prohibited "the buying and selling the bodies and souls of men, women or children with the intention of enslaving them," and provided a plan, to go into effect within twelve months, for the immediate or gradual emancipation of all slaves held by Methodist masters, the design being "to extirpate this abomination from among us." [7] This rule of 1784 represented the high water mark of anti-slavery legislation in the church, but it did not have the effect of freeing the church from slavery. After 1800, increasing moderation marked the course of Methodist legislation on this subject, and the General Conference of 1808 struck out from the *Discipline* all that related to slave-holding by private members of the church. The General Conference of 1816 adopted the so-called

---

[7] To properly evaluate this church law, however, one must remember that at this particular time in the history of the country there was a strong movement to abolish slavery throughout the bounds of the United States, a movement which resulted in the adoption of antislavery laws by all the states in the northern part of the country. But the invention of the cotton gin about that time, the introduction of the raising of short staple cotton on a large scale in the South, and the need of a large and cheap supply of labor in that part of the country halted the antislavery movement. The country thus became divided in its economic systems as far as labor was concerned, and this division was reflected in other phases of society including religious organizations.

"compromise law." This provided that "no slave-holder shall be eligible to any official station in our church where the laws of the State in which he lives will admit of emancipation and permit the liberated slave to enjoy freedom." This was the situation when the Missouri question arose.

A majority of the early settlers of Missouri had come from the slave-holding states of Kentucky, Virginia, North Carolina and Tennessee, and did not see anything morally wrong about the institution of slavery, and indeed had brought their slaves with them. While the plantation system of the more southerly states was not as a rule transplanted to Missouri, many of the immigrants did bring a few slaves with them to help clear the forests, till the land and work around the house. The settlers intensely disliked to have the national government interfere with their established customs and social institutions. There is no evidence that Methodists were different from other new settlers in this respect. But with the adoption of the "Missouri Compromise" by Congress, admitting Missouri as a slave state but prohibiting slavery in the other territories of the United States north of Missouri's southern boundary, the excitement abated. It is to be noted that this question of the admission of Missouri did not divide the church, but it helped to fix the attitude of Missourians on the subject of slavery when a church question involving slavery arose later.

Section IV
Building of the Union Church
and Organization
of Columbia Circuit

In the meantime, the population of Missouri as well as the membership of its churches continued to grow rapidly. New counties were being organized and new county-seat towns grew up. In 1820, the year of the admission of Missouri into the Union, Boone County was one of a number of new counties established by the General Assembly of Missouri, and Columbia was made its seat of government. When the fifth annual session of the Missouri Conference met in the fall of 1820, it was discovered that the Boonslick circuit, in which the Columbia region had been included, reported the largest number of members of any circuit in the district; and as a consequence, its territory was divided and the new circuit of Cedar Creek was established. This included the southern part of the Boonslick circuit and contained the area around Columbia, so that almost from the beginning of the history of Columbia, it was included in the new Cedar Creek circuit. The first minister appointed to this circuit was James Scott, with S. H. Thompson as Presiding Elder, and Scott may be thought of as Columbia's first Methodist minister.

After this first appointment of a circuit rider to the circuit of Cedar Creek in 1820, one was appointed for that circuit each year until 1834; and annual reports were made to the conference from the circuit. The report of membership on the circuit varied from about 200 to 325 but there was no regular growth in the membership. Some years it would be up and other years down, indicating probably changes in the meeting places for public worship or the emigration of settlers further to the West. The ministers were changed every year. Occasionally two men would be appointed to the circuit.

There was no Methodist house of worship in Columbia during that first decade of the history of the town. The preaching places were in the homes of the members or, if it were summer time, in a grove or in the front yard of one of the members. Sometimes,

Co-Builders of the Union Church—1837

Moses U. Payne   William Jewell

Early Preachers in Columbia

W. W. Redman   Andrew Monroe

as in 1831, the public services could be held in the courthouse.[8] Camp meetings were held almost every summer at different places on the circuit.[9]

How many Methodist communicants there were in the town of Columbia in its early years cannot be told definitely. There was no annual conference report, such as began to be published about thirty years later. The Bishops must have kept some sort of record and years later these records were gathered together and published,[10] but Columbia was only a "point" on the Cedar Creek circuit so that we cannot get this information from the abbreviated minutes published years later.

In the meantime, the growing importance of the Methodist population in and around Columbia was recognized in various ways. The *Intelligencer* in an editorial of July 19, 1834, had mentioned the growing influence of the Methodists and in the Annual Conference, meeting in September in 1834, the circuit was named the Columbia circuit and the Cedar Creek circuit was discontinued. To this Columbia circuit was sent Robert H. Jordan. It was a good appointment. Jordan had been admitted to the conference in full connection and ordained as a Deacon in 1831, and as an Elder in 1833. He was then sent to St. Charles for a year and now in 1834 came to Columbia as the first minister for the newly organized Columbia circuit. The next year he was given another appointment and then in 1836 returned to Columbia for another year.[11] In the interim of a year between his two appointments, J. F. Young and R. S. Reynolds together were the appointees on the Columbia circuit. In Jordan's second year, 1836-1837, he was associated with Condley Smith. The Columbia

---

[8] It was announced in the *Missouri Intelligencer* of April 2, 1831, the local newspaper published in Columbia at that time, that there would be "Methodist preaching" in the courthouse in Columbia on the second Sunday in each month; the preacher was announced as Rev. J. Edmondson. He was a prominent minister of the conference and was made Presiding Elder of the Missouri District the next year.

[9] One such was announced in the *Missouri Intelligencer* of October 5, 1833, as being in Sexton's Grove, and one in the *Intelligencer* of August 2, 1834, for the same place.

[10] *Minutes of the Annual Conferences of the Methodist Episcopal Church*. Volume I includes the minutes from 1773 to 1828, Volume II, 1829 to 1839, and further minutes were published later. The information published in these minutes was of limited value but included the number of memberships in each circuit of each conference, but not the number of members on each "point" of a circuit.

[11] Jordan later filled important appointments in the Conference. He died October 21, 1878 in Chillicothe, Missouri, age 78 years.

circuit at that time reported 453 members, including 68 colored. Jesse Green was Presiding Elder.

What the Methodists of Columbia most needed was a house of worship. The Baptists were in the same predicament. The Presbyterians had erected the first church building in Columbia, located on Walnut Street between Fifth and Sixth Streets, and seemed at that time to be the most influential sect in town. It was while Jordan was serving his second pastorate on the Columbia Circuit that the Methodists and Baptists together solved the problem for a few years of church buildings for their respective denominations. This was done by the two groups working together to erect a building which became known as the "Union" Church. It happened fortunately, that each group included a locally prominent and wealthy member, and the two together financed the purchase of a lot and the main portion of the construction. These two men, Moses U. Payne[12] for the Methodists and William Jewell for the Baptists, bought a lot from John and Emily Guitar, on February 11, 1837, located on the south side of Walnut Street about half way between Seventh and Eighth Streets on a short street named Guitar. The lot cost Payne and Jewell $150 and provided space for a building, 47½ by 56 feet.[13] The church building was erected that year and the hours for services of the two denominations were arranged satisfactorily.

For the next fifteen years this building was prominent in the development of Columbia. Not only did it provide a meeting place for the religious services of the two denominations, but it was the largest hall in the town, and many secular meetings were held there, so that in a sense it served as a "town hall." The first President of the University of Missouri, Dr. John H. Lathrop, delivered his inaugural address there in March, 1841, before the first University building was erected. There is no evidence that the Union Church was ever formally dedicated as a place of worship; indeed, the lot was purchased in the name of Payne and Jewell rather than in trust for religious organizations.

The growth in number of Methodists in the town of Columbia for the few years following the appointment of Jordan in 1834

---

[12] Payne was a local preacher in the Methodist Church.
[13] The records of this transaction are in the Recorder's Office in the Boone County Court House.

is impossible to determine.[14] There were several preaching points around Columbia, some of which were served by the person appointed to the Columbia Circuit, but the statistics of membership reported in the Annual Conference sessions never indicated the location of these country preaching places or the number of members of each. The appointments of ministers to the Boonslick Circuit were still being made; and in the Conference of 1835, 407 members were reported from that circuit. This may have included some of the communities in Boone County but how these country points were divided between Boonslick and the Columbia Circuit is not known.

It is not possible, either, to determine the identity of the members of the Columbia church. Except for Payne, no mention of the names of the members was made, either in official church publications or in publications such as newspapers. As far as is known, the local church never published a list of names of its members in this early period, and any manuscript list for the use of the pastor or the officers of the church has long since been lost or destroyed.[15]

An event in the history of the Church in Missouri which changed considerably the names and boundaries of the Districts in the Missouri Conference as well as the size of the Conference itself was the establishment by the General Conference of 1836 in Cincinnati, of the Arkansas Conference. This took from the Missouri Conference all of the territory of Arkansas as well as part of the region in Missouri south of the Missouri River. Thus it became necessary to reorganize district lines in the Missouri Conference, and in this readjustment a Columbia District was

---

[14] The following is the number of Methodists reported from Columbia (Columbia Circuit) from 1835 to 1844, but this included many from country points around Columbia.
1834-1835, 511; 1835-1836, 454; 1836-1837, 521; 1837-1838, 502; 1838-1839, 735; 1839-1840, 712; 1840-1841, 531; 1841-1842, 545; 1842-1843, 854; 1843-1844, 583

[15] *The History of Boone County*, published by William F. Switzler in 1882, includes a few paragraphs on church history. On page 823, referring to the Methodist Church this says that owing to the loss and destruction of its records, and there being no other source of information the author was compelled to depend upon the memory of some persons still living. From this source he says that some of the original members of the church were Turner Daniels, Samuel Austin and wife, Moses U. Payne and wife, Mrs. Eliza Matthews and her son Milton S., and Thomas Phillips and wife. These are all the names that come down from the earliest period of the Columbia church.

organized. This was continued until the Annual Conference session of October, 1852, when in another readjustment the Fayette District was organized and the Columbia District discontinued. Columbia and Rocheport were joined into one charge in 1842.

Section V
Slavery Questions Divide the Church in 1844: Columbia "Goes South"

Meanwhile the American people had found that the adoption of the Missouri Compromise of 1820 had not solved permanently all questions relating to the institution of slavery. Various new irritants in the "house divided against itself" kept appearing. The northern states one after another had forbidden slavery within their borders, leaving a small number of Negroes who were as free as were the white people. Moreover, particularly in the border states, an occasional master would provide by will for the manumission of his slaves. It was found, however, that the presence of these free Negroes had a disturbing effect upon the slaves. To get rid of this irritating condition, some good-intentioned citizens proposed that the free Negroes should be colonized in Africa, and an American Colonization Society was organized to provide the cost of transporting free Negroes to Africa. Religious institutions in the border and southern states looked upon this as a good solution to a touchy subject, and found also a pious argument in its favor, namely, the sending of these Americanized and Christianized Negroes to "benighted" Africa would be missionary work, carrying the Gospel to the uncivilized black races of Africa. But at the same time, a movement had been organized in the North to form "Abolition" Societies, not so much interested in sending free Negroes to Africa as in striking the bonds of slavery from all Negroes in America. These Societies were bitterly condemned in the states which still supported the institution of slavery.

The Methodists in Missouri took notice of these aspects of the slavery problem in the meeting of their Annual Conference in September, 1835. Resolutions were presented and adopted approving the plan of colonizing in Africa "free persons of color" as "the most practicable means of securing to that unfortunate class the blessings of civil and religious liberty." On the other hand, the Conference expressed its disapprobation of the abolition societies and their agents. It declared them mischievous in their character and work, not helping the situation of the people of color and sowing dissension among the citizens of the United States. The resolutions showed the attitude of people in Missouri in the middle thirties, and were prophetic of what would happen a decade later.[16]

After the building of the Union Church in 1837, when Jordan and Smith were ministers sent to the Columbia Circuit, the whole circuit continued to grow in membership. Following that year William Ketron and James L. Forsythe were appointed to the Columbia Circuit. The Columbia District had been organized in 1836, and the Missouri District discontinued. The bishops had the policy of switching the presiding elders from district to district, though usually with the term of service of two or three years in each district.

In 1836 the first presiding elder for the new Columbia District was Andrew Monroe who had been presiding elder for the Missouri District some years previously and was to serve in other districts later. The two preachers for the Columbia Circuit for 1838-1839 were J. F. Young and S. Grove. The next year the presiding elder appointed to the Columbia District was William Patton, with David Fisher and Daniel Sherman as the Columbia Circuit riders. Patton continued his service in that district in 1840-41, but with only one preacher appointed to the Columbia Circuit, Benjamin R. Johnson. He reported a membership at the end of his first year of 432 as compared to 610 the preceding year, indicating the division of the circuit in 1840. Johnson was continued as pastor for the next year (the first time a minister had been appointed on the circiut for two successive years), but Jesse Greene who six years before had been presiding elder of this district was now appointed to that position and was continued there for the next two years. Following Johnson's two years as minister, Asa McMurtry was appointed to the position for the year 1842-43.

Now there was another reorganization and Columbia and Rocheport were detached from the Columbia Circuit, and erected into a separate two point circuit. Walter Prescott was appointed as minister of the Columbia-Rocheport Circuit and was continued there through 1844-1845, with William Patton as Presiding Elder during the last year. Reflecting the last change in the size of the charge, the total membership in the two points of Columbia and Rocheport was only 177. What percentage of this total lived in Columbia is not known.

At this point, we must revert to the problem of slavery; and its influence on the church. The rise, growing strength, and

[16] *Missouri Intelligencer,* October 3, 1835.

continued agitation of the abolition societies in the north, naturally reacted upon the southern slave states. By the middle forties all of the southern states had passed laws forbidding the emancipation of slaves by any method whatsoever. This was the situation leading to a grave question in the General Conference of 1844, held in New York. It became known that both Bishop James O. Andrew of Georgia and his wife possessed slaves, though neither had bought nor sold slaves themselves. They had inherited slaves, but under the laws of Georgia, they could not emancipate them. This possession of slaves by such a prominent leader in the church led to a bitter and lengthy debate in the Conference, resulting eventually in the adoption of a resolution that the Bishop should desist from exercising the functions of his office "so long as this impediment exists." The day after the Conference adjourned the delegates from the slave-holding states held a meeting which proposed a convention of delegates from the southern states, to meet in Louisville, Kentucky, to take whatever action they thought was necessary. The southern annual conferences accordingly elected delegates to meet in Louisville at the appointed time, May 1, 1845.

In the meeting of the Missouri Annual Conference, September 25, 1844, eight delegates were elected to attend the Louisville Convention; namely, Andrew Monroe, Jesse Greene, John Glanville, Wesley Browning, William Patton, John H. Lynn, Joseph Boyle, and Thomas Johnson. Patton, who was Presiding Elder at that time in the Columbia District, had been a delegate to the General Conference of 1844 and was active in the movement to form a separate southern church. All of the other delegates also were sympathetic with that movement, and the Missouri delegates to the Louisville Convention were all in favor of the separation. The Missouri Conference, which elected these eight men, had instructed them to favor the separation of the church "if it was thought indispensable and unavoidable." That, indeed, might be a matter of judgment, but it appeared that the delegates elected had already made up their minds on that point.

The problems left unsolved by the General Conference of 1844 or created by the Louisville Convention of 1845 were discussed freely in the columns of the church papers, many of which were doubtless taken by the leading Methodists of Columbia.[17]

---

[17] For a discussion of the expressions in the church papers, see William Hauser Winter, *History of the Schism in the Methodist Church in Missouri, 1844-1855*.

This Louisville Convention organized the Methodist Episcopal Church, South, and called for its First General Conference to meet in Petersburg, Virginia, May 1, 1846. It was left, however, for each annual conference to decide for itself its future course in regard to the new church.

The Missouri Annual Conference of 1845, meeting in Columbia for the first time in the history of Methodism in Missouri, began its sessions on October 1, in the Union Church of Columbia. A large attendance was present, including many of the laity of Columbia, though the laity had no voice in the proceedings; it was well known that the exciting topic brought over from the Louisville meeting would be the chief question engaging the attention of the ministers. Bishop Soule, one of the two bishops who had upheld the position taken by the southern delegates in the General Conference of 1844, arrived the second day and presided during the rest of the meeting. Just what effect, if any, upon the final voting of the ministers his presidency of the Conference had, will never be known.[18]

A series of resolutions was presented by Patton, the third of which contained the heart of the matter under discussion and read as follows: "Resolved, that as a Conference claiming all the rights, powers and privileges of an Annual Conference of the Methodist Episcopal Church, we *adhere* to the Methodist Episcopal Church, South, and that all our proceedings, journals and records of every kind, hereafter be in the name and style of the *Methodist Episcopal Church, South.*" [19] The debate on this resolution was a warm one and protracted, lasting through several meetings. Those speaking against the resolution and therefore against the division of the church were James M. Jameson, Wilson S. McMurry, Nathaniel Waterman, and Thomas W. Chandler. They denied "in toto, the assumed necessity for a separation, never having yet seen evidence sufficient to convince them that the objects and purposes of the Christian ministry and church organization could not be peaceably, fully and satisfactorily accomplished without such separation." They denied

---

[18] Theo H. Wolff, in "A Narrative of the Saint Louis Annual Conference," page 5, says that presiding Bishop Soule used every effort to carry south the conference, that it was he who instructed every preacher to answer either "North" or "South." It may be that Wolff was prejudiced, himself.

[19] This account of the Conference proceedings is from the columns of the *Missouri Statesman,* and was furnished to the editor by W. W. Redman, Secretary of the Conference.

the identity of the southern organization with the Methodist Episcopal church and deemed it a secession. The other side of the question was ably and eloquently upheld by Andrew Monroe, Thomas Ashby, William Patton, Wesley Browning, Joseph Boyle and Jesse Greene, and possibly others.[20] When the roll-call vote was taken, the resolution was adopted 86 to 14. This total of 100 votes did not include quite all the members of the Conference, and a subsequent resolution allowed any who were absent to record their votes later, but there is no record of later votes. No list of the votes for or against the resolution was given out or kept in the records as far as is known. It is known, however, that in the appointments for the next year, none of those whose names were published in the newspaper as being opposed to the resolution received an appointment. To continue in the Methodist ministry, they either had to become pastors of local churches which were opposed to the action taken by the Conference, or transfer to a northern Conference. Both courses were followed by different ones.

The Missouri Conference thus became a Conference in the Methodist Episcopal Church, South, and the Columbia church a component part of that new denomination. There were several Methodist congregations in Missouri which refused to recognize the division in the church, and remained related to the Methodist Episcopal Church. There were also some communities which were so divided that both Methodist and Methodist, South, church organizations were established; but generally speaking, the Methodists of Missouri through their local societies, joined with the movement to establish a new church organization and were thenceforth members of the Methodist Episcopal Church, South; that apparently was the situation in Columbia. The evidence is too scanty to risk an opinion that the Columbia church was at all divided. There is no record of any discussion in the local Board of Stewards and there did not seem to be any doubt that the local members approved the vote of their representa-

---

[20] The prominent official positions these men occupied in the church in Missouri explains at least partially why the vote in favor of separation was so one-sided, and why there was no immediate movement to organize a northern branch of the church in Columbia. Three of the men, Monroe, Greene and Patton, were presiding elders of the region around Columbia (organized as the Columbia District in 1836) from 1836 to 1850, and must have been well-known and affectionately regarded by Columbia Methodists. Joseph Boyle had the reputation of being one of the greatest pulpit men in the Conference, and the other men had prominent committee appointments in the Conference.

tive, the minister of the Columbia church, in this important decision.[21] Columbia was a town in which many of the citizens held slaves, and the Methodists, like the majority of the citizens, believed that the South was in the right in this decision.

The loss in membership as the result of the action taken in the Annual Conference in October, 1845, was not great. The Columbia and Rocheport charge reported in 1845, before the vote on separation was taken, 167 members. The next year this charge reported 160 members when normally it would probably have increased rather than diminished by a few members. The number of members reported for the Columbia District in 1845 was 3,479 while in September, 1846, it was 3,212. After that there began a gradual rise for several years. The Columbia charge, Columbia and Rocheport together, in 1849 reported 194 members. It was definitely holding its own and growing at a small rate.

Before the Annual Conference of 1846 met, the first General Conference of the Methodist Episcopal Church, South, was held in Petersburg, Virginia, and that conference split the state of Missouri into two Annual Conferences; the Missouri Conference included all the territory north of the Missouri River in the state and the St. Louis Conference all the territory south of the Missouri River. When these conferences met in September and October, 1846, the two together reported 24,526 members. This was a loss of 1,535 for the territory covered by the two conferences where ordinarily there would have been an indefinite gain during that year. By the next year, October, 1847, when the wounds of division should have been partially healed, the membership reported for the Missouri conference was 10,924 but at the annual meeting a year later in 1848 the membership had fallen to 10,750. After that, the figures turned upward for a number of years. One cannot be sure of the figures reported

---

[21] From this date until 1939, the history of the Columbia Methodist church is related as a part of the history of the Methodist Episcopal Church, South, rather than of the Methodist Episcopal Church, and all references to the General Conference refer to the General Conference of the Methodist Episcopal Church, South. This was a quadrennial meeting, as in the case of the General Conference of the original church, but it convened in the alternate even years, 1846, 1850, etc., rather than in 1848, 1852, etc.

because there might have been mistakes made by the secretary of the conference.[22]

The connection of Columbia and Rocheport to be filled by one pastoral appointment ceased in 1849, and the two separate societies were again placed in the Columbia Circuit with Patrick M. Pinckard as the circuit rider. Pinckard was returned the next year, 1850-1851, to the same appointment but with a new Presiding Elder, Jacob Lanius.[23] The following year, 1851-1852, two ministers were appointed to the Columbia Circuit, R. P. Holt and E. K. Miller. Lanius, who was again appointed to the District, died of typhoid fever within a week after his reappointment.

---

[22] A note at the end of the General Minutes for 1845-1846 said that some of the minutes were so badly written and carelessly arranged that it was impossible for even the most experienced reader to decipher every word and accurately ascertain every proper name. It was suggested that the secretary of each Annual Conference prepare a "fair copy" of his minutes and include complete answers to all the questions before they were delivered to the President (Bishop) for his examination and safe keeping.

[23] Lanius had been one of the prominent men of the Conference. He had been ordained as a deacon in 1834 and as an elder in 1836. He was one of the delegates from the Missouri Conference to the General Conference of 1850, held in St. Louis. He died on October 8, 1851, leaving a wife and seven children. It is not known who was appointed as his substitute after his death, but possibly it was Richard P. Holt, the first of the two men appointed to the Columbia Circuit in 1851. Holt was regularly appointed to the position in 1852.

First Methodist Church Building in Columbia
1852-1870

Berry Hill Spencer
Pastor, 1852-1854

J. P. Nolan
Pastor, 1866-1867

SECTION VI
First Methodist Church Building in Columbia

A reorganization, interesting to Columbia, took place in the Annual Conference of 1852; the name of the district was changed from "Columbia" to "Fayette," but the appointment of Columbia was placed for a time in the St. Charles District, with Enoch M. Marvin [24] as Presiding Elder. At the same time, Columbia was raised for the first time to the status of a "station," [25] with its own pastor, Berry H. Spencer.[26]

This leads us to turn more particularly to the development of the Columbia Methodist Church. During the forties, the Methodist and Baptist congregations occupying the Union Church had been coming to the conclusion that each should have a separate edifice. The old Union Church was too small for the activities of two vigorous growing denominational groups. There is no evidence that they had any misunderstandings, but each

---

[24] Marvin later became the first native-born Missourian elected to the bishopric of the Methodist Episcopal Church, South. He was born in St. Charles County, June 12, 1823. Entering the Methodist ministry in 1841, he was assigned to preach the opening sermon of the Annual Conference held in Columbia in 1845. He served in various pulpits before his appointment as Presiding Elder of the St. Charles District in 1852, where he continued until 1854 when he was transferred to the St. Louis Conference and appointed minister of Centenary Church. The Missouri Conference chose him as a delegate to the General Conference of 1854. Transferring to the St. Louis Conference the next autumn, he immediately became a leader in that conference and was elected as a delegate to the next General Conference in 1858. In 1861, he was elected as the leader of the St. Louis Conference delegation to the General Conference in 1862, the Conference which did not meet because of the war. He was not elected as a delegate to the Conference of 1866 but went to that conference anyway and found when he arrived he had already been elected a Bishop. As Bishop he served in a number of Episcopal areas but chiefly in the Missouri area. He was well-known in Columbia where he had preached many times in his earlier career, and he dedicated in 1875 the new church building on East Broadway. He died November 26, 1877.

[25] This meant among other things that instead of dividing his time with other points on a circuit, the pastor would give his whole time to the Columbia congregation, and in reporting statistics to the Annual Conference, he would report for Columbia alone.

[26] This first minister sent to the Columbia "station" was a rather remarkable person. He had entered the ministry as a young man, and was ordained as a deacon by Bishop Soule in the Annual Conference which met in Columbia in 1845. He became one of the leaders in the Conference, and was sent as a delegate to six General Conferences. He died in Palmyra, August 2, 1883, and is buried there.

43

wished for various reasons to have its own church edifice. The Baptists eventually solved their problem by purchasing a lot from the county court on the courthouse square, a little further down toward seventh street, and erecting on the north side of Walnut Street a church building which served as their home for many years.

The Methodists studied the problem for some time, but finally bought a lot on the southwest corner of 6th Street and Broadway from William Jewell, paying him one hundred and forty dollars. Because this transaction appears in full in the Boone County Recorder's Office [27] one can find the first known official list in existence of a few of the members of the Methodist Church in Columbia. They were the Trustees, and under the terms of the *Discipline* of that time had to be members of the church; their names were as follows: James R. Boyce, Milton S. Matthews, Harvey G. Berry, David B. Cunningham, Brightberry McAlester, Fauntleroy Nutt, and Turner R. Daniel, prominent business and professional men of Columbia. They were "trustees in trust" for the parcel of land, 175 feet fronting on the south side of Broadway and running back 142½ feet to a fifteen foot alley. This land was conveyed to the trustees for the purpose of building a house of worship for the use of the members of the Methodist Episcopal Church, South, according to the Rules and *Discipline* of that Church; and they were to permit ministers who were duly authorized to preach within the building. When members of the Board of Trustees died or ceased to be members of the Columbia Methodist Church, vacancies were to be filled on the nomination by the pastor of the church of suitable persons, and elected by vote of the majority of the remaining trustees. The date of this deed was July 11, 1849, and the deed was recorded by Robert L. Todd, Clerk and Recorder, on October 12, 1849.

It was sometime before the trustees had funds great enough to proceed with the erection of the building. It was necessary to raise about $3,000 in cash and pledges to build the church, and the campaign to raise this fund lasted from 1849 to 1852. An interesting note in the *Missouri Statesman* for January 30, 1852, said that the edifice would be completed within a few weeks and then be dedicated. The building was described as follows:

---

[27] This record is in Book S, page 380, in the Recorder's Office, Boone County Courthouse.

FIRST METHODIST CHURCH BUILDING IN COLUMBIA

"It is a neat and tasteful brick, thirty-seven by forty-eight feet, with sixteen foot ceiling. It contains fifty-eight pews, painted in beautiful style and capable of seating three hundred persons. In addition, there is a gallery for the colored people, in which about one hundred can be comfortably seated. The pulpit, with altar in front, is tastefully painted, and is soon to be decorated with appropriate drapery. The base of the pulpit is painted in imitation marble—a very good imitation. The house is well lighted and ventilated, there being eight windows in it, each containing twenty-four lights, eleven by eighteen inches. The building has a basement story, valuable to a church for Sabbath school and prayer meeting purposes. This however, is in an unfinished state. On the whole, the new Methodist Church is a tasteful, beautifully finished edifice and is an ornament to our village."

The dedication services were held on April 18, 1852, when Rev. Andrew Monroe preached the dedicatory sermon.[28]

---

[28] The *Statesman,* April 16, 1852, reported that the ladies would occupy the center pews between the two aisles, the gentlemen those on each side. This was in accordance with the *Discipline* of 1850, on page 161 of which was the following: "Is there any exception to the rule, 'Let the men and the women sit apart?' Ans. There is no exception. Let them sit apart in all our churches."

Section VII
The Uneasy Fifties

The Columbia Methodist Church now entered upon a new period in its history. With a church sanctuary just completed for its own use, how did the members respond to this new challenge? It is difficult to answer this question, for it was a very complex and uneasy period through which the state and the country were passing. It is sometimes called the "Middle Period," but that term is not descriptive and merely defines that part of the nineteenth century. It was a very unstable period in social, economic and political affairs; it seemed as if the country were caught in some mighty maelstrom from which it could not extricate itself. Year after year with almost inexorable force it seemed to be rushing on to some dreadful climax, as indeed it was. One leading statesman ten years before the appeal to arms spoke of the approach of "an irrepressible conflict" and neither civil nor religious leaders seemed able to stay its advance. The division in the Methodist Church in the middle forties was but one phase of the division between the North and the South, and the crescendo kept rising in subsequent years.

Yet the initial local reaction after the erection in Columbia of the first Methodist church building was good. Items of church news seldom found their way into the columns of the secular press. But near the beginning of this decade of the fifties, the two conferences in Missouri of the Methodist Episcopal Church, South, had sponsored the publication of a four-page weekly Methodist church paper in the state known as *The St. Louis Christian Advocate*. It had been authorized by the General Conference of 1850, with the conditions that it should not commence until at least two thousand subscribers had been obtained, and that it should be under the control of a joint committee representing both Conferences in the state. The Conferences in the fall of 1850 appointed this joint committee; and it chose Rev. P. M. Pinckard, a leading minister of the Missouri Conference, to be the publisher. After filling the editorship with a temporary appointment, the joint committee elected Dr. David Rice McAnally to be editor.[29] The first number of the paper was issued

---

[29] David Rice McAnally, born in Tennessee February 17, 1810, entered the Methodist ministry as a young man and filled various pulpits in that

HISTORY OF THE MISSOURI METHODIST CHURCH

November 14, 1850; but then, fearing that the conditions of the General Conference had not been fulfilled, it suspended publication until the following August, 1851, and continued regularly thereafter. It published some official news for Methodist readers in the state, such as the dates for the various quarterly conferences in the Presiding Elders' districts, and generally the proceedings in an abbreviated fashion of the annual conference sessions. Just occasionally there were items of interest from local communities.

As already stated, the Columbia church organization was raised to the rank of a "station" in October, 1852, and the Rev. Berry Hill Spencer was appointed pastor. An item of news from Mr. Spencer appeared in the *Advocate* in the issue of January 30, 1853; telling of his first quarterly conference (which lasted, as quarterly conferences usually did at that time, for several days, and was devoted rather largely to evangelistic services), he wrote that there had been 15 additions to the church during the conference. Most likely, though it isn't mentioned, his Presiding Elder, Mr. Marvin, was present during the meetings and did much of the preaching. Marvin was a strong evangelistic preacher. Spencer mentioned also that there had been 30 additions to the membership since the Annual Conference in October, quite a remarkable growth, and that the Sunday School was in a flourishing condition.

With Columbia as a station, the statistics of membership reported to the Annual Conference at the end of Spencer's first year, October, 1853, would show for the first time how many members the Columbia church had; this was 94 white persons and 80 colored, not a large membership according to twentieth century standards, but Columbia was a small town at that time with a population of about 1,100. There were also at least three

---

state. He became interested in religious educational work and religious journalism, and in 1851 was elected by the Board of Managers of the new *St. Louis Advocate* as its editor. During the Civil War, he was accused of publishing material helpful to the Confederate cause, and he was arrested and imprisoned and the *Advocate* suspended, temporarily. When the paper resumed publication after the war, he again became editor, and with two short intermissions served until 1895. He died July 11, 1895. He had been a delegate five times to the General Conference. It is interesting to note that his son, David R. McAnally, Jr., was for a number of years professor of English in the University of Missouri at Columbia, and as such gave the first University course in Journalism ever taught at the University, or for that matter in the world; from that position he resigned to become an editorial writer for the *St. Louis Globe-Democrat*.

THE UNEASY FIFTIES

other active Protestant denominations in the town. But strangely, a year later, at the end of Spencer's two years there, his report showed a total of only 144, exactly divided between white and colored. The number of both white and colored memberships declined during his second year.

The smaller membership of the Columbia church reported at the end of Spencer's second year is difficult to understand, and no explanation is found in the records. Nevertheless, the presiding Bishop, H. H. Kavanaugh that year, continued Columbia as a station for the following year and appointed J. S. Todd to be pastor. Columbia was still in the St. Charles District, but M. G. Berryman followed Marvin as presiding elder, Marvin being transferred to the Centenary Church in St. Louis. The decline in membership continued under Todd, who reported at the end of his year, October, 1855, 68 white members and 75 colored. With the membership so small and becoming less each year, and with the membership of the Columbia circuit so large, the presiding Bishop in 1855 decided to add to the duties of the Columbia pastor the community of Nashville, a few miles southwest of Columbia. Thus Columbia became a part of a two-point circuit for the year 1855-1856 over which A. P. Linn was appointed as pastor. The Columbia appointment was now placed back in the Fayette district where it remained indefinitely.

This arrangement was evidently not satisfactory, for in 1856 Columbia again became a station with S. W. Cope as pastor. A year later Columbia became again a part of the larger Columbia circuit with William Penn as minister, and P. M. Pinckard as presiding elder. That lasted through 1857-1858 when B. F. Johnson was made minister, with W. G. Caples as presiding elder. For the last year of the decade, Columbia was made a station again, with W. G. Miller as the minister, and Berry H. Spencer as the presiding elder. But finally, at the next Annual Conference, the last before the Civil War, September 12-19, 1860 at St. Charles, and with Bishop Kavanaugh presiding again, Edwin Robinson became presiding elder of the Fayette District, and two men, W. G. Miller and Joseph Dines, were appointed on the Columbia Circuit of which Columbia was again a part. The report of the membership of the Columbia church in September, 1860, the last year before the war, showed 67 white members and 22 probationers, and 54 colored members and 18

49

probationers.[30] Before time for another Annual Conference, the United States was engaged in civil war and travel for the Bishop as well as for the ministers was difficult and indeed dangerous.

The oscillation back and forth in the fifties between being a station or a part of a circuit was certainly not good for the morale of the Columbia Methodist organization. Why this was done does not appear in any official publication; it may have been because the one church did not adequately support a minister financially, or because the number of Methodists on the circuit was larger than in the town, and a better division between town and country was attempted. It is likely that the instability of the times made it difficult for churches to preserve their unitary integrity, and to keep from being involved in political tensions.

There had been a number of developments in the church at large during these years which affected considerably the local churches. The great division of 1844-1845, instead of healing the troubles, had seemed to create more. When fraternal delegates from the Church, South, appeared in the General Conference of the Northern Church in 1848, instead of being received in a Christian spirit they were not even accorded a hearing; they finally left the seat of the Conference vowing the southern Church would never again take the initiative in establishing friendly relations. And when an effort to settle in an amicable fashion a division of the ownership of the great "Book Concern" broke down, an appeal had to be taken to the United States Courts which upheld in every important particular the claims of the southern Church. The exact location of the line between the northern and southern zones of activities was never settled, and frequent disputes arose over these matters in ensuing years. Missouri had several such jurisdictional disagreements, though no evidence has been found that Columbia had any such case.

The Methodist Episcopal Church, South, had started its separate career with two Bishops, Joshua Soule and James O. Andrew, both of whom had been elected in previous sessions of the General Conference of the undivided Church, but who

---

[30] The term "probationer" was used to mean that a person asking for membership, before being received "in full connection," had to complete a probationary period of a few months to prove that he would lead a Christian life.

THE UNEASY FIFTIES

adhered to the southern Church when it was established. In its First General Conference in 1846, at Petersburg, Virginia, Dr. William Capers of South Carolina and Dr. Robert Paine of Tennessee were elected Bishops, and were ordained on May 14.[31] In 1850, at the General Conference in St. Louis, one Bishop was chosen, Dr. Henry B. Bascom of Kentucky who, however, died the following September.[32] Three Bishops were elected in the General Conference of 1854 in Columbus, Georgia: George F. Pierce of Georgia, John Early of Virginia, and Hubbard H. Kavanaugh of Kentucky. An ordination service for all three was held on May 25, 1854.[33] Bishop Capers died on January 26, 1855. There were no Bishops elected in the General Conference of 1858. Therefore the group of southern Bishops just before the Civil War consisted of Soule, Andrew, Paine, Pierce, Early and Kavanaugh. All of these Bishops had presided in the Missouri Annual Conference at some time or other, and their names were household words among the Methodist families of Columbia.

It must be emphasized that the Methodists of the South were just as devoted to the Wesleyan principles of religion, and to the episcopal form of church government as were the Methodists of the North. The *Discipline* of the Methodist Episcopal Church of 1844 had been taken over almost in its entirety, save for a few verbal changes, by the First General Conference of the Methodist Episcopal Church, South. The great division of 1844-1845 had not come over the Articles of Religion, nor over forms of church government, but because of a dispute over the way the General Conference proposed to handle a question related to slavery. The southerners contended that slavery was not a subject for ecclesiastical legislation, and, as Bishop Pierce said later, "It is not the province of the Church to deal with civil institutions in her legislative capacity." [34] The Church, South, therefore, as a Church, proposed to have nothing to do with slavery questions.

One of the "restrictive rules" of the Methodist Church, how-

---

[31] Journal, *General Conference of 1846*, p. 61.
[32] Bascom was scheduled to preside in the Missouri Annual Conference of October, 1850, but because of his death in September no Bishop was present. As a result the Conference elected A. Monroe to preside.
[33] Journal, *General Conference of 1854*, p. 298.
[34] Bishop Pierce's statement is found in the *Proceedings of the General Conference of 1858*.

ever, from the begining of its history in America, had enjoined upon members to avoid "evil of every kind, especially that which is most generally practiced, such as . . . . the buying and selling of men, women, and children, with an intention to enslave them." Since according to the *Discipline* these rules could be changed only by a two-thirds vote of a General Conference followed by a three-fourths vote of all the members of the annual conferences, or *vice versa,* and especially since the members of the church professed to believe that the rule in question referred only to the foreign slave trade, which had already been made piracy by a law passed by the Federal Congress, there seemed to be no need to go through all the procedure to strike the words from the *Discipline*. In the first three of the General Conferences, little had been said about the rule.

As the rift between the North and the South had grown wider, however, this statement in the southern *Discipline* seemed to become more incongruous, and a movement had begun in certain southern conferences to get rid of the offensive reference to slavery. The Alabama Annual Conference voted in 1856 to send a memorial to the General Conference of 1858 to take action to expunge the statement from the *Discipline,* in the meantime proposing to the other annual conferences to take similar action. When the General Conference met in 1858, in Nashville, Tenn., it was found that nearly all the annual conferences had acted on the question, but three had not voted. Furthermore, five annual conferences (Missouri, Kentucky, Louisville, St. Louis, and Tennessee) had voted against concurrence for expunction.[35] This whole question was debated through much of the General Conference of 1858. A very large majority of the delegates favored the omission of the rule from the new *Discipline,* but an able minority argued that such action at that time, in view of the fact that three annual conferences had not voted, might not be consistent with the church constitution. Since more than two-thirds of the General Conference favored expunction, it was finally decided to refer the question again to the annual conferences, and when *all* had been heard from (if there were a three-fourths majority for concurrence), the Bishops were to have

---

[35] The vote reported from the Missouri Annual Conference was almost unanimous against concurrence, forty to one. This seems strange, remembering the great majority just a few years before in that Conference for the division of the Church. No explanation of the vote is known, and nothing has been found about the debate in the Conference.

the Book Editor publish a new edition of the *Discipline* with the statement about the "buying and selling of men, women, and children" omitted.[36] The final result was a new edition of the *Discipline* in 1859 without the objectionable statement which had caused so much debate. In view of the total abolition of the institution of slavery within a few years, one wonders at the futility of all of this discussion.

There was another problem which concerned the whole southern Church, and affected every individual member in the entire denomination; that was the name taken by the group of annual conferences breaking away in 1844-45 from the Methodist Episcopal Church. This had been determined at that time, apparently without much consideration as to its future impact upon the development of the denomination. One cannot think that the best minds of the First General Conference paid much attention to this problem. It was a geographical limitation that would become hurtful. It was discussed briefly in the General Conference of 1858, but without any positive action.[37]

---

[36] In its second vote on the question of concurrence, taken as a result of the action taken in the General Conference, the Missouri Conference voted in October, 1858, 49 to 14 in favor of concurrence. There was probably some influence brought to bear upon the ministers to induce them to change their vote.

[37] Reference to this subject will be made later. The name of the Church was positively hurtful in the border conferences during the war.

Section VIII
"Martyrdom in Missouri"

The caption for this section is the title of a two volume work written by the Rev. W. M. Leftwich, a Methodist minister of Missouri in the period during and after the Civil War. The books are descriptive of the sufferings endured by southern Methodist ministers during the war. The author of this monograph does not accept all of Leftwich's conclusions, but nevertheless it is true that in many parts of the state, and in many individual personal experiences, great hardship was visited not only upon ministers but also upon lay members of the Methodist Church, South. Part of this suffering stemmed from the residue of hard feeling caused in 1845 when the decision of the Conference to "go South" was made; in part it was due to the name which the southerners themselves had chosen for their new church (Methodist Episcopal Church, *South,*) a name equivalent to "secessionist" in the minds of many people; another factor was the rather natural movement of many thousands of young Missourians southward to join the Confederate armies, and southern Methodists made up their share of this movement; finally, the southern sympathizers suffered from the terrible character of the war as fought in Missouri, but northern sympathizers as well as southern suffered also; the raids of the "gray ghosts" were remembered for many years. To one who is unfamiliar with the internal character of the history of Missouri during the war period, it is difficult to understand the depth of the feelings which divided every phase of the political, social and religious life of those years.

Columbia and Boone County were in the region of Missouri known as Little Dixie, one of the most proslavery sections of the state. It was certainly because of this fact that a contingent of the Federal military forces was bivouacked in Columbia and on the University campus early in 1862. From this vantage point, the military authorities watched carefully the people of the town and surrounding region. Forays of cavalrymen were sent out more or less constantly, and men under suspicion were arrested and brought to a military court held in the University building. The military judicial procedure was short and settled with dispatch. The least sentence one under suspicion could hope to receive was to be forced to execute an oath of allegiance and to report regularly to the authorities. For a person to violate such an oath was dangerous; for if caught he would be subject to long imprisonment if not to death, and his property would be confiscated and his family left penniless. Many citizens were required in addition to give a bond to guarantee good behavior, while others were banished from their families and places of business or profession to some northern state. To the radical Federal partisans men who belonged to the Methodist Episcopal Church, South, were always suspicious characters.[38]

But all was not bad. No doubt some Methodist preachers in the Conference, perhaps with the knowledge of their Presiding Elders, left the assignments to which they had been appointed, because they felt there was a greater call of duty to become chaplains in the southern armies.[39] Other preachers stuck to their ministerial posts of duty, tried to hold their memberships together, preached the Word of God from Sunday to Sunday (as long as they were allowed by the civil authorities to preach at all), visited the sick and buried the dead. The members of the church in Columbia probably maintained a Sunday School, and must have had meetings of the membership even when preachers could not be present, but where a "class-leader" was present and a religious service was held.

Little is known of the actual church life during these years. No minutes of local church meetings have survived nor any Sunday School records. As far as the newspaper published in Columbia is concerned, one gets the impression that it became the studied policy of the editor to exclude from the columns of his paper everything pertaining to the local Methodist Church. One may read the *Missouri Statesman* from one year's end to

---

[38] Milton S. Matthews, Columbia Methodist, was arrested in March, 1862, and required to take the oath of allegiance and give bond for $1,000. Edwin Robinson, presiding elder of Fayette District, was arrested in April, 1862, required to take the oath and give bond for $2,000. B. H. Spencer, former Columbia pastor and later presiding elder of the St. Charles District, was banished to Indiana for nine months, with no formal charge against him. There were many others like these mentioned.

[39] Enoch M. Marvin was one of the Methodist pastors of St. Louis who left his appointment, secretly made his way south, and served as a chaplain in the Confederate armies during much of the war. Perhaps this was one reason why he had such strong support from the southern annual conferences for his election to the Bishopric in the General Conference of 1866.

the next without knowing whether there was a Methodist Church or minister in town.[40]

The annual assignment of ministers for their preaching appointments for the coming year is usually the last business at an Annual Conference. It has been related hitherto (page 49) that at the last Annual Conference held before the war, September 12-19, 1860, Edwin Robinson [41] had been appointed presiding elder of the Fayette District, and the Columbia Church was put back into the Columbia Circuit with two men appointed on the Circuit, W. G. Miller and Joseph Dines. At the next annual session at Glasgow a year later, the ministers must have assembled with mixed emotions. The election of Lincoln had occurred, the southern states had held their convention at Montgomery and had decided to secede, and the first battles of the war had occurred. Although Missouri, a slave state, did not secede, thousands of Missourians were in the armies on both sides of the conflict. There were few great battles in the state, but the war was fought in country lanes and stealthily by night rather than by armies in battle array, and no "rules of warfare" were observed. It was no time for Bishops of the Methodist Episcopal Church, South, to be travelling in Missouri, and none came to the state, either this year of 1861, nor until four more years had passed.

The ministers of the Conference, however, gathered on September 11, 1861, though in lessened numbers. With no "chief pastor" present, the ministers chose one of their own number to preside, William G. Caples, distinguished for his good sense, his fairness and his spiritual integrity.[42] The outline of business as laid down in the *Discipline* for an annual conference was followed through. There were eight districts in the Conference at that time, and Caples had the assistance of the other Presiding Elders in making out the assignments of ministers to the various preaching points. Edwin Robinson was reappointed to the Fay-

---

[40] There was one exception to this statement. The *Statesman* of March 13, 1863, published this news note: "A RELIGIOUS REVIVAL is progressing at the Methodist Episcopal Church in this place. The house is crowded each night and a deep interest seems to be manifested." There was nothing else published about the meeting, nor the name of any preacher. Note that the word "south" was left off from the name of the church.

[41] Robinson was shot by a squad of Northern soldiers in 1864, apparently for no other reason than that he was a southern Methodist minister.

[42] Caples was killed in 1864 when a cannon ball from a southern battery struck him during the battle in Glasgow.

ette District, Caples himself became Presiding Elder of the Brunswick District, and Berry H. Spencer, former Columbia pastor, was sent as Presiding Elder to the St. Charles District. Joseph Dines, on the Columbia Circuit the year before, was sent to the Rocheport Circuit, and W. G. Miller, the other minister on the Columbia Circuit the pervious year, was sent as pastor to the Louisiana station. A new man, William F. Bell, was sent to the Columbia Circuit. The number of assignments this year was about ten per cent less than the previous year, and many of the appointments were filled by "supplies," superannuated preachers or local preachers for the most part.

One item of business handled by the Annual Conference of 1861 was the election of delegates for the General Conference of 1862, scheduled to meet in May in New Orleans. The Missouri Conference was entitled to six delegates, and the Conference elected the following persons: W. G. Caples, Andrew Monroe, C. I. Vandeventer, W. H. Anderson, Tyson Dines, and Berry H. Spencer. Before the time for the General Conference came, it was realized that it would be difficult, if not impossible, to hold the Conference because New Orleans was in the hands of the Federal forces, and the Conference therefore was cancelled by the Bishops. The Missouri Annual Conference of 1862 had a comparable difficulty in being able to meet, and it was cancelled also. It is presumed that the presiding elders handled the various personnel problems within their respective districts during the following year of 1862-1863 as best they could; preaching services were held in as many of the pulpits as possible during the conference year of 1862-1863.

One must not think that the southern sympathizers, whether members of the Methodist Episcopal Church, South, or not were the only ones in Missouri who suffered from the war. There were thousands of Confederate partisans in the state who never joined the Confederate organized armies, but yet kept up a constant fight against the northern elements of the state. Some of these were known as bushwhackers who might hide by day in the wooded areas, or might be apparently quiet and peacable farmers, but under cover of darkness they would sally forth to wreck destruction upon the loyalist inhabitants, to burn their houses, confiscate their property, or even shoot those whom they knew to be supporters of the North. It was to hunt down such individuals or forces that the Federal authorities stationed small bodies of troops in various strategic places through the state.

"MARTYRDOM IN MISSOURI"

In such a war, innocent persons would be made to suffer in various ways, as in the destruction of their schools and churches. The Mount Zion Methodist Church north of Columbia was burned to the ground in September, 1862, by Federal troops because it was rumored to be a resting place for bushwhackers.

A grave attack on civil rights was the forced suspension in April, 1862, of the *St. Louis Christian Advocate.* This was done by the arrest and imprisonment of the editor, Dr. McAnally, without bringing any charges against him. He lay in a damp prison for months before being paroled without trial; he was subsequently re-arrested from time to time and threatened with banishment. The Federal authorities evidently feared the influence of the *Advocate* was derogatory to their success in Missouri. Early in the war the *Advocate* had published editorials explaining fully and perhaps rather sympathetically the constitutional position of the southern states, namely, that the Constitution had been ratified originally by the individual states as an act of sovereignty, but that they did not thereby surrender their sovereignty; they could now as sovereign states withdraw their ratification and declare their separation from the Union. They believed that if they remained in the Union it would be unconstitutional to nullify the laws passed by Congress, but that they could constitutionally withdraw from the Union. The *Advocate* did not give this as its view, but it explained it so fully and compassionately as to give southern partisans a constitutional argument to support their community of feeling with the South, and thus was said to encourage secession.

Perhaps there was another reason for stopping the publication of the *Advocate*. It was charged that prominent northern Methodists wished to get possession of the *Advocate* press and list of subscribers, and to use them not only as an aid to the Federal cause but as an attempt to swing the Methodists of Missouri back into the Northern Methodist Church. But in any case that purpose if it existed was frustrated by the publisher of the *Advocate,* Rev. P. M. Pinckard, who by legal maneuvers preserved their possession.[43]

The months dragged wearily by. By the fall of 1863 the area

---

[43] The suspension of the paper during the rest of the war was a distinct loss to the morale of the Methodist Episcopal Church, South, as apart from its political effect. Its publication, doubled in size, was resumed by that church, September 21, 1865, at the same price as formerly, $2.00 per year.

of the war in Missouri had retreated so far south that the church authorities felt that it would be safe to hold the Annual Conference again. The preachers, therefore, met at the pre-assigned place, Fulton, October 14, but of course, with no Bishop present. They chose the old war horse, Andrew Monroe, as their chairman, and John D. Vincil, who a few years later became pastor of the Columbia Church, as secretary. In the appointments for the following year, Edwin Robinson was continued on the Fayette District, and Robert H. Jordan and James S. Smith were sent as the team for the Columbia Circuit. Jordan was the same man who in 1834 had been sent as the first preacher on the Columbia Circuit, and was well known to many of the Columbia members. Spencer was not returned to the presiding eldership of the St. Charles District because he was under banishment by the Federal military authorities to Indiana. In fact, of the eight presiding elders of 1861, the last time Conference had met, only three were left in 1863. No reports were preserved from this session of the finances of the various churches, nor of the number of their memberships.

The last Annual Conference of the Civil War period was held in Mexico, September 11, 1864. Although the war west of the Mississippi River had been pushed south into Arkansas, a last great invasion of Missouri by Confederate armies was made late in the summer and fall of 1864. Entering southeast Missouri by way of Arkansas, the hostile forces drove up through the Ozark region to central Missouri with the intention of seizing Jefferson City, but that place was too strongly fortified and the force turned westward. Boone County lay in its path, and Columbia was terror-stricken. All business, including the opening of the University for the fall semester, came to a halt, and a blockhouse, with cannon pointing every direction, was erected at the corner of Eighth and Broadway. A force of all able-bodied men in the town, known as the Columbia Tigers, was formed, and a company of Federal cavalry was hastily summoned from Iowa. As it turned out, Columbia was also too well defended, and the Confederate force turned aside from the town.

The invasion came about the time that the Missouri Annual Conference planned to meet in Mexico. Whether the military dangers made the Sub-District Provost Marshall unusually jittery is not known, but before the preachers could organize they were met with a peremptory order forbidding the meeting even to organize until the members severally subscribed to the following oath:

"I. . . . .of the County of. . . . .in the state of Missouri do solemnly swear that I will bear allegiance to the United States and support and sustain the Constitution and laws thereof; that I will maintain the national sovereignty paramount to that of all state, county or Confederate powers; that I will discourage, discountenance and forever oppose secession, rebellion and the disintegration of the Federal Union; that I disclaim and denounce all faith and fellowship with the so-called Confederate Armies and pledge my honor, my property and my life to the sacred performance of this my sacred oath of allegiance to the government of the United States of America."

The members of the Conference refused to take this new oath. They had taken a similar oath, the "Convention" oath of June 10, 1862, and they refused to conform to this new test. They placed their case before the Provost Marshall General, who after some delay instructed the Sub-District Provost Marshall to allow the Conference to organize and to proceed with its business. This was done September 16, 1864. In the absence of the Bishop, Monroe was again elected president pro tem, and Vincil, secretary. Horace Brown was named presiding elder of the Fayette District, and Robert H. Jordan was returned to Columbia, with Thompson Penn as his assistant. The few records of the Conference were as devoid of statistics as the previous Conference records had been. Within a few months the war was over, and a new era began.

Section IX
Back to Normalcy

"*Normalcy*" as an attribute for a Christian church means to move forward. That certainly had not been done by the Methodist Episcopal Church, South, during the destructiveness of the Civil War. It was, perhaps, remarkable that the Church had not been stamped out completely as many people in the North expected it to be. In Missouri, as throughout the South, many local congregations had been scattered and impoverished, their leading members killed or moved to some distant state, and their places of worship despoiled or destroyed. What more natural than for the northern Church to "move in," to "assist" these stricken southern communities by "honest missionary work." But in southern Methodist history the early part of these years of the "Reconstruction Period" seemed to be characterized by a rather bare-faced attempt by some of the leaders of the Methodist Episcopal Church, not the entire Church, to take over the congregations and buildings of the Church, South, an attempt to *confiscate* a religious organization as a piece of property is confiscated in time of war.

To this end an order was secured from U. S. Secretary of War, Edwin M. Stanton, directing Bishop Ames of the northern Church to take possession of the southern church buildings, and to dispossess the "rebel" ministers and appoint "loyal" ministers to fill their pulpits. This was a very serious infraction of religious freedom for many of the local congregations in the South, including also many of those in Missouri. It was eventually stopped by the local resistance of the members of the Church, and in the end the whole scheme was crushed through decisions of state and federal courts. But it left a residue of hard feelings even in those communities such as Columbia where no such attempt was made. The Columbia Methodists were generally from the South, either immediately or by descent, and too sympathetic with the South for such a movement to succeed, and it wasn't even tried. The southern church papers published in their columns these attempts at "grand larceny" as they were called. This policy of appropriating the property and organizations of the southern Church, pushed by different church leaders in the North, certainly did not sweeten the relations between the two great branches of Methodism; it helped to postpone the day of "union" for seventy-four years after the war.

But the transfer of churches from one denomination to the other was not a one-way street, The southern Church did not use the same tactics as the northern Church did; but when just after the war, quite a large majority of the districts in the Baltimore Conference voted to leave the northern Church and join the southern, they were joyfully and officially welcomed by the southern General Conference of 1866. That was bitter medicine for the northern Church.

Another serious problem affecting more or less all denominational churches in Missouri, but thought to bear most heavily upon the Catholic and the southern Methodist clergy, was a provision in the new radical state constitution of 1865 requiring all clergymen of whatever church or rank to take a certain oath that they had not done or would not do certain things prescribed in the new state constitution.[44]

As long as the oath provision was binding, clergymen could not exercise the functions of their offices without first executing the oath before a notary public, under penalty of six months imprisonment and a fine of $500. Patently unconstitutional, it was yet sporadically enforced through the rest of 1865 and 1866 until declared unconstitutional by the United States Supreme Court. Its enforcement depended largely upon local public officials and local public opinion, and since southern Methodists and Catholics were unpopular with the radicals, warrants were sworn out against them more frequently than against other denominations. In St. Louis, on the other hand, Grand Juries refused to indict ministers for declining to subscribe to the oath.[45]

In the spring of 1865, three leading members of the Missouri Conference, realizing the civil disability under which the south-

---

[44] The state constitutional convention which met January 6, 1865, grew out of the intense personal and political feelings, general disorder, and rapidly growing demand for violent and radical measures marking the last months of the war. It was controlled by the rabidly anti-slavery factions, and among other things wrote into the constitution this oath applying to clergymen of all denominations.

[45] The constitutionality of the oath provision was questioned in the case of Cummings, a Catholic priest who was arrested for performing Mass soon after the Constitution went into effect. The district court decided against Cummings, and the case was appealed to the State Supreme Court which also decided against Cummings. He took an appeal then to the United States Supreme Court which decided in December, 1866, that the oath provision was unconstitutional. (See *4 Wallace, 277*.)

ern Methodist clergy would work, called for a meeting of the prominent members of the Conference, to convene at Palmyra June 22, 1865. They were to consult on "the state of the church," and report their findings to the public in appropriate resolutions. The work of this unofficial conference was of great significance not only for southern Methodist churches in Missouri but for the entire denomination throughout the South. Bishop Kavanaugh was present, appearing for the first time since 1860 in a meeting in Missouri and gave great encouragement to the group of ministers. After careful consideration and discussion, resolutions and reports were adopted unanimously and were sent out in an eight-page leaflet, not only to every southern Methodist minister in Missouri but to leaders of the denomination throughout the nation.

To understand the acidity of the Palmyra reports against the Methodist Episcopal Church, one must remember that this was just the time when Bishop Ames of that Church was trying to take over the southern churches in the Mississippi Valley. The Palmyra meeting declared it to be "of paramount importance" and the "imperative duty" of the clergymen to maintain the distinct organization of the southern Church. Denying the smug assurance of the northern aggressors that their church was the parent church, the southern clergymen declared that in descent and "original paternity" from the first establishment of Methodism in America, no other church was prior to their own, and anyone claiming such priority "was trying to deceive the people;" to the plea that the end of slavery had swept away all differences between the North and the South, it was replied that the question which had divided the church was not whether slavery was right or wrong but whether it was a legitimate subject for ecclesiastical legislation. The ministers gathered at Palmyra found that about two-thirds of the appointments in the Conference had been regularly supplied with preachers and called upon the Presiding Elders to appoint supplies as far as practicable to vacant pulpits until the next Annual Conference met.

The next session of the Missouri Annual Conference met at Hannibal a few weeks after the Palmyra meeting, August 16, 1865, with Bishop Kavanaugh presiding and John D. Vincil as secretary. The proceedings of this Conference were published in a printed pamphlet; in an abbreviated form the Annual Conference Minutes had been published more or less regularly since 1852 in the *St. Louis Christian Advocate* until its suspension in

1862.[46] These Minutes of 1865 included a long report on "The State of the Church," taken quite largely from the resolutions adopted at the Palmyra Meeting a few weeks earlier:

> In calling attention to this subject, the first thing worthy of note is, its imminently perilous condition. Never were the signs of a violent persecution of the Church and Ministry of God more manifest. Never since the days of bloody persecution has opposition to the Church and Ministry, and to our common Christianity, been so bold, so defiant, so well organized, and so bitter and determined as now. . . . In the afflictions which have come upon the Church of God in Missouri, our denomination has had a double share; and in persecutions yet to come we are singled out for special attention. We have been denounced as a 'secession, traitorous, and rebel organization; as unworthy of civil protection; and, indeed, as only deserving to be suppressed and destroyed by the Government.' . . . .some of our houses of worship have been burned, others dismantled and otherwise injured or destroyed. Of the use of others we have been forcibly deprived for months, and even for years; and the most painful fact in this bill of complaints is, that the latter has frequently been done by men professing to be Christian Ministers! . . . . Some of our own ministers and members have fallen by the hands of violence, while others had to flee for their lives. The principle reason for the bitter persecution with which we have been assailed is the word, SOUTH, affixed to our ecclesiastical name. The charge has been made . . . that this word in our name means *secession, treason,* and *rebellion,* and hence there is nothing more common than for our enemies to call us *The Rebel Church.* . . .We wish to say, then, distinctly and emphatically that the word *South* as it attaches to our ecclesiastical name, *never did, and does not now, have any political significance whatever.*

The statement went on to say that a change of name could be effected only by the General Conference which was not to meet until April, 1866. The committee proposed, therefore, to hold to the present organization, and to obey the 23rd Article of Religion

---

[46] In even more abbreviated form, they had been published in *Minutes of the Annual Conference of the M.E. Church, South* since 1845.

as set forth in the *Discipline* of the Church, *viz.* "The President, our Congress, the General Assemblies, and the Councils of State, as the delegates of the people, are the rulers of the United States of America, according to the division of power made to them by the Constitution of the United States, and by the Constitutions of their respective States."

Other reports of committees to the Annual Conference of 1865 urged the reorganization of the schools and colleges of the Church, and a better supply of religious books and periodicals for the members of the Church. Relative to the latter subject, it was urged that the time was ripe for the resumption of the publication of the *St. Louis Christian Advocate.* "The necessity of the church demands it and our people are anxious for it." In response to this request, the former editor of the *Advocate,* Dr. D. R. McAnally, resumed its publication September 21, 1865. The subscription price was still two dollars per year, but the paper was enlarged to eight pages a week. The initial number of the new series of the paper contained the recent Pastoral Address of the southern Bishops to the Church at large, the plan of Episcopal visitation for 1865-1866, and among other things a long argument from the *Richmond Christian Advocate,* which had also resumed publication, against union with the northern Church. The paper was sent to all who had been subscribers when the *Advocate* was forced to suspend in 1862.

There were no financial statistics given in the published minutes of 1865, and no reports on the number of members of the different churches. The appointments for the coming year included, for Columbia (still as it had been all through the war on the Columbia Circuit), John R. Taylor and R. A. Claughton. The venerable Andrew Monroe was appointed Presiding Elder of the Fayette District. There were five districts at this time where there had been eight in 1861. Many of the circuits or stations were left without appointments and were "to be supplied" later as far as possible. Finally, the Conference charged the preachers to take up collections to defray the expenses of the delegates to the next General Conference. The delegates elected to that Conference were as follows: Andrew Monroe, P. M. Pinckard, William M. Rush, C. I. Vandeventer, and B. H. Spencer. All except Pinckard had been serving rather regularly for years past as Presiding Elders, and Pinckard had been publisher of the *Advocate* and head of the supply house in St. Louis for religious literature.

This General Conference of 1866, held in New Orleans, was one of the most important Conferences in the annals of the Methodist Episcopal Church, South. In any history of the local church, down to the smallest point in any circuit, the actions and constructive policies of this Conference were most influential. It will be remembered that no General Conference had been held since 1858, and vast changes had taken place since that time. In the realm of the general supervision of the church, no Bishops had been elected even in 1858, so that the College of Bishops was depleted and many had become less effective because of advancing age.

In their opening Address to the Conference, the Bishops admitted that they had been compelled during the last few years to confine their Episcopal supervision to the conferences east of the Mississippi River, but for the most part those conferences had been held regularly. They declared that the Church had not become complicated with political affairs. They had issued a Pastoral Address in August, 1865, giving advice and encouragement which seemed necessary at the time. The publication of the church papers had been revived generally since the war had closed; but the missionary work of the church had been almost ruined.[47]

To make the supervision of the Church more effective, this General Conference elected four new Bishops: William M. Wightman of South Carolina, Enoch M. Marvin of Missouri, David S. Doggett of Virginia, and Holland N. McTyeire of Tennessee. In connection with the College of Bishops, the first outline of the territorial division of the church into Episcopal Districts was made. These Districts were numbered, and the Fifth included the Annual Conferences of Missouri, St. Louis, Indian Mission, Arkansas, and Little Rock. An effective Bishop was to reside within each District.

Another question which caused considerable discussion in the General Conference was that of the modification of the name of the Church. Before the war, in the General Conference of 1858, that question had been considered briefly, but no proposi-

---

[47] It will be remembered that the missionary work had been quite largely with the colored population of the South, but with the change of the status of the colored people from slaves to free persons, that work now needed reorganizing. The missionary work of the church was reorganized and divided between two separate boards, The Board of Domestic Missions and The Board of Foreign Missions.

tion for discussion had reached the floor of the house from any committee. One suggestion at that time had been to change the name to "The Methodist Church in America." After much discussion, it was now in 1866 proposed to change the name to "The Episcopal Methodist Church of America," but this change had to be approved by a three-fourths vote of the members of the annual conferences. Some of the conferences later approved the change almost unanimously, but others were divided or opposed. *The St. Louis Christian Advocate* in various editorials vigorously opposed the change (despite the strictures on the word "south" in the Annual Conference of 1865); and when the vote was taken finally in the Missouri Conference, it stood 28 for the change and 30 against. Eventually, the total vote of the church was 1,168 in favor of the new name to 409 against. This was slightly less than the required three-fourths majority.

Another constructive measure of the General Conference of 1866, which also affected every unit of the church by making its government more democratic, was the proposition to introduce Lay Representation in the General and Annual Conferences.[48] This also had to be approved by a three-fourths vote of the members of the annual conferences. It eventually carried throughout the church by a vote of 1,199 in favor to 371 against. To make the local membership still more conscious of the organization and work of the individual units of the Church, the General Conference of 1866 provided for the holding of local church conferences. An order of service was suggested for these meetings, with reports from the preachers, class leaders, Sunday School superintendents, and stewards. These meetings were to be held at least every three months, but were not to interfere with the preaching services or other stated services of the local church. Thus was introduced the Local Church Conferences.

There were two other interesting changes affecting the local church. First, the probationary system was stricken out of the *Discipline* entirely. A person either belonged to the Church or did not. Second, the time limit for preachers on charges was extended from two years to four. This did not mean that the preachers were to be appointed for four year terms. They were still appointed, as they had been since early in Methodist history,

---

[48] District Conferences were not formally constituted in the Methodist Episcopal Church, South, until the General Conference of 1870, though they were held in some Annual Conferences before that time.

for one year terms. But under the law of the church for a number of years past, they could be reappointed for a second year. Now, under this new provision, they could be reappointed three times, making four successive years on one charge. As a matter of fact, for some 20 or 30 years after this change in the length of pastoral tenure was made, ministers for Columbia were reappointed usually only twice and served no more than three years generally. The changes made by the General Conference for the introduction of local church conferences, for the abolition of the probationary system for membership, and for the extension of the time limit for pastors were not referred for approval or disapproval to a vote of the members of the annual conferences.

Following the General Conference of 1866, local pastors were notified by their presiding elders to prepare their annual statistics with care. Circumstances had been such during the past few years to make this impossible, but now it could be done. A long letter from Andrew Monroe, presiding elder of the Fayette District, printed in the *Advocate* of July 18, 1866, told of the gains made in that district during the past year. The only reference he made to the Columbia Church, however, was to report the addition in membership of three "clever young men," but gave no names. Monroe frequently wrote letters to the *Advocate,* but seldom gave much information of historical value.[49]

The Missouri Annual Conference of 1866,[50] convening in Richmond, September 5, was an unusually important meeting of that organization, because it had to vote on the changes proposed by the recent General Conference and conform its administrative practices to other changes made by the General Conference. Bishop Doggett presided, and opened the Conference with an address of an inspirational and informational nature. He told of some of the changes made in the *Discipline* of the Church. He referred to the proposed change in the name of the Church and to the provision for Lay Representation, both of which proposals the General Conference had passed by more than a two-thirds vote and had been referred to the annual conferences for approval or disapproval.

Lay Representation was a change which, if approved by the Church at large would affect the administration of the Church

---

[49] *The St. Louis Christian Advocate,* July 18 and August 8, 1866.
[50] Although the Proceedings of this Conference were printed in a pamphlet, a better and more complete account of its work appeared in the *Advocate* of September 19.

from top to bottom; but since this had not yet been approved by the Church at large, it would not come up for discussion in this Annual Conference except to vote on the measure.

Since Columbia was still only a point on the Columbia Circuit, there were no statistics from the Columbia congregation. In the appointments for the year of 1866-1867, Andrew Monroe was returned as presiding elder of the Fayette District, and Thomas DeMoss and Henry D. McEwin were appointed to the Columbia Circuit. It is quite evident that the Bishop and his cabinet at that time did not think of the Columbia church as sufficiently important to appoint a stationed minister there. This conclusion is based also upon a notice in the *Advocate* of December 16, 1866, which told of an apportionment of $700 for Central College among the churches of the Fayette District. Columbia was to raise only as much as Rocheport or Huntsville, and less than half as much as Glasgow.

Needless to say, the Columbia membership was disappointed when the appointments were announced. This appears in a letter printed in the *Advocate* of April 17, 1867. The letter also told of other difficulties which some churches had at that time. "Our church record was not left with anyone here and cannot be found," the letter said. As a result, they had no official record of the membership of the church. In regard to a minister for the church, the writer of the letter wrote: "We needed a zealous, active man here last fall so much, and fearing Conference would serve us as it had previously done, we concluded to take our case in our own hands and so corresponded with one of the preachers." They had nearly reached an agreement by which he would become their pastor, provided he were appointed, when they received a letter from Monroe begging them to do nothing further. He wrote that he had his eye on a young man with commanding talents and deep piety, whom he would send to Columbia if they would agree to support him. They agreed; but when the notice of appointments came out, they found that they were thrown on the circuit again with two preachers. "One we have never seen, the other preached once for us up to the first Sabbath in January." (From early September to early January!) "We were all delighted with him but owing to the distance where he lives, it is impossible for him to take care of us here as a shepherd ought to watch over his flock. He was not at his appointment in March nor last Sabbath, so you can see how seldom we receive the Bread of Life. We have had our church repaired and carpeted and by way of inducing Conference to pay more attention to us, we ladies are raising means to build a parsonage."

Emphasizing the desire of the Columbia Church to become a station church another correspondent in July, 1867, wrote to the *Advocate* that he had just attended the Commencement Exercises in Columbia of the University of Missouri, and that while there he had made the acquaintance of many of the Methodist people. He had found the ladies of the church busily engaged in conducting a bazaar to help secure funds for building a parsonage. They thought that if they could supply a parsonage it would help to secure a station appointment. When conference met in September, 1867, however, the Columbia people were again disappointed for they found they were still left on the Columbia Circuit. At this point they must have brought strong pressure upon the Bishop, for in the *Missouri Statesman* of October 4, 1867, a notice appeared that the Bishop to accommodate the wishes of the Methodists, had made the local church a Station and had appointed Rev. J. P. Nolan pastor for the present year. Nolan was to preach for the first time on the following Sabbath morning, October 6, at eleven o'clock.[51]

There was no information of a statistical nature about the individual charges in the earlier printed proceedings of the Annual Conference. There was nothing in the Minutes of this character until 1867 but even that was only the report of collections for Domestic and Foreign Missions. Nothing was reported from the Columbia Circuit for either. There is a statistical summary, however, for the Districts which gives the following information for Fayette District: white members, 2,726; colored members, 71; local preachers, 19; number of churches, 19; Sunday Schools, 29; number of scholars, 1,955; volumes in all the

---

[51] This Mr. Nolan had been appointed at the Conference in September to St. Charles but was evidently changed afterwards to Columbia. He had been a member of the Conference for some years and seemed to be something of an educator for he had been sent the previous year as principal of Macon High School, owned by the church. To show that the appointment of Nolan was a sudden change in the interim between conferences another notice in the same issue of the *Statesman* gave the itinerary of Rev. DeMoss for preaching services on the Columbia Circuit during the month of October and this had DeMoss at Columbia on the second Sabbath of October.

The reason Nolan's name does not appear on the usual list of Columbia pastors is that he was appointed after the Annual Conference had adjourned, and was not reappointed to Columbia the next September.

libraries, 3,430; preacher's salaries for the district, $5,375; but collected for salaries, $4,075; conference collections, $252.16; spent for church repairs and buildings, $13,860; value of churches and parsonages, $266,175. If those details could have been shown for the individual churches, it would have given a good picture of the work in each local church.

The Columbia congregation at this time was evidently an active group but it was largely a feminine group. A letter from Thomas DeMoss, appearing in the *Advocate* of October 9, 1867, apparently written before Nolan's appointment was known, told about the work on his Circuit and mentioned a series of Revival Meetings at Mt. Zion Church with 30 additions to the Church. At that place the members had erected a fine church on the same spot where the old Zion Church stood, burned down by the Federal soldiers during the war. DeMoss spoke briefly of Columbia where he said the membership was not large, "especially the male portion of it, but I think it is more than made up by the noble band of ladies that belong to the Columbia Church. They have cleaned the old sanctuary and have made it look like the House of the Lord. They are in need of a parsonage, and in this they must and will succeed for they have now some $700 or $800."

One must realize the pride and joy of the Methodists of Columbia as soon as it became known that their church had been raised in rank to a station church; they would have a minister living in their midst and preaching services every Sunday as other Protestant denominations had. It was almost like passing from childhood to adolescence. They redoubled their efforts to raise money to build a parsonage, and by 1869 the small congregation had bought a good location near the end of Price Avenue and had built a two-story frame residence for their pastor. The necessary funds had been raised largely through the efforts of the women of the church. The construction of a parsonage had been one of their main projects ever since the fifties. From this time, October, 1867, Columbia was never placed back on a circuit again.[52]

---

[52] The following editorial from *The St. Louis Christian Advocate* of September 18, 1867, will show something of the feelings of ministers and laymen about annual conferences at this time, and probably for many years before and after:
The season for our Conference is at hand . . .
For weeks preceding our annual convocations of Methodist preachers

how frequently does the word "Conference" occur with pastors and people? The last great effort to raise the preacher's salary is made just before "Conference." He is all industry in gathering up the statistics to be reported, and the moneys for missions, widows, orphans, superannuates and bishops, to be paid over at the approaching "Conference." Preachers and people alike look with interest to the coming "Conference," and if a "new preacher" be expected, who will "the conference" send us? is a question often asked by the people. If the preacher must change his field of pastoral labors, where will his destination be, is a question often considered by him.

At "Conference" the answer will be furnished, and with a light or heavy heart, he will to his home return for the inevitable "move."

At Conference every preacher will report himself unless providentially hindered, for the Conference season is to all one of the most pleasant occasions it falls to the lot of the itinerant preacher to enjoy. From every part of the Conference territory they come at the appointed time by all available modes of conveyance—by river steamers and rapidly rolling cars; by lumbering stage coaches and smoothly going buggies and carriages, and some slow plodding on the faithful horse, the sharer with his rider in a year of toil and travel. Here and there a wife accompanies her husband, and now and then a juvenile or infantile member of a clerical household swells the number of the gathering company, and occasionally a blooming daughter accompanies her fond father to see more of Methodism and Methodist preachers than she has seen in her own quiet parsonage home.

Of the clerical company, we find the observed of all observers. "The Bishop"; the venerable, gray-haired fathers; the stalwart men in the vigor of mature years and powers, and the "sons of the prophets"—"the young men"—the first arrivals, to undergo their annual examinations in their theological studies. What beaming smiles! What joyous countenances! What words of kindly greeting! What cordial "hand shaking!" What real pleasure abounds, when all these brethren meet at "conference" after another year of pastoral labor.

The hour of meeting arrives. The Bishop "in the chair" conducts the religious exercises. With swelling hearts and tremulous voices, and some with tearful eyes, they sing:

"And are we yet alive,
And see each other's face?"

How fervent the responses to the fervent prayer which follows—prayer for the preachers, their families and charges; for the Church at large, and the citizens among whom they temporarily abide. But the time and space would fail us to record the thoughts that rapidly crowd upon us in connection with a Conference season from the gathering of its members till the final consummation of its work; the reception in the last moment of the appointments for another year—appointments on which the success of the Church and the destiny of immortal beings rest in many places. Let the people at home follow their preachers with their prayers, invoke for the Bishop Divine guidance, and receive as the messengers of God the preachers assigned them, and let the year to follow be a year of peace, of love, and of prosperity.

Section X
The Columbia Methodist Congregation Outgrows Its First Church and Builds Its Second

The history of church denominations as well as of other institutions may be divided for the sake of convenience into periods, though contemporaries do not generally recognize that they are passing from one period to another. It is not always possible either for later historians to name an exact date for the end of one period and the commencement of another. But if such a date were needed to mark the end for the Columbia Methodists of the harassments of the war years and the discouragements in subsequent years, it would be October 4, 1867, when it was announced that the Columbia Church had been made a station church with Rev. J. P. Nolan as pastor. Nolan evidently had a successful year at Columbia. He made a new roll of the membership in the place of the lost roll, and stirred up the interest of the local congregation in missions. Little information of a statistical nature appears in the minutes of the next Annual Conference, but the collections for missions from the individual charges were given; Nolan had raised $15.35 for domestic missions and $122 for foreign missions, the first such report of the interest of the Columbia congregation in missions.

The missions of the Church at large were in financial straits during and after the war.[53] A report made to the General Conference of 1866 disclosed that the Board of Missions was in debt about $60,000, due to the impossibility during the war of collecting and sending funds from the South to the foreign fields. Under these conditions, a New York City friend had come to the rescue of the Board by loaning the amount necessary to keep the mission fields active. The amount of this debt was now apportioned among the annual conferences, and the share of the Missouri Conference was $1,000. It will be seen, therefore, that Nolan raised from the Columbia congregation over one-tenth of the entire amount apportioned to the Conference.

The domestic work of the Board of Missions, that among the former slaves, involved not so much the paying of a debt as the

---

[53] General Conference Minutes, 1866, page 61. See also *St. Louis Christian Advocate,* December 15, 1869, article on missions of the church.

entire reorganization of that work. This problem consumed considerable time in the General Conference of 1866. Whether it was understood by the leaders of the Church as being a part of the whole problem of the reorganization of society in the southern states after the war is not known; but it was believed the colored people could not, and would not, remain members of the local churches, as in slavery days. Therefore, eventually, the Negroes were encouraged to organize a separate "Colored Methodist Episcopal Church, South," though after organization they themselves would determine the exact name of their church. This was the beginning of segregation in the church, a problem still unsolved after the passing of a century. The net result at the time was a meeting of leading colored preachers at Talladega, Alabama, in November, 1869, with two Bishops from the Methodist Episcopal Church, South, to advise them and to ordain those elected as Bishops. The work of this Church was organized in Missouri the same year. The name the Negroes chose for their Church was "The Colored M. E. Church of America." This was only one of the several colored church denominations organized after the war, but it was the one in which the Methodist Episcopal Church, South, was most interested.

Since the Columbia Church was now a station church, its membership would be reported at the Annual Conference of 1868. This was 72, only 72! When one recalls that eight years before, in 1860, Columbia reported a membership of 89 white persons and 72 colored, one can realize the unhappy effect of the war, and perhaps of the downgrading of Columbia by the Bishop and his cabinet. It may be also that since the roll of the members had been lost the previous year, not all the names on the previous roll had been placed on the new roll. The Bishop at the Conference in 1868 appointed Nolan to be in charge of the Macon Female Seminary, owned by the Church, and left the Columbia church "to be supplied." Finally, in November, the supply was announced, Rev. T. J. Gooch, a transfer from the Memphis Conference. The presiding elder of the previous year, D. A. Leeper, had suffered a long illness during the winter and died in March, 1868. To fill his place the new presiding elder was W. A. Mayhew. Gooch was happily received by the Columbia congregation and evidently made an able preacher and a most excellent pastor. In January, 1869, the church bought a handsome organ. This

THE COLUMBIA CONGREGATION OUTGROWS FIRST CHURCH

added to the interest of the congregation in the public services.[54] It was reported at this time in the *Statesman* that the congregations were much larger and the interest manifested in the welfare of the church much greater than had marked its history for years.

At the end of the conference year of 1868-1869, Gooch reported a membership of 91, which was a good increase over the preceding year. Gooch was transferred to Glasgow in 1869 and in his place the Rev. M. B. Chapman, another transfer into the Conference, was appointed to Columbia, while Mayhew was reappointed as presiding elder. Chapman, assisted by the other Protestant ministers of Columbia and by Bishop Marvin, held a series of revival services in January and February, in which there were over forty conversions.

In the meantime during the late sixties, the church at large was having its first experiences with the election of laymen to the various councils of the church and with their presence in those bodies. An address had been issued to the Church by the Bishops in May, 1867, saying among other things that the annual conferences had approved by the necessary three-fourths majority the admission of laymen to the conferences. When the Missouri Annual Conference met at Macon in September, 1867, therefore, there were a number of lay delegates present for the first time.[55] To provide a regular way for their election and admission thereafter, this Conference approved a resolution that during each conference year the presiding elders were to call a meeting in their respective districts, to be composed of all the traveling and local preachers, Sunday School superintendents, exhorters,[56] and two other laymen from each appointment within their districts. The laymen of this meeting were to elect four lay representatives to the following annual conference, and to attend to any other matters referred to them.

Among the results of lay representation was the development on the part of the laity of greater interest in church finance. The Bishops and connectional officers of the Church and the General

---

[54] The use of instrumental music in Methodist church services had not been common before this time. The General Conference of 1858 had considered a resolution to ban such music, but the resolution was laid on the table.

[55] *Missouri Statesman*, September 20, 1867. This gives the names and addresses of a few of the laymen who were present; apparently none was from Columbia.

[56] "Exhorters" were laymen, appointed to exhort but not to preach.

Conference could decide the amount of money needed for church-wide enterprises and levy assessments against the annual conferences; they in turn could add the amount they needed and levy assessments against the districts. The districts might divide their shares among the local churches, and the churches assess their individual members. But if they did not pay, the whole project failed. Bishop McTyeire in an article published in the church press [57] in 1871 came to the conclusion that the assessment plan, all the way down to the person who eventually paid the money, was the best and most satisfactory plan that could be devised for raising money for church enterprises. He wrote that the only alternative was the renting of pews, something which has been foreign to Methodist economy throughout the history of the Church. Otherwise, the amount needed in each community would have to be squeezed from a few liberal persons.

Closely related to this problem was the lack of funds raised for the support of superannuated preachers and their widows and dependent children, a condition which often led to pathetic situations. In an effort to improve such pitiful conditions, some of the annual conferences were gradually adopting a plan to assess each active clerical member of the conference with a certain percentage of his salary for the support of the superannuates. Though opposed by some of the preachers, this was slowly extended throughout the Church, and became known as the "five per cent plan." It was tentatively approved by the Missouri Annual Conference in 1867, and went into effect finally in 1870. The result for a number of years practically revolutionized the support of the superannuates and their families. It was a type of "social security" years before that term was commonly used. The amount required from each preacher was supposed to be added to his salary and raised by the local congregations, but be it said with shame many local congregations failed to do this, and it became a "5% tax" on the preachers.

The clerical members of the annual conferences took very seriously that item of their business of passing on the character of the preachers. In the Missouri Annual Conference of 1869, there were two interesting cases, one involving a man who afterwards became the pastor of the Columbia church, and the other a man who later became presiding elder in the Fayette District. Against the first it was charged that he falsely interpreted the

---

[57] See *St. Louis Christian Advocate,* November 1, 1871.

Articles of Religion of the Church. It was charged that he taught that the simple resolution to do better and to join the church was regeneration; on the "witness of the spirit," he taught that the Spirit does not primarily witness to the fact of regeneration; on the spiritual condition of children, he taught that children are born regenerate and pure. He was tried by a committee which decided that his answers were not satisfactory and that he should be admonished in open conference by the Bishop. The Bishop performed this task kindly, and then the man's character was "passed," that is, approved.

The second case was that of a preacher who had been prominent in the conference for some years, and was one of the leading members in later years. A committee brought charges that while he was in sympathy with the Articles of Religion, yet he was unfortunate in use of terms and modes of expression and that if he would be more cautious, he would render greater service to the church. His character was afterwards passed with approval by the whole conference.

At the end of the next conference year in September, 1870, the Columbia minister, Mr. Chapman, reported a membership of 138, an increase of more than 50 per cent over the previous year, due to the revival services held during the previous winter. This Conference of 1870 was held in Columbia, the second such meeting held there in the history of the local church. The business sessions were in the comparatively new Presbyterian Church at the corner of Tenth Street and Broadway, but preaching services every afternoon and evening were conducted in the Methodist Church building on lower Broadway. Among the extra features of this Conference was an invitation from President Daniel Read of the University for the members to visit the University (composed at that time of the original main building, a small observatory west of the main building, and a wooden normal building in the northwest corner of the campus.) In the chapel of the University President Read made a short address, to which Bishop McTyeire responded.

According to the financial records of this Conference, over $12,000 was needed for the superannuates and to bring up the salaries of those preachers whose congregations had not paid their salaries in full, while only $2,031 was reported for such purposes. From this time forward, however, the needs of the superannuates were reported separately from the salary deficits, and unless the appointment was a mission church a preacher was expected to secure his salary from his own congregation.

The appointments for the coming year returned Mayhew as presiding elder of the Fayette District but the pastor of the Columbia Church was again changed. John D. Vincil,[58] Secretary of the Conference and one of its leading members, was sent to Columbia. He was the first in a line of several three-year pastors for Columbia. Vincil's introduction to Columbia was most sad; his wife was taken ill, and died on November 9, 1870. He went ahead bravely with his work, however, and was supported loyally by his congregation. In March, Vincil held a series of evangelistic services, and reached a class of people in the community which had hitherto been untouched. Several University students and a number of heads of families in Columbia were converted. The congregations became uncomfortably large for the little church building, and thus in his first year Vincil was introduced to a problem faced by many church organizations, and one which was to face the Columbia congregation again in future years—too small a building in which to hold public services.

After the revival services, held in the spring of 1871, the official members of the church decided to dispose of the building on lower Broadway, secure a new location, and erect a new church home. The new site finally chosen was about five blocks east of the old building, on the north side of Broadway, nearly opposite the entrance of Hitt Street.[59] On this new location, a splendid brick structure was erected in 1871 and 1872. Its spire reached heavenward, higher than any other building in town.

---

[58] Vincil had been secretary of the Missouri Annual Conference in 1863, and was reelected annually for 41 years. He died October 12, 1904, and W. F. McMurry, afterwards Bishop, presented his memoirs at the Conference of 1905. McMurry said that Vincil "had much to do with laying the foundation of Methodism in Columbia, and until his going away, he had a large place in the hearts of that city." While he was pastor there, in 1873, the State University conferred upon him the degree of Doctor of Divinity. Vincil served for two terms as a member of the University Board of Curators. He married for his second wife after he left Columbia, Miss Emma Norwood, daughter of one of the eminent professors of the University. His standing among his fellow ministers is shown by the fact that he was elected as a delegate to seven General Conferences of the Church. "There was never a time," McMurry said, "in all his connection with the Church that he did not stand ready to defend her policy, preach her doctrines, and forward her interest in every possible way."

[59] The old church building was sold to the Columbia School Board in 1871 and converted into a four-room school building for white children. A building for the colored children, the beginnings of Douglas School, had been erected previously.

The Methodist Church in Columbia
1870-1904

Bishop Enoch M. Marvin

Thomas J. Gooch
Pastor, 1868-1869

J. D. Vincil
Pastor, 1870-1873

THE COLUMBIA CONGREGATION OUTGROWS FIRST CHURCH

The cost was about $20,000 and construction was commenced with only about $4,500 subscribed. As it happened, and might happen again in the future, by the time the building was completed and before it was paid for, one of the great depressions in American history shook the country; and the growing amount of interest on borrowed money threatened to bankrupt the church. The members did everything conceivable to wipe out the indebtedness so that the church could be dedicated, but they failed.

Under Vincil's successor, W. H. Lewis, the church found itself in dire financial straits. It had even sold its parsonage to get funds to relieve the pressure, but that was far from enough. Finally, in June, 1875, it was decided to ask Bishop Marvin to come to Columbia and, with his flair for persuading people to make contributions, to hold a series of public services to which all the people of the town would be invited. If this were successful in raising the indebtedness, the dedication of the church would follow. The date chosen for the meeting was Sunday, June 27, 1875. It was a fine day and a large crowd of representative citizens was present. The amount of cash and pledges needed was thought to be about $9,000. During the forenoon service, featured by a sermon by Bishop Marvin on the power of money and followed by a person to person canvass of the entire congregation, about two-thirds of the debt needed was raised. The entire evening service was spent by the Bishop in pleading for the remaining third; he announced that the church could not be dedicated unless the full amount was raised. Finally it was announced that all of the debt was covered by pledges. Calling the officers of the church to meet him at the pulpit, the Bishop held a short dedicatory service and then the benediction was pronounced. The members of the church, some with streaming faces, crowded to the front and congratulated the Bishop and each other. It was one of the great days in the history of Columbia Methodism.[60]

---

[60] *The Missouri Statesman,* July 2, 1875, described fully these services in the church and gave the entire list of subscribers even down to the one dollar contributors. One person contributed a woman's gold ring which, however, was to be returned to her as soon as her name was known. There were about 150 names on the subscription roll ranging all the way from $600 to $1. While this list undoubtedly included most of the names of the heads of families and many of the women and children of the church, it could not be regarded as a roll of church members because many were present and contributed who were from other churches. The finance committee was composed of B. McAlester, G. W. Henderson, W. T. Anderson, G. W. Riggans, and F. D. Evans.

But there was a depressing postscript to this meeting of June 27th. Evidently the financial records had not been well kept, for it was discovered that an item of a thousand dollar indebtedness had been overlooked. Then one of the best members of the church died, and his subscription of $400 could not be collected from his estate. Moreover, in the continuing hard times, several of the subscribers to the debt fund failed in business, and the interest charges kept increasing. It began to be whispered on the street that the Methodists after all were going to lose their new church building. Under these conditions a committee of responsible business men was appointed in 1878 to make an accurate survey of the financial situation and report to the church. It reported that $4,300 was needed; a new subscription campaign was quietly begun, and $3,400 was pledged, but they seemed to be able to go no further. Then the pastor at that time, George W. Horn, wrote a letter to the *St. Louis Christian Advocate,* appealing to its subscribers for aid. The response was large enough finally to pay the entire debt.[61]

---

[61] *Missouri Statesman,* March 8, 1878.

SECTION XI
Growth of the Church Through the Last Third of the 19th Century

The publication in pamphlet form of the Minutes of the sessions of the Missouri Annual Conference began just after the Civil War. This was an important event historically because it preserved much information about the local churches of the Conference otherwise unavailable. Improvements were made from year to year in the amount, quality and accuracy of this information. Especially in 1871 there was introduced specific and interesting data in the form of statistical tables giving information from each and every charge in the Conference. These tables showed for each charge the number of members, the number of adult and infant baptisms during the past year, detailed information about the Sunday Schools, the amount of money spent in building or repairing churches, money raised for the salaries of preachers, presiding elders and bishops, amount raised on conference assessments for specific purposes, number of church periodicals taken on the charge, the value of church buildings and the number of their seatings, the value of church parsonages, and from time to time other items of interest.[62] These tables would be summarized for the districts, and then the district tables would be summarized for the conference.

The following statistical table, constructed from the Minutes from 1871 to 1899, shows a few of the more important items for the Columbia church during this third of the century. The name of the pastor for each year is shown at the beginning of his conference year, usually about mid-September, while the statistics are those reported at the same conference the minister was appointed, and, therefore, were at the end of the previous conference year.

Statistics may not be interesting, but many interesting stories could be told from this table of statistics. It is found, for instance, that while during the early years, after 1870, the pastors

---

[62] A resolution was adopted in the Annual Conference of 1883 that the statistical secretary thereafter should prepare blanks for statistics embracing the amounts assessed for various purposes, showing the deficiencies or excesses. In this way one could tell from the tables after that time whether any church was paying its assessments in full. The Columbia Church usually paid its assessments in full.

for Columbia were sent back to the town for three years, after Mr. Watson's time their tenure was irregular. Why did Mr. Grimes, Mr. Chapman, and Mr. Glanville stay on the Columbia charge only one year each, while in other cases the appointee remained in Columbia for two or three years, or even as in the case of Mr. Jackson for four years? [63] The circumstances in each case before and after Jackson's time, explaining the reasons for the change, are only speculative.

Year	Pastor	Church Members	Baptisms	S. S. Members	Salary of Pastor	Paid for Missions	Value of Parsonage
1870-1871	J. D. Vincil	149	18	155	$1,000	$ 50	$3,000
1871-1872	J. D. Vincil	153	11	110	1,000	25	2,500
1872-1873	J. D. Vincil	119	0	87	1,000	50	
1873-1874	W. H. Lewis	220	40	150	940	40	
1874-1875	W. H. Lewis	245	29	154	1,025	7	
1875-1876	W. H. Lewis	240	12	161	600	34	
1876-1877	G. W. Horn	148	4	150	800	30	
1877-1878	G. W. Horn	162	2	147	800	0	
1878-1879	G. W. Horn	170	13	130	200	60	
1879-1880	H. B. Watson	170	0	95	800	65	
1880-1881	H. B. Watson	150	0	111	900	85	250
1881-1882	H. B. Watson	155	2	110	782	90	
1882-1883	E. K. Miller	165	1	137	1,000	121	
1883-1884	E. K. Miller	181	16	137	800	48	
1884-1885	Chaney Grimes	187	2	145	1,000	70	
1885-1886	M. B. Chapman	209	20	97	1,000	150	1,700
1886-1887	J. A. Beagle	220	8	137	1,000	140	1,800
1887-1888	J. A. Beagle	234	14	166	913	112	1,800
1888-1889	J. H. Jackson	279	70	226	1,075	220	1,800
1889-1890	J. H. Jackson	317	35	240	1,000	310	1,800
1890-1891	J. H. Jackson	309	22	190	1,000	228	1,800
1891-1892	J. H. Jackson	291	16	190	1,000	222	1,800
1892-1893	T. E. Sharp	339	12	196	1,200	240	1,800
1893-1894	T. E. Sharp	409	66	334	1,200	204	1,800
1894-1895	T. E. Sharp	431	13	331	1,200	270	1,800
1895-1896	W. F. Packard	465	37	255	1,200	225	1,800
1896-1897	W. F. Packard	506	40	166	1,200	311	1,800
1897-1898	J. H. Glanville	490	0	266	1,000	276	2,500
1898-1899	M. H. Moore	399	3	174	1,200	225	1,500
1899-1900	M. H. Moore	406	7	260	1,200	225	1,500

The reasons for the changes in the number of members each year are a little better known. The measure of success in a series of evangelistic meetings, held irregularly but every two or three years, might account at intervals for a large increase in the reported number of members. The number of baptisms also each

---

[63] Mr. Jackson was the first minister in the history of the Columbia Church to remain for four years. According to the *Discipline* at that time, a minister could not be returned to one congregation for more than four years, and that explains at least why Jackson was not returned for a fifth year. We know that a very large petition was sent from the Columbia congregation to the Bishop and his cabinet at the end of Jackson's third year asking for his return for one more year.

year reflected in a certain degree the success of the revival services. On the other hand, since Columbia was a town in which the turnover of the population was large on account of the changes in the faculty and students of the educational institutions, this would partially account for decreases in membership of the Church. It became customary also to prune occasionally the church membership list of those who were not attending services, or of all those who had moved away without leaving a change of address. At times as many as a hundred names were taken off the list.

The changes in the number of Sunday School scholars enrolled, which in this table includes the teachers and officers, is not explained so satisfactorily. Indeed the information about the Sunday School attendance is a depressing feature of this table of statistics. The number of scholars was almost as large in 1870 as at the end of the century, nearly thirty years later. The decreases or increases from year to year may have been due to careless methods in keeping the roll of attendance, but one suspects that at times this phase of church work was emphasized less than at other times. But why the total size of the Sunday School attendance showed so little growth while the church membership was growing during almost a third of a century is hard to understand.

The salary paid to the pastor affords an interesting study. Generally speaking, he was paid less than other professional men of equal ability. It is true, however, that during this period the cost of living index was declining, so that the pastor was considerably better off in 1899 than in 1870, but so were other professional men. There were fluctuations, however, in the salaries among the pastors themselves which should be noticed. In 1874, Lewis received $1,025, the highest ever paid up to that time. But in 1875, he received only $600, and in 1878 Horn was paid $200 (surely a mistake in the report or a misprint.) In 1882 Miller was paid $782, probably all the congregation paid that year though it was not a period of hard times. Again, we know from other statistics not printed here that in 1888 the church agreed to pay $1,000, but it paid $1,075, nearly making up for the deficit the previous year. Commencing with Jackson in 1891, the salary was usually fixed at $1,200. This was one of the larger salaries of the Conference. It is difficult to understand how some of the preachers in poorer communities lived on the salaries they were paid.[64]

The column of figures for missions includes the amounts paid for both domestic and foreign missions. It was small but it will be noticed that gradually the amount was raised. The column which shows whether or not a local congregation had a parsonage indicates there was none in Columbia from 1872 to 1885. The church in 1872 had sold its new parsonage, built in 1869, to help reduce the indebtedness on the new church building. Whether the congregation paid rent for a house for the pastor during those years is not known. The amount of $250 shown for 1880 was probably parsonage rental, and leads one to wonder whether any parsonage was provided in other years. After 1885, there seems to have been a parsonage owned by the church, but whether it was one house owned continuously, or where it was located in Columbia is not known. By 1889 nearly all the charges in Fayette District had parsonages or furnished parsonage rent.

There were other activities and organizations within the church, not shown by the table of statistics, but generally reflecting similar activities throughout the church at large. The women of the church, without whom there could have been no effective religious organization, could hold at that time no official position. "Laity rights for women" had not yet been granted by the men. They could not be delegates to annual or general conferences, nor even be members of local boards of stewards. Yet they were important in every local church organization. In Columbia, they were interested in getting the first Methodist church building, and in holding the congregation together in the dark days of the Civil War; and afterwards, they kept working to collect a fund to build the first parsonage so that the Columbia Church might become a station church.

Women in the church at large, as well as in Columbia, had been working effectively, but not as a solid, cohesive body,

---

[64] Letters in the *St. Louis Christian Advocate* of November 7 and November 21, 1877, gave an analysis of the amounts received as salaries by the preachers in the Conference for the past year. The nine presiding elders had received an average for the year of $729; the preachers of the Conference had received an average of $404. Several charges paid less than $150. Of the 25,860 members of the churches in the Conference, the average paid on preachers' salaries was not quite two dollars a year, less than four cents per week. Columbia members paid an average of $5.40 each on salaries annually. For all church purposes as reported in the Minutes, Columbia members paid $6.70 each annually. That was about an average figure for the Conference.

GROWTH OF THE CHURCH—19TH CENTURY

almost from the beginning of the southern Methodist Church. They included most of the Sunday School teachers, but they were also interested in the missions of the church, foreign and domestic. But it was not until 1878 at the General Conference at Atlanta that a report from the Conference Committee on Missions, May 14, recommended a constitution for the Woman's Missionary Society of the Methodist Episcopal Church, South. This report was unanimously adopted on May 22. The constitution had the fewest possible provisions so as to allow the women to have great latitude in developing their work and organization, but their work was to be done in connection with the General Board of Missions and subject to its advice and approval. The women immediately organized by the election of Mrs. Juliana Hayes as President, and made plans to extend their organization to the various annual conferences.

Thus, when the next session of the Missouri Annual Conference met in Macon in September, prominent women were present from several local societies of women's organizations and formed the Missouri Conference Woman's Missionary Society. They elected Mrs. Adam Hendrix of Fayette as president.[65]

Meanwhile, following the General Conference of 1878, the women of other annual conferences throughout the South organized Conference Missionary Societies. At the subsequent first meeting of the General Executive Association, held May 16 and 17, 1879, at Louisville, Kentucky, delegates were present from twelve annual conferences, including two from Missouri, Mrs. Witten McDonald of Kansas City and Mrs. Watkins of Fulton. Nine auxiliaries were reported as having been formed in the Missouri Conference, with names of the towns in which they were established.[66] None had been formed in Columbia.

At the Second Annual Meeting, in 1880, the report from the

---

[65] Mrs. Hendrix was a very able and devoted member of the group of women at Fayette, mother of Eugene R. Hendrix who at this same Conference was appointed president of Central College, and a few years later was elected Bishop. The Minutes of this meeting were published in the Minutes of that Annual Conference, page 24. The original hand-written secretary's book of this meeting as well as of several subsequent meetings was afterwards deposited in the Library of the State Historical Society of Missouri for safekeeping.

[66] The Minutes of this Louisville meeting as well as of subsequent meetings of the General Executive Association were published by the Southern Methodist Publishing House at Nashville. Miss Maria L. Gibson of Louisville, afterwards of Kansas City, Missouri, was one of the "Managers." She became well-known in Columbia.

Missouri Conference showed 29 auxiliaries but still none was in Columbia; but at the Third Annual Meeting, held in St. Louis in 1881, the report from the Missouri Conference showed that an auxiliary had been established at Columbia with 17 members, so we may conclude that a society had been established there sometime during the previous year, 1880-1881. This was during Mr. Watson's second year at Columbia. At the fourth annual meeting of the General Executive Association, the report from the Missouri Conference Woman's Missionary Society showed that the Columbia society had 19 senior members and 62 junior members. From this time forward the Woman's Missionary Society was active in the Columbia church, and was organically connected with the women's societies in the other churches of the Conference and thus with the general organization of the church. Eventually, when the parent organization was divided into the Home and the Foreign Missionary Societies, the Columbia society was likewise divided into two organizations, but they worked in harmony and became very prominent in the activities of the Columbia Church.

The men of the church were not organized so effectively as were the women. Except in the small Boards of Stewards and in the Boards of Trustees, there was no general organization of men within the church. A "Laymen's Association" had been organized in some local churches to promote the usefulness of the laity in aiding the pastor in the spiritual and financial interests of the Church and this group was organized in the Annual Conference of 1890, with a vice-president in each district. But except for a reference to it in the Minutes of the Conference of 1892, it seemed to have disappeared. No reference to it has ever been found in the Columbia Church.

The young folks of the church, just emerging into adulthood, were not recognized officially by the church until 1890, except as they were in Sunday School classes. Nevertheless, Methodist young people over the country in many communities under various names, more often than otherwise under the name of a Christian Endeavor Society, had organized, but without any connectional unity with each other. The miscellaneous names and character and purposes of these local organizations were not satisfactory to the general church authorities; and at the General Conference of 1890 held in St. Louis, a report was presented from the Sunday School Board providing for the organization of young people's leagues, with the objects of promoting loyalty to the church organization, education in church history, and the encouragement of "works of grace and charity" among the young people. The report was approved and the Board which had made the recommendation was charged with the formation of this new arm of the Church. It proceeded at once to draw up the framework for the organization of the young people of the Church into local, district and conference societies, and gave as the name of the new organization The Epworth League; this name recalled the Epworth Parish in England and the connection of the Wesley family with its history. That name had been adopted also by the other branches of Methodism, and it is likely that the southern Church was simply putting itself in line with a similar movement elsewhere. But for the first two or three years the organization grew very slowly. The Missouri Annual Conference did not even mention in its Minutes the Epworth League until the session of 1893 when, in connection with a Sunday School report it was told that there were 70 chapters of the League in the Conference, with a membership of 2,358 persons. The preachers, busy with their other work, had been rather indifferent about this phase of their pastoral labors.

But in Columbia, Rev. J. H. Jackson, pastor at the time, called together on Sunday evening, September 12, 1891, the young people of the church, and organized an Epworth League chapter, with a full complement of officers as follows: George A. Cooper, president, George H. Beasley, first vice-president, J. A. Krummel, second vice-president, W. D. Lockwood, third vice-president, Frank Norwood, secretary, and Rosa Smith, treasurer. This was at the beginning of the new conference year and also of a new University school year, and part of the officers were students in the University.[67] Meetings were to be held each Sunday evening, forty-five minutes before preaching service.

The General Conference of 1894, held in Memphis, recognizing what the Sunday School Board had done in the formation of the Epworth League organization and in the establishment

---

[67] Columbians will recognize part of these names as belonging to prominent families in the town and Church. Beasley was very active not only in the League but in the Sunday School and Church for years to come; his niece, Mary Searcy, was a missionary in Japan for many years. Lockwood's family was also prominent in Church and University affairs; a sister was afterwards president of the Epworth League and also of the University YWCA; another sister married President Walter Williams. Their mother was a most faithful member of the Church and of its missionary society.

of many local chapters throughout the country, appointed a General Conference Standing Committee on the Epworth League. This Committee brought in a report which was later approved, providing for the complete organization throughout the country of the League, with a general board of the Church to encourage and direct its activities. The general board was authorized to publish a weekly paper and to draw up uniform details for the organization of local chapters. Two new questions, numbers 24 and 25, were to be asked at annual conference sessions, and made a part of their records, namely, "What is the number of Epworth Leagues?" and "What is the number of Epworth League members?" The number of local chapters grew rapidly thereafter.

In the next session of the Missouri Annual Conference, September, 1894, it was reported that there were 124 Epworth League chapters in the Conference with 4,687 members. There were two Epworth Leagues in the Columbia Church, a senior and a junior chapter, with a combined membership of 180. The League became as important for the young people of the Church as the missionary societies were for the women. It provided social entertainments, engaged in a study course, and held weekly devotional meetings led by different ones of the members. By 1899 an annual conference report stated that the League had passed successfully from the period of infancy into that of a vigorous youth.

There is another class of source material for the history of the Church which so far has not been mentioned. This is the manuscript minutes of official Board meetings of the stewards, and of the Quarterly Conferences. Had this all been preserved from the earliest period, it would have been of inestimable value to the historian. Unfortunately, nothing has been found back of 1884.[68] These quarterly conference records are notable for three things. First, they contain the names of the stewards, trustees and other officials who were elected annually and who generally made up the working force of the church, at least as far as its administration was concerned. They attended the quarterly meetings with more or less regularity, and were familiar with every phase of church activities. Second, these records contain the quarterly reports of the pastor as to the Sunday School and the

---

[68] These earliest extant manuscript records are only for the Quarterly Conferences, and even they have some serious gaps after 1884. The minutes of the monthly Board meetings have not been preserved back of the first decade of the twentieth century.

Some Methodist Pastors prior to 1900

E. K. Miller, 1882-1884

C. Grimes, 1884-1885

J. H. Jackson, 1888-1892

T. E. Sharp, 1892-1895

W. F. Packard, 1895-1896

Some leading lay members during the Church's History

B. McAlester

J. P. Horner

Mrs. James D. Bowling

W. T. Maupin

Dr. A. W. McAlester

general state of the church; they were more or less routine with oft repeated statements, but generally mentioned the more important developments during the preceding quarter. Third, these records contained the names of all those who had joined the church during the preceding quarter, as well as the names of those who transferred their membership to other churches, or those who were dropped from membership by a church conference because they showed no interest in the church or because they had moved away without leaving a change of address.

This record of the meeting of October 22, 1884, is, as far as is known, the first Quarterly Conference record for the Columbia Church in existence. It contains the first known official list of stewards and trustees and, therefore, because of its historical value, this list is given here in full: the Presiding Elder was J. A. Mumpower and the preacher was C. Grimes. The secretary was John P. Horner who was also a steward and trustee. The other stewards were: J. M. Baker, B. McAlester, J. C. Orr, A. Reese, Dr. Riggins, and F. D. Evans. The trustees present were: Evans, McAlester, Riggins, Orr, J. B. Douglas, and W. G. Anderson. James M. Lyons was the Sunday School Superintendent. Of these men, McAlester was one of the oldest and one of the most trusted members of the church. He had come to Columbia in 1846 and became a lumber merchant and a contractor and had erected many of the buildings in Columbia. J. M. Baker was a younger man but had been active in the church for some years, and his active service was extended into the future for the next forty years. Horner had been active in the church since the Civil War and had filled many of the more important offices of the church. Evans was a member of the Boone County National Bank firm; he usually was on the board of stewards or the board of trustees.

In subsequent years, other men were added to the board to take the place of those who were removed by death or who left the city. W. B. Nowell became a member of the board September 6, 1889, and continued to serve faithfully for the next thirty-five or forty years. There were two members by the name of Maupin not closely related to each other both of whom were active in the church and served in various capacities. W. T. Maupin was a delegate to several Annual Conferences and was a local preacher. He frequently went to some country church Sunday morning to preach. W. D. Maupin was not quite so active but was a steward for a number of years.

Ever since the provision for lay delegates to the Annual and General Conferences, Columbia had usually furnished one of the four delegates from the Fayette District to the Annual Conference, but seems never to have had a representative among the delegates to the General Conference. There were two men in the Columbia Church, one of whom was sent quite regularly to the Annual Conference, Horner and W. T. Maupin. In 1879, G. W. Riggins was sent to the Annual Conference as a delegate from the Fayette District; he had served in the Mexican War as a doctor and in the Civil War as a surgeon in the Confederate army, but had returned to Columbia after the war and had become active in the Methodist Church. In 1884, D. R. McAnally, Jr., son of the editor of the *St. Louis Christian Advocate* and professor of English at that time in the University of Missouri, was elected a delegate to the Annual Conference.

The Missouri Annual Conference of 1885, for the third time in its history, met in Columbia. It was invited by the executive committee of the Board of Curators of the University to hold its sessions in the University chapel; the invitation was graciously acknowledged but not accepted because the church building at that time was large enough for the needs of the conference sessions.[69] This session of the Conference marked the second time within 20 years that the ministers discussed the question of a change of name for the church. The General Conference of 1882 meeting in Nashville, had proposed that the name be changed from "Methodist Episcopal Church, South," to "Methodist Episcopal Church in America," provided it was approved by a three-fourths vote of the members of the Annual Conferences; but it was disapproved by a large majority. The Missouri Conference, while voting against the change nevertheless voted to ask the General Conference to eliminate the word "South" from the name, but that had to wait for the organic union of the denominations in 1939.

---

[69] The separation of church and state was not so distinct as it became half a century later. There seemed nothing inappropriate for prayers to be said at the opening of University faculty meetings or at meetings of the Board of Curators, and as late as 1901 the Board of Curators voted to establish a chair of Christian Morals in the University—prevented only because of the lack of money. President S. S. Laws, a Presbyterian minister, appeared before this 1885 session of the Annual Conference, bringing the good wishes of the University faculty. Thirty years before this time, President James Shannon of the University, a Christian minister, had gone over the state holding revival meetings, but that was too much even for that time, and he was forced to stop his preaching or resign the presidency. He chose to resign.

GROWTH OF THE CHURCH—19TH CENTURY

During this third of the century, the general organization of the Methodist Episcopal Church, South, had recovered from the ruinous effects of the Civil War. It had added rapidly to its membership and to the number of the Annual Conferences,[70] and had enlarged and strengthened the administration of the church to meet changing conditions. Several new Bishops were elected and (to use the word used in the Journals of the General Conferences) were "ordained"; the younger leading men of the Church were beginning to object to the use of that term, holding that the Bishops were not a separate order in the hierarchy of the church, but that they were simply Elders set apart through election and were "consecrated" to perform certain functions. At the General Conference of 1870, held in Memphis, John C. Keener of Louisiana was added to the list of Bishops. None was elected in the General Conferences of 1874 and 1878, held in Louisville and Atlanta, but by 1882 the passing of time and the ravages of death had so weakened the College of Bishops that four new Bishops were chosen: A. W. Wilson of Maryland, Linus Parker of Louisiana, J. C. Granbery of Virginia, and Robert K. Hargrove of Alabama. At the Conference of 1886 held in Richmond, four more Bishops were chosen: William W. Duncan of South Carolina, Charles B. Galloway of Mississippi, Eugene R. Hendrix of Missouri, and Joseph S. Key of Georgia. In 1890 at St. Louis, two were elected: A. G. Haygood of Alabama and O. P. Fitzgerald of California; and in 1898 at Baltimore, Warren A. Candler of Georgia and H. C. Morrison of Kentucky were chosen. None was elected in the General Conference of 1894.

In another way the church at large was showing development of maturity and Christian character; this was in accepting advances made by the northern Methodist Church for the establishment of fraternal relations between the two Methodist bodies. Fittingly, the first advances were made by the northern Church, since that Church, in its General Conference of 1846 had refused even to give southern fraternal messengers a hearing. But the northern General Conference of 1872 had spent considerable time and heart searching on this subject, and as a result had appointed a board of commissioners to approach a similar board

---

[70] *St. Louis Christian Advocate* of June 26, 1872, and *Minutes of the Annual Conferences of the Methodist Episcopal Church, South*. The West St. Louis Conference, afterwards named Southwest Missouri Conference, was formed in 1870.

to be appointed by the southern Church to try to clear up the problems and allay the hard feeling. Thus, when fraternal and distinguished delegates approached the southern General Conference of 1874 they were given a respectful hearing, and in turn the southern General Conference appointed a delegation of distinguished churchmen to the next northern General Conference. In this way friendly relations were established, and henceforth, the two denominations worked in harmony on many problems. This reacted powerfully on many local communities, particularly in the border states. In towns like Columbia, to which members of the northern Church frequently moved, membership in the local Church could be established as easily as if transferring to their own denomination. Before long it was possible for commissions representing both denominations to publish a common hymnal.

In the meantime, the Church at Columbia was growing constantly, if a bit irregularly, through this closing third of the nineteenth century. One can find many notes of interest from the records of the quarterly conferences. The additions to the membership, name by name, were cataloged in the pastors' reports on the state of the church; and in this way, the degree of success of the revival meetings can be determined as far as numbers were concerned. It was a matter for regret and apology by the pastor if such a series of meetings were not held every year. One realizes from reading these reports how much the Columbia Church depended upon evangelistic meetings for its growth, but these lists of new members do not tell at all of the re-awakening in their religious life of those who were already members. One comes to the conclusion, though, that even if the Methodist Church does not believe in "backsliding," it does believe in re-awakening of backsliders. In December, 1888, the pastor, Rev. Mr. Jackson, mentioned 96 additions as the result of his recent revival efforts; but in addition to the names added, there were many members of the church whose religious life was quickened.

The date for the appearance of many individuals who were important in the later history of the Church is found in these quarterly reports. Thus, Prof. and Mrs. E. A. Allen joined in the fall of 1885; Mr. Allen had just come from the faculty at Central College to take the chair of English at the University of Missouri in the place of Prof. D. R. McAnally, Jr., and Mrs. Allen became quite prominent in the Woman's Missionary Society in later years. In the quarterly conference of December

30, 1888, W. B. Nowell was reported to have been baptized and to have joined the Church. He and his family became faithful and efficient members and officers in the Church for many years to come. The Gribble family seems to have appeared in the spring or summer of 1896 and among others of the family who joined the Church at that time the names of Lois and Alta appear; these sisters became prominent in the music of the Church for over two decades.

The deaths of prominent members were mentioned also; and if the person were a member of the board, resolutions recognizing his services would be adopted. In 1894, the death of J. C. Orr, long a member of the board and "one of the most popular and best beloved men in Boone County" was related with grief. In 1885, the death of the wife of John P. Horner was mentioned; and ten years later the death of Horner himself, on September 25, 1885, was told, with the notation that the Church had lost one of its most faithful members; even that was an understatement for the services of Horner. The death of the wife of B. McAlester was mentioned in October, 1888. She preceded in death by almost fourteen years her faithful and beloved husband. They were the parents of the man to whom, more than to any other person, was owed the honor for reestablishing the School of Medicine in the University of Missouri, Andrew W. McAlester, a loyal Methodist. In the first month of 1895, the pastor, Rev. T. E. Sharp, noted with great sorrow the death of his own daughter. Later in the same year, August 9, 1895, Moses U. Payne died. He had been a prominent business man in Columbia and Boone County almost from the beginning of their history. He was a local preacher in the Methodist Church, and was fond of holding protracted meetings in which he usually led the singing. Earlier in this history it has been shown that he was one of two men to build the Union Church of 1837. He was buried in Rocheport.

Every pastor spoke at one time or another of the religious education of the children. At every quarterly meeting, they reported on the work of the Sunday School; Mr. Chapman spoke of taking the children through the Wesleyan catechism, and after the formation of the Missionary Society and Epworth League, every pastor was interested in the functions of junior missionary societies or Junior Epworth Leagues. The children were not neglected. Yet, Mr. Jackson, in 1890 feared that the young people were not being educated in the foundations of Methodist doctrine. He doubted whether ten per cent of the Sunday School scholars could repeat the Apostles' Creed and suggested that the Creed be repeated and explained in the opening exercises of each Sunday School session.

The Church was usually "up" in its finances, that is, had paid the salaries of the minister and presiding elder. Usually at the end of the conference year it was reported that all conference collections had been paid in full. One year, 1888, it was reported at the end of the year that the pastor and presiding elder would have to wait until after Conference before they were paid in full. In the Fourth Quarterly Conference of 1891, it was reported that the Church had raised a total amount of $2,274.05 during the year but that was during the financial depression. Three years later it was reported that for all purposes during the year, the Church had raised $4,338.90. This was told as evidence of the financial prosperity of the Columbia Church. The year after that the report read: "We have had a total expenditure of $2,883.12; and if the church owes a dollar, I am not aware of it. On the contrary, we have $1,500 loaned out on interest, awaiting the time of the new church building." [71]

The Church during these years nearly always paid the conference assessments for missions in full, and sometimes overpaid. The Church was interested, not only in keeping up the payment of its assessments but in conducting home missionary activities in surrounding communities; thus, a Sunday School was organized and staffed by the Columbia congregation at Persinger, north of town. The pastor reported in 1890 that a Sunday School "under our supervision" had been organized at the Grindstone School House on the Ashland Gravel Road.

The great fire which destroyed the main University building on the night of January 9, 1892, and the subsequent uncertainties as to whether the University would be transferred to another city affected not only the University but all other town organizations. Rev. Mr. Jackson, making his report to the quarterly conference of February 29, 1892, said: "If from our last conference we could have seen adown the future even two short months, it would have called for amazing grace to steady us in the way. An almost unprecedented amount of sickness, amount-

---

[71] It had already been decided that although their present church building was only about twenty years old, they had outgrown it and would soon need a new one.

ing to almost an epidemic, unusually severe weather, two large and disastrous conflagrations, and as the crowning trial to this people a well organized and strenuous effort to wrest from them the State University, their purchase and pride, all conspired to affect church interest and to render fatal our special efforts to secure revivals of religion and save souls. But through the epidemic of sickness the death angel's hand was not lifted over any of our homes, and we are exempt from making any report in the death list. Out of the flames we did not come unscorched as to material loss, (Columbia had to pay $50,000, into the building fund, and guarantee a water system sufficient to protect the buildings from fire) but unscathed I believe as to moral shriveling and purpose to stand by the right and sustain the Church of God. As to the effects of the effort that is now put forth to wrest from us the result of the victory of 50 years ago, and of half a century of fostering care and consequent development, this people possessed their souls in patience and trust in the arbitration of our interests to do right. Through the first three weeks of this quarter and in the midst of these events we held our protracted meeting and made war on sin. God was with His people. He burdened souls, tears, rejoicing, prayers, songs, and conversions can be referred to but not tabulated. . . . Attendance on public worship is good. We take heart to go forward."

Thus, through the closing years of the nineteenth century, the Columbia Church gradually became one of the leading appointments of the Missouri Conference and its pastors always influential members of the body of the ministry. The first year book (church directory) ever published by the church, as far as is known, was distributed in 1899.[72] Rev. Matthew H. Moore was in his second year as pastor and lived at 117 College Avenue. His picture appears as a frontispiece for the booklet. The full list of official members of the church is given, including for the board of stewards: Major F. D. Evans, Thomas W. Westlake, W. B. Nowell, J. M. Shaefer, G. W. Harrell, Jr., B. M. Lockwood, M. W. Coffey, J. M. Baker, J. T. Perkins, Dr. J. W. Carryer, Milton M. Dearing, and George H. Beasley. The trustees included: B. McAlester, F. D. Evans, T. W. Westlake, Charles Matthews, C. W. Bowling, W. D. Maupin, and C. B. Sebastian. Mrs. M. E. Dearing was president of the Foreign

---

[72] A copy has been preserved in the library of the State Historical Society of Missouri.

Missionary Society and Mrs. J. D. Bowling president of the Home Mission Society. George H. Beasley was Sunday School Superintendent and B. M. Lockwood president of the Epworth League. Even the organist and the list of six ushers were named. There were 403 members listed in the pamphlet but without their Columbia addresses. Directories published the three following years all included the Columbia addresses.

Section XII
Building of the Broadway Church

Among the towns of Missouri, Columbia during the 1880's had lost ground relatively in population. In 1880 it had ranked nineteenth but in 1890 it ranked thirty-first. While other towns were installing sewer systems, water works, electric lights and paved streets, Columbia had none of these marks of a progressive city. Its public schools were poor, and its travel connections with the rest of the state depended upon a poorly built branch railroad line and rough toll or dirt roads.

Then, on the night of January 9, 1892, the main building of the University had burned down. This seemed a colossal blow to any further growth, for there was doubt as to whether the state would furnish the money to rebuild the University in Columbia. If it did not, Columbia would soon sink into insignificance. The lower house of the General Assembly, called into session to provide money for rebuilding, came within two votes of a constitutional majority for transferring the University to Sedalia. But the senate stood fast to rebuild at Columbia, and in the end that was what was done. The campus was expanded, more buildings erected and more curricula added, and with one of its great presidents in office the University began a period of remarkable growth in its standards of scholarship and in the size of its student body. With the growth of the University came an immediate growth in the population of the town. Thus the fire turned out to be a blessing for Columbia.

The churches of Columbia all felt the new life which coursed through the town. The Baptists whose church had been located on the courthouse square for nearly fifty years had already secured a location nearer Stephens College (the Baptist Female College), had sold their old building to the county court for $2,500, and had erected a new brick church at the corner of Waugh Street and Broadway at a cost of $20,000; it was dedicated October 18, 1891, just before the catastrophe to the University. The Presbyterians erected a new stone church on their location at Broadway and Tenth Street, costing also about $20,000; it was dedicated October 7, 1894. The Christian church, a frame building located at the corner of Tenth and Walnut Streets not far from Christian

College, was dismantled and a fine new stone structure erected at a cost of about $30,000; it was dedicated in 1892. The Episcopal Church had been organized in Columbia in 1855; its church had been located on lower Broadway until 1899 when a new building was erected on Ninth and Locust Streets not far from the University campus at a cost of about $12,000. The Catholics of whom there were not many in Columbia at first had finally erected and consecrated for Catholic worship a church at the corner of Locust and Waugh Streets, and began to grow in influence. Several other smaller denominations were being established one by one and building houses of worship.

This period of church building must have had some influence on the Methodists. Yet they were slow to enter a construction program, for less than thirty years before they had faced the same problem, had sold their first building to the city to be converted into a public school building, and had started construction on a location further east on Broadway. The basement story had been completed in 1872 and used for three years before the superstructure was completed and dedicated in 1875. Bishop Marvin had spoken of that church as having one of the best auditoriums in which he had ever preached. There did not seem to be anything fundamentally wrong with it except that it was too small, even when it was dedicated. In the nineties, in their reports to the quarterly conferences, the pastors frequently mentioned the crowded conditions for preaching services. In June, 1894, the minister, Mr. Sharp, reported that at a Sunday morning service during the previous quarter, the congregation voted unanimously to set aside each year a considerable sum of money for the inevitable day of construction.

It has been mentioned that Matthew H. Moore was pastor of the Columbia Church at the turn of the century. The quarterly conference records for that period have been lost, so that many items of church interest during Moore's pastorate normally appearing in those records are unknown. The Pastor's quarterly reports on the Sunday School and on the state of the church, including the additions and deletions in membership of individuals, are thus lost also. There were, however, the church directories mentioned in the closing paragraph of the last section, and from these one may find the names of all the members of the church for each year during Moore's pastorate, as well as the names of all the officers of church organizations and societies.[73]

There were also the statistical reports made to the annual conference from each preacher at the end of each conference year and published in the conference Minutes. These reports had gradually become more complex and detailed as the years went by, perhaps required by different sessions of the General Conference. They contained, however, no personal information about the members of the local churches, but were a graphic summary in figures of the work of each charge for the past year. The accompanying table, culled from the annual reports of the Columbia ministers from 1900 to 1930, shows some of the more important information about the Columbia Church during that period. One must remember that the minister appointed always for one year, would make his report at the end of his conference year.

Half way through Moore's years of service in Columbia, in 1900, the Annual Conference met for its 84th session [74] in Fulton, with Bishop John C. Granbery presiding.[75] The pastor at Fulton at the time was J. H. Jackson who had been the preacher in Columbia ten years before. There were 206 clerical members on the conference roll compared to 37 in the first year after the Civil War. Among the members admitted on trial at this Conference was Charles W. Tadlock, several years later a pastor in Columbia. On the other hand, a preacher just finishing his active service and being admitted to the superannuate relation

---

[73] The directories were published annually from 1899 to 1902, Moore evidently preparing the copy for the last one before he was transferred to Moberly. None as far as is known appeared after that until 1910 when one was published by Rev. C. M. Aker, pastor at that time. The directories were important not only for their source value on individual Church membership and on the lay officials of the church, but for their information on the social, economic and genealogical history of Columbia. Every other page was filled with advertisements of Columbia business firms. Copies of the directories for all four years are in the library of the State Historical Society of Missouri.

[74] The sessions were numbered consecutively from the first in 1816 until 1844. Then the Conference joined the newly formed M.E. Church, South, and commenced numbering the sessions over again until 1870 when it decided to go back to the original numbering.

[75] Since the Civil War there had been 16 Bishops to preside in different sessions of the Conference. The action of the General Conference of 1866, establishing Episcopal Districts with a Bishop residing in each District (see page 68), did not set up these Districts for a quadrennium, and so did not require a Bishop to preside over any particular Conference for a full four years.

Church Statistics—1900-1930
Continued on page 207

Conference Year	Pastor	Salary of Pastor	Church Members	Baptisms	Epworth League Members	S. S. Members	Paid for Missions	Total Collections
1900-1901	M. H. Moore	$1,200	416	6	70	260	$ 285	$ 3,222
1901-1902	M. H. Moore	1,250	422	2	77	260	285	2,724
1902-1903	S. P. Cresap	1,200	375	6	100	292	305	2,991
1903-1904	S. P. Cresap	1,300	396	3	70	316	315	35,815
1904-1905	S. P. Cresap	1,400	550	115	85	488	320	3,902
1905-1906	C. M. Bishop	2,100	607	21	200	522	371	4,614
1906-1907	C. M. Bishop	2,000	638	11	229	422	344	4,268
1907-1908	C. M. Bishop	2,000	678	52	226	361	340	5,407
1908-1909	C. M. Bishop	2,000	744	41	211	451	343	5,963
1909-1910	C. M. Aker	1,764	776	57	150	478	376	6,188
1910-1911	C. M. Aker	1,620	859	56	152	453	409	6,247
1911-1912	C. M. Aker	1,700	878	28	162	534	436	4,269
1912-1913	C. W. Tadlock	2,000	830	8	120	795	530	6,590
1913-1914	C. C. Grimes	2,130	818	29	205	685	571	5,899
1914-1915	C. C. Grimes	2,130	835	27	172	680	500	6,797
1915-1916	C. C. Grimes	2,150	875	12	85	493	548	6,143
1916-1917	C. C. Grimes	2,250	931	2	135	844	515	6,404
1917-1918	S. W. Hayne	2,250	943	31	175	827	525	6,755
1918-1919	S. W. Hayne	2,400	875	58	205	851	4,048	11,927
1919-1920	J. D. Randolph	2,500	975	21	217	763	3,865	13,470
1920-1921	J. D. Randolph	2,750	949	10	430	951	3,864	16,325
1921-1922	J. D. Randolph	3,250	1,002	14	401	1,117	4,024	21,264
1922-1923	J. D. Randolph	3,250	1,013	11	424	841	4,968	25,801
1923-1924	M. T. Haw	4,000	1,140	44	400	846	2,648	24,896
1924-1925	M. T. Haw	4,000	1,200	51	462	890	2,312	26,818
1925-1926	M. T. Haw	4,000	1,031	28	483	1,032	2,139	30,786
1926-1927	M. T. Haw	4,000	1,113	49	505	1,073	2,078	25,216
1927-1928	M. N. Waldrip	5,200	1,156	26	525	1,132	2,621	30,270
1928-1929	M. N. Waldrip	5,200	1,131	19	350	835	2,694	46,392
1929-1930	M. N. Waldrip	5,200	1,146	2	300	1,100	1,051	46,787

BUILDING OF THE BROADWAY CHURCH

was Alonzo V. Bayley. Before the Conference ended, on September 17, Bayley was excused to go home to the bedside of his wife who was seriously ill, and special prayers were offered by the Conference for Mr. and Mrs. Bayley.[76]

Moore's pastorate in Columbia lasted until 1902; he was the second man in the history of the Columbia Church to be returned for a full quadrennium.[77] He was sent to Moberly and to take his place in Columbia the Bishop appointed Dr. S. P. Cresap, a vigorous and thoughtful preacher, an influential man among the members of the Annual Conference, and popular with the members of his congregations. According to the polity of the Methodist Church, the lay officials of the local church are always chosen at the fourth quarterly conference. If, therefore, there is a change of preachers in the ensuing annual conference, as there was on this occasion, the various official lay members for the coming year will always be chosen before the arrival of the new preacher. Cresap's first boards, therefore, were nominated by Mr. Moore in the summer of 1902.

The two boards of the Church were composed of able, competent men. The functions of the two boards were quite different. The board of trustees, a body which might include from three to nine men but usually in practice in the Columbia Church having a membership of nine, had charge of the legal relationship of the Church with the civil government, and held the property, the real estate, "in trust for the Methodist Episcopal Church, South." The trustees were to be substantial citizens, preferably

---

[76] Mrs. Bayley died three days later. Her memoirs appear in the Annual Conference Minutes of 1901, page 62. She was born in Boone County and educated in Stephens College, and was well known in Columbia. Mr. Bayley moved to Columbia with his family of young children. He was active in the local church until his death in 1935. His memoirs were published in the conference Minutes of 1936, page 62. One of his sons, Ernest R. Bayley, entered the Methodist ministry and joined the Missouri Annual Conference in 1924.

[77] Matthew Henry Moore was born in North Carolina, October 31, 1857. He entered the Methodist ministry in 1878 and served eleven years in North Carolina before being transferred to the Denver Conference, and then later to the St. Louis Conference before coming to the Missouri Conference in 1898 to be appointed to the Columbia Church. Leaving Columbia in 1902 he was appointed to other charges in the Missouri Conference until his superannuation in 1923, having served 45 years in the ministry. He was much interested in church history and philosophy, and wrote an authoritative book on the early history of Methodism in North Carolina. He died in his native state April 6, 1932, where he had been in retirement with his wife. His memoirs are in the *Minutes of the Missouri Annual Conference,* M.E. Church, South, for 1932, page 63.

though not necessarily members of the Church. As a board they had little to do with the ordinary work of the Church and usually met not more than once a year. The board of stewards on the other hand guided and regulated the ordinary affairs of the Church, and were presumed to be familiar with all the phases of church work. The size of this body depended upon the number of members in the local Church, one steward for every thirty members on the church roll. The qualifications for membership on the board of stewards were described in a rather famous one-sentence paragraph in the *Discipline:* "Let the stewards be men of solid piety, who both know and love the Methodist doctrine and *Discipline,* and of good natural and acquired abilities to transact the temporal business of the Church." [78]

The 1902 Board of stewards consisted of the following persons: W. T. Anderson, Hugh E. Baker, Ed F. Beasley, C. H. Conger, G. H. Harrell, Jr., F. B. Mumford, W. B. Nowell, J. T. Perkins, E. M. Price, John A. Stewart and William Walker. Anderson was a prominent business man of Columbia who had been a leading member of the church for several years past. Hugh E. Baker was quite evidently placed on the board in 1902 at the suggestion of his father, J. M. Baker, who had been active in church life for a number of years; upon Hugh's resignation several months later his father was restored to his former position on the board. One cannot think of J. M. Baker without remembering his sincerity, loyalty, friendliness and dependability throughout his long life. Beasley, always loyal to the church, came from a family which furnished numerous other church leaders.[79] Mumford had joined the University faculty rather recently and was placed on the board of stewards when he joined the church, and for over forty years continued to serve the church in various capacities. Nowell has already been mentioned for his

---

[78] There were no women members on either board nor in the quarterly conference. This seems strange from the point of view of a half a century later, but this was before the day of "Women's rights." A bishop's decision in 1898 had held that while a woman might be a Sunday School superintendent, she could not thereby become a member of a quarterly conference. In 1906, in another decision it was held that it was unlawful to elect a woman a steward. But in many other ways they were very active in church work and life.

[79] A brother, George Beasley, was specially active in the Sunday School organization; he was a teacher and became Superintendent of the Columbia Normal Academy. A sister of Ed's married a Methodist minister, Rev. B. P. Searcy, and became the mother of Mary Searcy, for almost a lifetime a missionary in Japan.

BUILDING OF THE BROADWAY CHURCH

services to the church.[80] Price, more active usually on the board of trustees than as a steward, was an officer in his father's bank. Harrell was a merchant tailor in Columbia and Walker a prominent plumber. Conger and Perkins, long active in the Columbia church, subsequently moved away from Columbia. Stewart had just transferred his membership from a country church to Columbia and was nominated for membership on the board of stewards at once, and for thirty years or more he and his wife were active in various phases of church life; he was at one time a member of the county court and bore the title of judge the rest of his life.

It was customary to place on the board of trustees some of the more prominent stewards. This first board of trustees under Cresap's tenure included Anderson, Nowell, Perkins and Price, and in addition J. M. Baker, Charles B. Bowling, F. D. Evans, Dr. A. W. McAlester, and Charles Matthews, all prominent business or professional men of Columbia.

It may be that Cresap was sent to Columbia for the primary purpose of inducing the membership to erect a new church. He saw that the Columbia Church was cramped for room for holding its services. In February, 1903, he called a meeting of the church members and discussed the problem with them. At the next quarterly meeting, March 19, 1903, he reported: "The membership has decided to rise and build a new church edifice. I have pleasure in reporting that the enterprise is now practically assured." It was agreed that three-fourths of the funds should be subscribed before the building work was started, and the church adopted the motto, "Owe no man anything." Cresap himself led the subscription list with a pledge of $1,000. Matching his subscription were several members and friends of the church: Turner McBaine, W. T. Anderson, John A. Stewart, Charles Bowling, Mrs. J. D. Bowling, Dr. A. W. McAlester, and others. They wanted no such financial difficulties as those which had followed the building of the previous church.

In May a building committee was elected, consisting of Dr. Cresap, C. B. Bowling, W. T. Anderson, J. A. Stewart, Charles Matthews and E. W. Crouch. This committee employed the firm of Matthews and Clark of St. Louis as architects, and in June the general plans were completed and accepted by the committee. The seating capacity was to be 725. The walls were

---

[80] See page 95.

to be of local stone and the roof of slate. Connected with the sanctuary by folding doors was to be a chapel. To the rear was to be the pastor's study, rest rooms, a choir room with an entrance to the choir loft, and a stairway to the basement or ground floor. On that floor was to be a furnace room, a kitchen, and room for Sunday school classes. A new pipe organ for which Mrs. Sarah Dameron, sister of J. P. Horner, had left $1,000 in her will several years before, and which had been well invested and now amounted to $2,000, was to be installed. All of the interior woodwork and furnishings, the cost of which was provided from the proceeds of the sale of the old church building, were to be of oak.

The contract for the new building was let about the middle of July, 1903, and construction began at once. The Missouri Annual Conference meeting in Palmyra that year decided on invitation to meet in Columbia the next year, and this acted as a stimulus in the building program. The corner stone of the new building was laid on Tuesday afternoon, September 22, with the Masonic Lodge conducting the ceremonies. The pastor of the Presbyterian Church, Rev. W. W. Elwang, himself a Mason, acted as Grand Master. A number of articles which might be interesting in future years were placed in the corner stone; included were copies of Columbia newspapers of that date, current coins, Methodist Church papers, directories of the church and of the lodge, and a few miscellaneous articles.

The site chosen for the new church seems to have been determined some time previously when two or three prominent members, foreseeing that the time was coming when it would be necessary to build again, personally bought a lot at the corner of Broadway and Short Street, just a block east of the old building. It was a poor location, just across the street from the new Baptist Church, but this was before the day of parking trouble for cars. It would have been better, however, to have built nearer the University, where so many Methodist students were attending. A better location might have been at the head of Cherry Street on Hitt Street where the Presbyterians built a generation later.

The construction of the church went along rapidly through the winter, and it was ready for the dedication ceremony on May 11, 1904. Bishop Charles B. Galloway of Mississippi was the preacher for the occasion. The sermon was on the topic, "Rebuilding the Temple." In an interesting, forceful and eloquent address, the speaker dwelt upon the influence of church building on church work and religious life. After the sermon a collection was taken to complete the amount necessary for the building enterprise, $4,600. This was quickly raised, and the regular dedication ritual was then observed.

The members of the church were proud of their new and handsome church home. The memorial windows added to the beauty of the sanctuary. One window given by Mrs. Payne in memory of her husband, Moses U. Payne, represented Christ in Gethsemane. Another window, given by Captain and Mrs. S. A. Smoke represented Christ as the Good Shepherd. The cost of the chapel was provided by the McAlester family. It seemed that in all respects as to beauty, harmony and utility (except only in size) the building was well nigh perfect. Thus the new church home was dedicated and inaugurated on its comparatively short but fruitful history as a Methodist meeting house.

At the morning service a week after the dedication, the congregation by a unanimous vote adopted resolutions presented by Major Evans testifying its appreciation of the leadership of Dr. and Mrs. Cresap in the construction program. A properly authenticated copy of these resolutions was furnished to Dr. and Mrs. Cresap, and the resolutions were placed also in the written proceedings of the last quarterly conference of the year.

At this quarterly conference also the trustees gave a final report of the cost of the church, $31,732.12. This did not include the pipe organ, for which $2,000 had been spent, nor the cost of the lot upon which the church was built, which the trustees valued at $2,500. They had been instructed to sell the old church and it soon passed out of their hands.[81]

The Annual Conference of August 31, 1904, met in the new church in Columbia, with Cresap as its host pastor, and with Bishop E. R. Hendrix presiding. The secretary was John D. Vincil, elected at this time for the 41st consecutive year.[82] An

---

[81] The sanctuary of the old church was used for a while as an entertainment hall, and a printing press was moved into the basement upon which the *University Missourian* was printed. The building was soon torn down, however to make room for a commrecial establishment.

[82] Within six weeks after the close of this Conference, Vincil died in St. Louis. He had been a splendid secretary for 41 years. A committee of the General Conference in 1902, criticizing the annual conference Journals, speaking of the one from the Missouri Conference, said: "This journal is well-nigh perfect in all respects." At the time of his death, Vincil was president of the University Board of Curators, and his body was brought back to Columbia where it was met by the faculty in Cap and Gown and followed to the University Auditorium for the funeral exercises. He was buried in the Columbia Cemetery.

interesting feature of the Conference was the introduction of the veteran Columbia editor, William F. Switzler, who told of attending as a reporter the Conference of 1845, when the preachers decided to join the M.E. Church, South. An emotional feature for Columbia visitors at the Conference was the reading of the memoirs of Rev. E. K. Miller who had died on the previous March 14; Miller had been pastor of the Columbia Church in 1882-1884. In making the appointments for the coming year Cresap was returned to Columbia for his third year.

Section XIII
The Broadway Church Moves Forward With Methodism

With the building of the new church in Columbia, Cresap could have rested on his laurels, but he believed an even greater spiritual victory was just ahead, and all through the fall of 1904 he kept urging his parishioners to prepare for a series of Gospel meetings which were scheduled to begin about the middle of January. An evangelistic team consisting of John E. Brown to preach and C. F. Curry to lead the music was engaged. There followed the greatest revival meeting ever held in the Columbia Methodist Church. The building was crowded to capacity night after night, even through zero weather. There were many professions of conversion. Even though Cresap had reported 53 new members to the first quarterly conference in December to join the church, he now reported to his second quarterly conference after the close of the revival meetings the names of 161 persons who had joined on profession of faith or by certificate. Among the new members were John W. Vesser and Mr. and Mrs. J. F. Brossart, and many others who became prominent in the church later. And as a result of the meetings as many persons joined the other churches in town. The moral and spiritual atmosphere in Columbia was appreciably changed.

The Church congregation wanted and expected Cresap to be returned to Columbia in 1905 for his fourth year, but the inscrutable judgment of the presiding Bishop transferred Cresap to St. Joseph and sent to Columbia Charles M. Bishop, a preacher with a clarion voice in the pulpit. Bishop's standing among his fellow Methodist preachers is shown by his having been the first man among the clerical delegates elected at this annual conference to the next General Conference, to meet the following May, 1906. Another of the delegates chosen at this time was Cresap himself, indicating the high class of men being appointed to the Columbia Church. The presiding elder of the district, B. D. Sipple, was also elected a delegate.

The General Conferences of 1902 and 1906, at Dallas and Birmingham respectively, elected several new Bishops, including, in 1902, Coke Smith of Virginia, and E. E. Hoss of Tennessee, and in 1906, J. J. Tigert of Kentucky, Seth Ward of Texas, and James Atkins of North Carolina. In 1902, W. F. McMurry of

Broadway Methodist Episcopal Church
Broadway at Short Street

the St. Louis Conference was elected a member of the Board of Church Extension; this began his long connection with that Board, a circumstance which was important to the Columbia Church, years later, when it became necessary to build the next church edifice, and when McMurry became *ex officio* chairman of the building committee.

Recognizing the rapid establishment of public high schools throughout America, characteristic of that period in the educational history of the country, the General Conference of 1902 recommended that the annual conferences should put less energy and money in that phase of education, and more in college education which prepared students for the ministry. Forty years before this time the Missouri Annual Conference had opened and managed a number of high schools, and principals for them, usually taken from the ranks of the active preachers, had been appointed to administer and teach in them. One after another of those schools had disappeared, in some cases sold to the school districts in which they had been located, in other cases simply closed for lack of patronage.

In 1902, upon request of the Woman's Home Mission Society, the General Conference authorized the establishment of the office of Deaconess. Such trained persons were needed for special home mission work, usually in the poorer sections of the South. The candidates were to be members of the Methodist Church, and at least 23 years of age. They were to pass a special course of training and were to be examined by an executive committee.

A significant movement in denominational cooperation in which the Methodist Episcopal Church, South, participated took place in the opening years of the twentieth century. It is difficult to determine the very beginning of great historic developments, but cooperative work rather than competitive efforts had been a dream of many church leaders for a number of years. On February 1, 1900, several persons from local and state federations of churches gathered in the rooms of the Young Men's Christian Association in New York. A committee was formed to explore the question of the formation of a national federation. This meeting led to several subsequent annual meetings, and finally to the proposal for denominational bodies to elect or appoint official representatives to a constituent meeting. Under the plan the Methodist Episcopal Church, South, would be entitled to 36 representatives. The College of Bishops in 1906 approved the plan, and the General Conference accepted their recommendation with the provision that six of the Church's representatives would be chosen from among the Bishops, fifteen from the laity of the Church and fifteen from the clergy. Those finally appointed from the Church included Bishop Hendrix who had been prominent in the movement from the beginning, and Dr. S. P. Cresap.[83] It was not until December, 1908, that the organization was finally completed by the adoption of a constitution, the choice of its first president, Bishop E. R. Hendrix, and the selection of a name, The Federal Council of the Churches of Christ in America.[84]

It was such influences as this which were to lead eventually to the union of the northern and southern Methodist Churches and the Methodist Protestant Church into The Methodist Church. Before this could be done there was a long period of incubation, perhaps beginning with the agreement to exchange fraternal delegates to the General Conferences of each. In 1894 the Southern General Conference provided for the appointment of a committee of fifteen to which all questions relating to federation could be referred. A similar committee was appointed by the northern Church, and the two committees held joint meetings at intervals, and made reports to their respective General Conferences; thus, agreements were made for the interchange of ministers, and for each denomination not to enter the local territory of the other without the permission of a Bishop when the other was already there with an organization and building. In this way the bitterness following the Civil War gradually gave way to cooperation, and this was to lead eventually to reunion.

Meanwhile, the local Church in Columbia under Bishop's pastorate was running along smoothly. As had been the practice, the lay officials were generally continued in their offices from year to year with few changes. In 1905 W. T. Anderson became a trustee instead of a steward, and E. F. Beasley had moved from the city. In their places as stewards, J. W. Vesser and S. W. Nairn were chosen. Dr. Bishop throughout his four-year pastorate made few changes in church officials except to add to the number of stewards because of the growing membership of

---

[83] The names of all thirty-six representatives are in the *Journal of the General Conference* of 1906, page 254.

[84] After about forty years the Federal Council, which at that time included 28 communions, was merged with several bodies of interchurch organizations, and became the National Council of Churches.

the church. Thus, at different times, the following persons were nominated and elected: George H. Beasley, brother of Ed F. Beasley, Dr. J. B. Cole, a practicing osteopathic physician, A. B. Coffman, a grocerman who afterwards entered the ministry, D. T. Mitchell, a retired business man, T. J. Riley, a University instructor, and perhaps two or three others who did not continue long on the board. Senator Charles J. Walker, who had been superintendent of the Sunday School since 1902, was continued in that office from year to year.

New members of the church continued to be reported at every quarterly conference. There would not be room here to name all of them, but among those who became active in the church later were Mrs. Laura E. Evans and her children, Mr. and Mrs. D. T. Mitchell and their daughter, Josephine, Dr. and Mrs. Frank F. Stephens, Mr. and Mrs. Ben R. Shore and their daughter, Margaret, and the Ed McDonnell and Emmett McDonnell families.

The subject of a parsonage for the minister occupied the attention of the quarterly conference occasionally. At one time a committee was appointed to purchase a parsonage; whether it was done does not appear in any recorded action. Moore's directories show a parsonage located on College Avenue but whether it was owned or rented does not appear. Cresap bought his own house on College Avenue, and after he moved away it was voted in the quarterly conference to purchase it, but there is no record that this was done. For many years after the new church was built, the statistical report from Columbia in the Conference Minutes left blank the subject of a parsonage, thus leading to the conclusion that the church did not own a parsonage. Whether the church paid the rental for a house for the minister, or left him to hunt his own house and pay the rent does not appear in any surviving records. The church board in a perfunctory way seemed to recognize its responsibility in this regard, and voted at one time to "buy or build" a parsonage, but the good resolution seemed to evaporate. It may have been that the Woman's Home Mission Society, which seemed to have some connection with the parsonage question, and which raised considerable sums of money for "home work" each year, paid the rental for a parsonage house.

Throughout the first two decades of the twentieth century, beginning almost as soon as the new church was built, there was difficulty in finding room for all who wished to attend the Sunday School or the regular Sunday morning preaching services. In the last quarterly conference of his first year, Bishop told the church officials that it was a matter of concern and perplexity how to provide room for all who might attend the Sunday School through the coming winter. The building had not been planned for separate classrooms for the large number of classes. In the sanctuary where the adult classes were scattered about, it seemed that each group was trying to out-do the others, and attention was always attracted to the teacher who talked loudest. In the basement where there were no partitions, a dozen or more groups of little folks were gathered in a semi-circle around their teachers, and it was a bedlam of noise. It was noted in a quarterly conference in the early part of 1907 that a great improvement had been made in the basement when, through the generosity of Judge Stewart who paid the expense, the classes had all been curtained off from each other.

Despite the inadequacy of space and its poor planning for Sunday School work, the church continued to grow and prosper throughout Bishop's pastorate. His sermons attracted the interest and attention of a growing number of University students who more than ever before made up an increasing proportion of the congregation. This was before the day of "associate membership" or of a student pastor and there was no headquarters for student activities in the building. But at the beginning of each fall semester Bishop would send a letter to each student who had indicated on his registration card that he belonged to or preferred the Methodist Church, inviting his attendance and participation in church activities. He also paid special attention to town boys between the ages of fourteen and eighteen years who were not University students. In his report to the First Quarterly Conference of 1908-1909, he wrote that he regarded this class of boys as being the most important group being reached in any Sunday School. It was during his last year and with the devoted assistance of A. B. Coffman that an organization of boys began to take form under the name of the IXL. They came to have an execllent influence on the later life of the Columbia church.

The membership of the church, which at the beginning of Bishop's pastorate was reported as 550, was 744 at the end, a 35 per cent increase. The collections for all purposes had increased from $3900 to $5963, and the pastor's salary had been raised from $1400 to $2000. The Epworth League membership (roughly corresponding to the Wesley Foundation at a later time) had increased from 85 to 211. The missionary societies had grown in membership from 90 to 156, and their annual collections from $450 to $854. Dr. and Mrs. Bishop and their family were popular with the congregation; his sermons were thoughtful and spiritual, and in his meetings with the board of stewards and the quarterly conference he was constantly urging greater devotion of church officials and more loyal service to the work of the church.

The Annual Conference which met in Savannah, Missouri, September 1, 1909, marked the end of Bishop's four years of service at Columbia; this was still the limit for which a minister could be reappointed annually to the same charge. This Annual Conference chose delegates to the next General Conference, meeting in May, 1910, in Asheville, North Carolina. Dr. Bishop was elected again as leader of the clerical delegation to the General Conference. That Conference was notable for the election of seven new Bishops for the church.[85] It refused the plea of Miss Belle Bennett, president of the women's organizations of the Church, to grant laity rights to the women. That was to come, however, at a later time.

To take the place of Dr. Bishop at Columbia in 1909, Bishop W. A. Candler who was presiding at the Annual Conference of 1909 sent Cecil M. Aker, formerly of Mexico, Missouri. Mr. Aker introduced a number of new helpful features, though he always consulted the official board before embarking on a new course. At the first meeting of the Board, the pastor's salary was cut from $2,000 to $1,764. This would seem to have been a retrogression, though it represented a substantial increase over what Aker had been receiving at Mexico. At his suggestion it was agreed to publish a weekly four-page bulletin, giving the program for the Sunday services and church news of interest to the congregation. It was not sent out through the U. S. Mail, but was handed to the members as they arrived for services. This little bulletin usually contained also the names of the members of the board, and officers of the other organizations of the church, with the regular time of their meetings during the month. This publication was not continued during Aker's second year, but was published during his third year again.[86]

[85] The seven were: Collins Denny, John C. Kilgo, W. B. Murrah, W. R. Lambuth, R. J. Waterhouse, E. D. Mouzon, and James H. McCoy.
[86] An incomplete file of these bulletins has been preserved by the Library of the State Historical Society of Missouri.

Another innovation was the organization of the men of the church into a club, to be known as "The Methodist Brotherhood of Columbia." A constitution was adopted which provided that any man who was 21 years of age and a member of the church was eligible for membership, and men not members of the church could become associate members of the organization. Meetings were to be held on the last Thursday night of each month. As far as is known, no officers were elected at first, but in a called meeting in April, 1910, the following officers were chosen: President, F. F. Stephens; Vice-President, J. M. Whitesides; Secretary, Wm. Yochum; and Treasurer, J. A. Stewart.

One of the first things the new officers of the Brotherhood undertook to have done was the publication of a church directory. None had been published since 1903 when Moore's last one had appeared. With the Brotherhood's approval and assistance, a new directory was published in May, 1910. This booklet contained the names of 753 members with their street addresses and indicated which ones belonged to the Men's Brotherhood, to the Woman's Foreign Missionary Society, and to the Woman's Home Mission Society. There were 40 members of the Brotherhood, 62 of the Foreign Missionary Society, and 58 of the Home Mission Society. A brief and rather inaccurate historical sketch of the Church was given, together with lists of the officials of the various organizations. There was also a directory of the streets of the town, showing the families of the Church living on each street.

The board of stewards elected in Dr. Bishop's last quarterly conference and therefore serving in Aker's first year included eleven who had served previously and two new members to take the place of two who had left town. The two new members were F. F. Stephens, who had joined the Church by letter two years before, and James W. Schwabe who had just joined the Church by profession of faith. Schwabe became especially helpful in the business affairs of the Church for the next two decades. After his first year in Columbia, Aker increased the size of the board by nominating 24 members, but this was still a fewer number than the disciplinary regulation of one steward for each thirty members of the Church would have allowed at that time.

In the meeting of the official board in October, 1909, Mr. Aker proposed the employment of his younger brother, Grover C. Aker, as an assistant pastor on part-time. Grover was a senior student in the University, and would therefore be unable to give his full time to the Church work. The proposal was approved by the board.[87] Among Grover Aker's duties as assistant pastor was to organize a "junior" church, which was to meet for its services every Sunday, after the Sunday School hour, in the basement of the building while the regular morning Church services were in progress in the sanctuary. The plan turned out rather successfully. The junior church enrolled about fifty members, and had its own organization of officials, including ushers, stewards, a junior choir, and a sermon by the assistant pastor every Sunday morning.

Perhaps the most important development as far as Methodism in Columbia was concerned during Aker's pastorate of three years was the beginning of a project to establish in Columbia a second Methodist congregation. This project started as a result of an evangelistic series of meetings held by Mr. Aker and his brother in June and July, 1910. They secured a large tent and had it spread on an open space north of Christian College, and the meetings were held there night after night for two or three weeks. Mr. Aker reported to the Fourth Quarterly Conference of August 15, 1910, that there had been 83 conversions and that 57 people had joined the church.

This posed a problem: if these new converts attended the Broadway Church, it would become even more difficult to provide room for preaching and Sunday School purposes, for that Church was already overflowing with its membership and with the Methodist students who wished to attend its services. After some desultory discussion it was suggested that a second Methodist Church ought to be organized and located in the north end of

---

[87] The records do not show how much salary was paid to Grover. According to the quarterly conference reports, and also to the statistics reported to the Annual Conference, Cecil M. Aker was paid $1,764 for his first year, but the quarterly conference records also show he was paid $525 for each quarter of the year making $2,100 for the year. Perhaps there was an unrecorded agreement that the extra $336 would be paid for parsonage rent and for a salary he would pay his brother Grover. Grover graduated from the University in June, 1910, and then joined the Annual Conference the next September, but was transferred to the Southwest Missouri Annual Conference. After two years he returned to the Missouri Conference and had a successful four years pastorate at the Excelsior Springs Church. He was then appointed to the Church at Lawson but became very ill there and died on November 1, 1918. His obituary is on page 108 of the Minutes of the conference of 1919. Cecil Aker moved to Southern California for his health in 1920, transferred to the Methodist Episcopal Church there, and was appointed to various charges in the Los Angeles District.

town. This idea appealed to the members of the Quarterly Conference, and a large committee of 24 members of the Broadway Church, with James W. Schwabe as chairman, was appointed to solicit funds, purchase a lot in the name of the trustees of the Broadway Church, and contract for the erection of a new Church there. Even then, only the basement covered with a temporary roof was provided at first, and the Methodists of the surrounding area organized and held their various services there until the superstructure could be added.

In the Quarterly Conference of the Broadway Church of August 4, 1915, on motion of F. F. Stephens, the trustees of the Broadway Church were authorized to transfer this new church property to the trustees of the Wilkes Boulevard Church, to be held by them in trust for the Methodist Episcopal Church, South. The first regular occupant of the pulpit of the "North Side" Church, as it is called in the Annual Conference Minutes of 1914, was a layman, A. B. Coffman, an earnest and dedicated member of the Broadway Church, who was appointed as a "supply." Coffman was admitted to the Annual Conference of 1915 "on trial," and was reappointed to the Wilkes Boulevard Church, as it was named after that first year. He continued to serve as its pastor until 1919.

Returning to Aker's pastorate in the Broadway Church, his first year had shown the helpfulness of having an assistant pastor there, but since Grover Aker, the pastor's brother, was no longer available because he had been sent to a pulpit of his own, the presiding Bishop was persuaded to appoint another young man to divide his time between his studies in the University and the work of the Church. This was James Thomas Budd who was appointed as "Junior Preacher," the first such appointment in the history of the Church. He was admitted to the Annual Conference on trial at this session.[88]

It is unfortunate for the history of the Broadway Church that there are no surviving records of the quarterly conferences nor of the meetings of the board of stewards for the immediate years after Aker's first year. There was also no weekly bulletin published during his second year, and few of the bulletins published

---

[88] Not much is known of Budd and he seems to have left little impression on the life of the Church. He did not continue in the University longer than the first semester. There is no record as to his salary in Columbia. The Annual Conference sent him in 1911 and 1912 to the Prairie Hill Circuit, and he was transferred to the South Georgia Conference in 1913.

during his third year have been saved. There were, however, the Minutes of the annual conferences from which a little information may be extracted, and the local newspapers occasionally included items of church news in their columns.

The Ninety-Fifth Session of the Missouri Annual Conference was held in the Broadway Church, August 30 to September 4, 1911, with Bishop Collins Denny of Virginia in charge. This was the fifth time in the history of the Columbia Church that the Conference had come to Columbia. The women of the Church served meals in the basement of the Church to the delegates. An interesting feature during the meetings was an address by President A. Ross Hill of the University on the place of church-related colleges in higher education. The statistics reported to this Annual Conference showed that the Broadway Church paid in full the conference and general assessments levied against it, and had added about one hundred new members during the year. On the other hand it had lost nearly as many through death, and by transfer of memberships. The appointment of ministers returned Aker to Columbia for his third year, but sent no junior minister there.

The IXL Club, an organization of teenage boys formed during Bishop's pastorate and similar in many ways to the later troops of Boy Scouts, wanted a place in the crowded Church where they could have their headquarters during the week as well as on Sundays. They discovered an attic over the choir room in the rear of the Church in February, 1912, and with the permission of the board of stewards constructed a stairway to the attic from the back hallway, floored and sealed the room, installed electric lights, and were given articles of furniture by various members of the Church. They held their programs there every Friday night.

The Methodist Brotherhood, previously mentioned, continued its meetings from month to month. The list of officers for the second year included J. M. Hughes, president; Dr. S. D. Smith, vice-president; William Yochum, secretary; and George Brady, treasurer. The full lists of officers thereafter are not available, but for the third year W. H. Hays was president, and for the fourth year Dean F. B. Mumford was president.

During these years from 1910 to 1914 the Board of Missions of the Church at large was being reorganized so as to include all the different mission organizations of the Church, including the missionary societies of the women. It will be remembered that the General Conference of 1878 approved the establishment of a Woman's Foreign Missionary Society, that a general organization was immediately formed, and that during the next few years this new society had been extended to the formation of conference missionary societies, and gradually local auxiliaries had been formed throughout the church.[89] In 1886 the General Conference authorized the organization of a woman's department of the Board of Church Extension, the objects of which were to raise funds for the building of parsonages where they were most needed and for home missionary purposes. This new organization, like the older one, organized conference societies as well as local auxiliaries, and held annual conventions the first of which was in St. Louis in 1893. It changed its name, however, to the Woman's Parsonage and Home Mission Society. In many of the annual conferences, as in the Missouri Annual Conference for a number of years, the annual meetings of both societies would be held at the same time and place, the programs being dove-tailed with each other. On the other hand, competition sometimes developed between the two organizations, especially on a local scale.

The Missouri Conference organization of the younger society was formed at a meeting in Chillicothe, May 17, 1889, and it held regular annual meetings beginning in 1891. The annual meeting for 1895 was held in the Columbia Methodist Church, May 8-9, before an auxiliary had been formed there, but the ladies of the Columbia Foreign Missionary Society of the local church served as a reception committee and helped in the entertainment of delegates. Shortly after this meeting and probably as a result of it, a local auxiliary of the Woman's Parsonage and Home Mission Society was formed in the Columbia Methodist Church.[90]

As a result of action in the General Conference of 1898, the collection of funds for the building of parsonages was taken over by the General Board of Church Extension, and the Woman's Parsonage and Home Mission Society became simply the Woman's Home Mission Society, with Conference organizations and local auxiliaries as before. Four years later, in the General Conference of 1902, it was suggested in a committee report,

---

[89] See page 89. The first Columbia society of the Woman's Foreign Missionary Society was apparently formed during 1880-1881.
[90] Quarterly Conference Record, May 20, 1895. This was a very active society in the Columbia Church for a number of years.

though not made definitive by Conference legislation, that the Foreign and Home Societies ought to be unified. Actual unification of all the missionary efforts of the Church became the objective when legislation was passed in the General Conference of 1910 at Asheville, North Carolina; this provided for the creation of a General Board of Missions in the management of which women were to participate. The two women's societies were to reorganize into a Woman's Missionary Council which was to nominate representatives in the General Board of Missions. But all the work carried on by the two former women's societies was to be carried on by a Foreign and a Home department of the Woman's Missionary Council.

It took some time for this new woman's society to extend its organization throughout the Church. The first annual meeting of the Woman's Missionary Council after the organizing meeting at the General Conference of 1910 was held in the St. John's Methodist Church in St. Louis in April, 1911. The membership of the Council included the corresponding secretaries of all the various Conference Woman's Foreign Missionary Societies and Woman's Home Mission Societies. The representatives from the Missouri Annual Conference Societies were Mrs. F. F. Stephens [91] and Mrs. Turner McBaine, both of Columbia. This meeting ordered leaflets to be prepared and sent out to all conference and district officers of both the Foreign and Home Societies, explaining the plan of unification of missionary efforts adopted by the General Conference. In the Missouri Annual Conference in May, 1912, the two former organizations held their last annual meetings and united to form the Missouri Conference Woman's Missionary Society with Mrs. W. L. Reed of Mexico as president and Mrs. Stephens as corresponding secretary. The local auxiliaries throughout the Conference were unified soon afterwards. At the midyear meeting of the executive committee of the Woman's Missionary Council, February 4-11, 1914, a resolution was adopted to the effect that the union of the two Societies had been formed in most conferences and auxiliaries satisfactorily, and that therefore the General Conference of 1914 was asked to make no changes which would disrupt the union. The General Conference of 1914 at Oklahoma City

---

[91] Mrs. Stephens began her connection with the Woman's Missionary Council at this first annual meeting and continued it until her sudden death in February, 1931.

heeded this request and named the ten women who were nominated by the Council as members of the General Board of Missions. The Council was made to include as *ex-officio* members various men who occupied important positions as officials in the General Board.[92]

---

[92] See *Fourth Annual Report of the Woman's Missionary Council* for 1914, page 26; *Journal of the General Conference,* 1914, Reports number 16 and 17 of the Committee on Missions.

Presiding Bishops, Missouri Conference, 1901-1956

W. A. Candler
1901-1909

A. W. Wilson
1902

C. B. Galloway
1903

E. R. Hendrix
1904-1905, 1914-1917

J. S. Key
1906-1907

H. C. Morrison
1908

Collins Denny
1910-1911

E. D. Mouzon
1912

E. E. Hoss
1913

W. B. Murrah
1918-1921

William F. McMurry
General Chairman
Building Committee
Missouri Methodist Church
1922-1929

A. F. Smith
1930-1933

John M. Moore
1934-1937

W. T. Watkins
1938

Ivan Lee Holt
1939, 1944-1956

J. C. Broomfield
1940-1943

Section XIV
Growth Circumscribed by Lack of Space

The problem of insufficient space for church services and Sunday School activities was faced by the Broadway congregation almost from the time the church was built. That was before anyone had suggested holding two identical Sunday forenoon preaching services, but even if such services had been held, it would have left unsolved the question of room for the large Sunday School classes of University and college students and the manifold activities of many groups of children below the college age. In a very real sense this pressure for space was the difficult problem running all through the life of the Broadway Church. Concern had been expressed over this situation in a Quarterly Conference as early as in Bishop's pastorate, and in Aker's first year a committee had been appointed in the Quarterly Conference of May 2, 1910, to consider this question and report to a later meeting.

In those days religious instruction and moral education were presumed to be within the sphere of legitimate activities for state supported schools and colleges. This was shown in occasional discussions in University faculty or board meetings, as when the curators ordered the establishment of a professorship of Christian Morals in 1902, or when the faculty in 1904 asked for the appointment of a man whose work would be to organize and lead all the moral, spiritual and religious forces in the University. Funds were too short in either case to provide for the appointment. But a religious denomination had made the attempt to fill the gap when the Christian Church performed the pioneer service in 1895 of establishing "The Bible College of Missouri." It invited students to enroll in its courses free of cost, but for ten years its courses were not accredited by the University. Moreover, that solution was not precisely what other religious denominations desired. Though they were not opposed to the instruction the students received in the Bible College courses, they wished to keep their student members related to their own churches.

Among the Methodists, the problem was first raised on a Conference-wide scale in the Missouri Annual Conference of

Columbia Methodist Pastors, 1898-1913

M. H. Moore, 1898-1902

S. P. Cresap, 1902-1905

Charles M. Bishop, 1905-1909

C. M. Aker, 1909-1912

Charles W. Tadlock, 1912-1913

1911,[93] when its Board of Missions reported that it had carefully investigated the situation resulting from the rapidly growing number of Methodist students in the University. It had come to the conclusion that special provisions should be made for relating this large number of students to the Church in Columbia, but that the burden of this work should rest upon the Methodists of the entire state and not simply upon the local Church. As a temporary measure it proposed that the Conference should employ an assistant for the Columbia pastor and that cooperation in this project should be sought from the mission boards of the two other Annual Conferences in the state. Its proposals were approved, but no assistant was appointed for that year.

At the next Annual Conference, September, 1912, the Mission Board reported that it had secured the cooperation of the other conferences in the state and that they would employ a part-time University student, to be known as the student secretary, working under the direction of a committee composed of the presidents of the three mission boards, the presiding elder of the Fayette District, and the pastor of the local Church. The person employed was Rush H. Limbaugh, afterwards a prominent attorney in St. Louis and Southeast Missouri. He was a fine worker and performed his duties satisfactorily.

Meanwhile, at this Annual Conference in 1912, Aker was moved to the Fayette Church and Charles W. Tadlock [94] was sent to Columbia. He proved to be a strong pulpit man and was admired and loved by the Columbia congregation. The crowds attending the Sunday morning church services were so great that it was difficult at times to provide seats for all. This again emphasized the need for a larger church auditorium as well as room for the various large student classes in the Sunday

---

[93] It is not known how this problem came before the Board of Missions, for there is no reference to it in the daily Minutes of the session nor in the Minutes of the preceding Annual Conference. Since this session of 1911 was held in Columbia where the ministers could see the crowds of students, it is quite likely that the pastor, Mr. Aker, had talked to the members of the Conference Board of Missions about the situation.

[94] Tadlock remained at Columbia for only one year. He was transferred to the St. Louis Conference in 1913 and appointed as General Secretary of the Board of Finance, a church-wide organization which was working to raise a large endowment for the support of the superannuated ministers and their dependents. He became prominent throughout the country, and was sent as fraternal messenger to the General Conference of the northern Church in Des Moines in May, 1920. He died from a heart attack in May, 1942.

School services, but whether to enlarge the Broadway Church or to build a new church was seriously considered for the first time during Tadlock's pastorate. It was the topic for discussion in a meeting of the men's Brotherhood January 30, 1913, when Dean Mumford was its president. He suggested the building of a student church, governed by students and with its own pastor. Dr. Tadlock, on the other hand, thought the best way to handle the problem was to enlarge the Broadway church building and have an associate pastor; he thought the students liked to meet with the regular congregation on Sunday mornings. The Board of Stewards had recently appointed a special committee consisting of Messrs. Nowell and Stephens, Dean Mumford, Senator Walker, and Judge Stewart to make a thorough investigation of the student problem and to report the most effective way for its solution. This committee decided to send a delegate from the Church to the Sixth Annual Conference of Church Workers in State Universities. This was a cooperative organization of various denominations, with membership in a number of state university communities and holding a conference annually in one of the university towns. The conference met that year on February 4-6 in Lawrence, Kansas, and Stephens was sent as the delegate. He reported when he returned that it appeared there was no uniform practice in state university communities in caring for the student problem.

With the transfer of Tadlock in 1913 to the St. Louis Annual Conference, Rev. C. C. Grimes[95] was appointed pastor at the Columbia Church. The Columbia congregation was disappointed that Tadlock had not been returned but soon found that Grimes also was a great pulpit man. To the entire satisfaction of the Columbia congregation, he was left as the pastor for four years, which was still the disciplinary limit for the reappointment of pastors to one charge. The Board of Missions of the Missouri Conference in September, 1913, had reported the necessity for a more earnest effort to meet the needs of the Methodist students, and with the help and cooperation of the two other conferences in the state, it would support a full time minister for the students, to serve as assistant pastor at Columbia. For this

---

[95] He was the son of Chaney Grimes who had been pastor of the Columbia Church, 1884-1885. Grimes did not spend much time visiting members of his congregation but sat in his study during the week reading and thinking and when he appeared before the congregation Sunday mornings he had something to say that forced their attention.

position, it asked for the appointment of A. C. Zumbrunnen who had been pastor in the St. Joseph Hyde Park Church for the past four years. He was the first full-time assistant pastor appointed to the Columbia Church.

During that conference year, the General Conference had held its quadrennial session in May, 1914, in Oklahoma City. This had been a period of the rapid growth of student bodies in state universities throughout the country and everywhere there were similar problems to the ones which existed in Columbia. The Committee on Education of the General Conference, considering this situation, brought in a report, which was approved by the Conference, placing the responsibility for assistance to Methodist churches in state university centers upon the annual conference Boards of Education rather than upon the Boards of Missions. In the Missouri Annual Conference of September, 1914, there was a report, therefore, from the Board of Education, recommending that a special commission be appointed to devise and propose plans a year later for aiding the Columbia Church. This commission was to be composed of one layman and one clerical member of each annual conference in the state. For the Missouri Conference, the commission nominated Dr. Stephens and Rev. J. C. Handy.

This temporary commission composed of six persons representing the three conferences in the state, met during the next year, consulted with various persons and finally reported that the tasks were too great to be handled by a temporary commission. It recommended the formation of a permanent commission, named "The Methodist Commission on Religious Work at the State University" similar in composition to the temporary commission, to make reports from year to year. During the next few years the membership of this Commission changed more or less from time to time though Stephens continued through the life of the Commission as the lay representative from the Missouri Annual Conference and as secretary of the Commission. Appropriations were made annually to continue the work begun by Zumbrunnen though the latter was appointed as student pastor only for the years 1913-1915. He was succeeded by Rev. W. L. Halberstadt. The Commission reported in 1916 that there was need for a type of church work in Columbia "that we are as yet unprepared to do. An adequate church building suitable for religious, educational, and social purposes is now an immediate need."

By that time the United States was drifting into World War I, and all thought of a new church building was temporarily abandoned. The permanent commission, however, continued to hold meetings all through the war period and years of recovery immediately after. All three of the annual conferences through these years made annual appropriations for the support of a clerical or lay worker in the Columbia Church.

During the spring of 1918, Halberstadt was moved by the Bishop to Cape Girardeau to become pastor of the church there, and Fred Gutekunst, a student, filled his position for a few weeks. He was succeeded in the fall and winter of 1918 by Jesse H. Smith who became also temporary Sunday School superintendent. By that time all male students of military age, except those who were classified as 4F (physically unfit), were in the armed services. The Spanish influenza epidemic came along in the fall of 1918, and for several weeks boards of health closed all public meetings, including church meetings. But by the summer of 1919 the country was well on the way back to "normalcy," and the educational institutions were filling up again. Churches could resume their normal programs of work. Grimes, as pastor, had given way in 1917 to Stanley W. Hayne, and he in 1919 to Joseph D. Randolph, a young man who had served through the war as an army chaplain. At the same time with his appointment, the Commission was fortunate to secure the services of Ernest H. Newcomb as student secretary, and he and Randolph worked together as a good team during the quadrennium of Randolph's service as pastor.

In the meantime, but extending far back into the nineteenth century, the Church was gradually changing from an ecclesiastically controlled body to one in which the laity had more voice. Perhaps the first step, or at least the one which was of most significance, was the General Conference legislation of 1866 which provided for lay representation in the annual and general conferences. Four laymen from each presiding elder's district were to be sent to the Annual Conference, and these laymen were to elect to the General Conference an equal number of delegates as were elected by the clerical members of the Annual Conference. It is conjectural whether or not this Conference action was to insure the solid support of the laity in resisting northern attempts to break up the southern Church just at that time. There were some details left to be worked out later, such as the creation of the District Conference in 1870.

A similar period of turmoil in the military, political, and social life of America occurred in the second decade of the twentieth century. Among its effects was the adoption of the 19th Amendment to the national Constitution granting universal suffrage to women. In the Methodist Church an analogous and contemporary demand led to the campaign for "laity rights for women." Ever since 1866 the word "layman" had been interpreted to exclude women from any official capacity in the Church.[96] A progressive element had been trying for some years to expand laity rights to women as well as to men. The question had arisen in the General Conference of 1910, when on invitation Miss Belle H. Bennett, president of the newly created Woman's Missionary Council, had appeared before the Conference and had made a stirring appeal for this extension of the suffrage in the Church. The College of Bishops, representing a more conservative attitude, recognized this movement for the demand for equality but said in their address to the Conference, "We believe that the spirit of this movement is against the view which our people at large have held and still hold in regard to woman's place in the Church and in society, and that such a step would not, therefore, make for the greater efficiency of our Church as a whole in any of the regions occupied by it." Later, in the Conference, a minority report of the Committee on Revisals granting laity rights to women was rejected by a vote of 188 to 74. The majority report was then adopted; "we do not believe that the fullness of time has come when, in fairness to them (women) and in justice to the Church, we can put upon them the official burdens of the Church so long and so rightfully borne by the men of the Church."

The same question came up again in the General Conference of 1914, when the Bishops, in their opening address repeated *verbatim* their opposition as expressed four years before. The Committee on Revisals reported that among many other memorials on the subject of laity rights for women was one from the Woman's Missionary Council "asking that the women be granted the privileges of the lay members of the Church, thereby entitling them to sit as members in Quarterly, District, Annual, and General Conferences, and to be elected as stewards and trustees." A minority report, in favor of granting these rights,

---

[96] See note 78 on page 108.

was lost by a vote of 105 to 171, and the majority report against the movement was adopted.

Finally, in the General Conference of 1918 in Atlanta the question came up a third time with a greater demand than ever before for the expansion of laity rights to women. A report from the Committee on Revisals granting laity rights to women in all levels of Church government was adopted by a roll call vote of 265 to 57. The next day the Bishops, with Collins Denny as their spokesman, vetoed the action on the ground that it was a change in the constitution of the Church which could be made only by a three-fourths vote of the members of all the annual conferences. Upon motion of Marvin T. Haw, a clerical delegate from the St. Louis Conference (some years later pastor of the Columbia Church), the question was submitted to the annual conferences for their decision. The vote in the annual conferences was 4,280 in favor of the change to 467 against. Several of the annual conferences, including the Missouri Conference, were unanimously in favor. Thus the change was approved simply by changing "layman" to "lay member."

In Columbia when notice of the approval of the change by the annual conferences was received, the pastor, Mr. Randolph, on November 6, 1919, nominated for election to the board of stewards four women, namely, Mrs. Turner McBaine, Mrs. R. H. Emberson, Mrs. F. F. Stephens, and Mrs. W. T. Stephenson. They thus became the first elected women officials, except for the officers of the Woman's Missionary Society, in the Columbia Church. This was an historic date for the women of the Church. An associated change was made by the General Conference of 1922 by enlarging the membership of the Quarterly Conference to include the president of the local Woman's Missionary Society.

The General Conference of 1918 further democratized the government of the Church by doubling the number of lay delegates in the annual conferences. This was done by providing that the district conferences should elect eight delegates to the annual conferences, instead of four as formerly. In the Fayette District Conference in subsequent years, it became almost a matter of amusement that one of the delegates from the Columbia Church, J. Emmett Hawkins, nominated all eight members of the delegation to the Annual Conference, but Emmett was not the kind of man who wanted to "run things" and he always consulted laymen from the other churches before making the nominations.

Many proposed changes in the *Discipline* affecting the local churches came to the various sessions of the General Conference for its approval. These suggestions or "memorials" as they were called, were generally referred to the Committee on Revisals which sifted and classified them and then generally recommended their rejection. Sometimes, though, the Committee recommended approval. As an example, quite a large number of members throughout the Church were still dissatisfied with its title, although efforts to change it had failed previously; they wanted to eliminate the word "South" at the end of the title. They felt that this word limited the activities of the Church, both in this country and in its foreign missions. The Committee on Revisals finally in the General Conference of 1910 proposed that the title be simply "The Methodist Church," and this was approved by a vote of 150 to 63. The College of Bishops vetoed the change, however, on the ground that the name of the Church was a part of its organic law, and could not be changed by a simple resolution of the Conference. Subsequently, not to be denied by the action of the Bishops, the delegates voted to submit the change to the annual conferences, proposing this time that the name be "The Methodist Episcopal Church in America." The annual conferences later refused the change by a vote of 3,396 to 1,310, thus for the third time in the history of the Church refusing to change its title. In the Missouri Annual Conference where there had always been some opposition to the word "South" in the title the vote was 83 in favor of the change to 43 against.

A proposal to amend the Apostles' Creed as used in the services of the Church was submitted to the annual conferences from the General Conference of 1918. The amendment would have stricken out the words "the holy catholic church" and have substituted the words "Christ's holy Church." It was held that many members misunderstood the former wording. The Bishops ruled that this was a question relating to "standards of doctrine" and to become effective had to be approved by a majority vote in every annual conference. But in the annual conferences, some members thought this was almost like changing the wording of the Bible, and nine conferences voted against the change and, therefore, the amendment failed.

A change made by the General Conference of 1914, meant to

increase the efficiency of the administration of the Church, provided that the Bishops were to be assigned for a quadrennium to specific areas in the Church. The Bishop assigned for the years 1914-1917 to the area including the Missouri Annual Conference was E. R. Hendrix, a native Missourian; for the years 1918-1921 it was W. B. Murrah, and the next two quadrenniums, 1922 to 1929, it was W. F. McMurry, another native Missourian. In the General Conference of 1918 six new Bishops were elected —John M. Moore, W. F. McMurry, U. V. W. Darlington, H. N. DuBose, W. N. Ainsworth, and James Cannon, Jr. Four years later, in 1922, five Bishops were elected—W. B. Beauchamp, J. E. Dickey, S. R. Hay, H. M. Dobbs, and H. A. Boaz.

A development of importance throughout the Church, apparently coming from the body of the laity itself, led eventually to the establishment of a new General Board in the Church, the Board of Lay Activities. This development was known originally, however, as the Layman's Missionary Movement and probably started as an interdenominational celebration of the centenary of the Haystack Prayer Meeting.[97] The Movement was recognized in the General Conference of 1910 by the appointment of a committee consisting of one layman from each annual conference delegation to discuss among themselves and to propose to the Conference a program of action for laymen.[98] The committee brought in a resolution, which was approved, to recast the schedule of the annual conference business to give increased emphasis to the activities of laymen. It provided for the appointment in each annual conference, each presiding elder's district, and each pastoral charge of a missionary leader. Thus began the office of lay leader, though at first the word "lay" was omitted.[99]

---

[97] This was a term applied to the meetings of a small group of students at Williams College, Williamstown, Massachusetts, early in the nineteenth century. The group of students was led by Samuel J. Mills who was intensely interested in foreign missions.

[98] It will be remembered that the word "laymen" still meant only the masculine members of the Church, but that this General Conference of 1910 had reorganized the missionary activities of the women by providing for the organization of the Woman's Missionary Council. The Layman's Missionary Movement was at that time also emphasizing missionary activities for the men.

[99] A question to be asked thereafter in all annual conferences was "who is appointed lay leader?" The lay leaders of the Missouri Conference for the next several years were Judge B. J. Casteel of St. Joseph from 1909 to 1912, C. M. Hay of Fulton in 1913, Paul M. Culver of Gower from 1914 to 1917, and Judge Martin E. Lawson of Liberty for fifteen years following 1918.

GROWTH CIRCUMSCRIBED BY LACK OF SPACE

In the General Conference of 1914 the committee on the Layman's Missionary Movement became one of the standing committees of the Conference. The emphasis was still on missionary work; it was provided that each annual conference was to establish a board dealing with questions relating to missions, and consisting of the conference leader and the district leaders. Likewise, there was to be a district committee organized by each presiding elder with the district leader as the chairman and including the leaders of all the charges in the district.

The General Conference of 1918 more fully organized the work of the laymen, but at that time, since the United States was engaged in World War I, it seemed that the activities were directed more to the problems growing out of the War, such as food conservation, war relief work, and support of YMCA work in the armies.

Finally, in the General Conference of 1922, held at Hot Springs, Arkansas, and as a result of a memorial from the executive committee of the Layman's Missionary Movement, a constitution for a Board of Lay Activities was adopted and placed in the *Discipline*. This new General Board was to be directed by a General Secretary elected by the Conference, and was to include all annual conference lay leaders. The committee of the General Conference on the Layman's Missionary Movement was to be known thereafter as the Committee on Lay Activities. The duties of the General Board were to develop and promote all possible methods for securing and increasing the interest of the laymen in all the activities of the Church. The Conference Board of Lay Activities was to be composed of the conference lay leader, elected by the annual conferences on nomination of the conference board, and the district lay leaders and associate lay leaders from each presiding elder's district.

The district board of Lay Activities was to be organized in the same way as the district board of the Layman's Missionary Movement had been. Thus, down to the local church the work of the men of the Church was to be organized and channeled into a definite program of lay activities. It was a grand organization but how effective it would be would depend upon the ability and consecration of the various officials from the General Secretary down to the local charge lay leader.[100]

---

[100] The lay leaders of the Layman's Missionary Movement in the Columbia Methodist Church as far as the records which have been preserved show were J. W. Schwabe in 1910, Manuel Drumm in 1914, C. O.

During these same years of the second and third decades of the century there were several other local developments in Columbia which must be mentioned. The officers of the Broadway Woman's Missionary Society had come to the conclusion that a general meeting once a month in the basement of the Broadway Church was not securing the interest of nearly all the women of the church, and that some way must be devised to develop and more widely distribute leadership among the women and to enlist them more deeply in the work of the Church. As a result of the discussions, the town was divided geographically in 1916 into four parts, and the women members of the Church in each part formed an organization known as a "Circle." The members of each Circle elected their own officers and had their own programs once a month but all were expected to come together for an all-day meeting once a month. The Circles were named for prominent women leaders in missionary work. Thus there were the Cunningham, Combs, Gibson, and Perkinson Circles, each with its own group of officers.

The men of the Church had allowed their Brotherhood organization to lapse during the War years. At the regular meeting of the board of stewards, February 2, 1919, the pastor of the Church at that time, S. W. Hayne, proposed that the Brotherhood be reorganized and after comments by several different members of the board, a committee consisting of Dean Mumford and four others was appointed for this purpose. But Mumford was too involved in his work as dean of the College of Agriculture just at that time to call the committee together. The next November, after a change of pastors, the question was again brought up in the board meeting, and a new committee was appointed, consisting of Dr. S. D. Smith (lay leader at that time), F. F. Stephens, J. A. Stewart, H. M. Craig, and J. D. Randolph (pastor).

The committee reorganized the men into a Methodist Men's Club, and from that time forward the men of the congregation met at the Church once a month, except for the two summer months, had dinner together, usually prepared by one of the

---

Hanes in 1915, E. E. Windsor in 1916, F. B. Mumford in 1917, W. H. Rusk in 1918, and Dr. S. D. Smith from 1919 to 1921. After the reorganization of the Layman's Missionary Movement into the Board of Lay Activities, the Lay Leaders in Columbia were B. E. Miller in 1922, E. B. McDonnell in 1923 and 1924 and J. E. Hawkins for a number of years following 1924. Hawkins was also District Lay Leader.

women's circles, and listened to a prepared program.[101] The Club was responsible for many good things that occurred in the Church during the succeeding years including the sponsorship of Boy Scout Troop 5, a group of boys always closely related to the Church. Among the members of the Club who contributed largely to the success of this troop of Scouts were A. A. Jeffrey, E. A. Trowbridge, H. M. Wren, C. C. Coffman, A. J. Meyer, M. F. Miller, L. R. Grinstead, Marshall Clark, Earl E. Deimund, and Jas. E. Crosby.

---

[101] An unpublished monograph written by T. T. Martin gives a short history of this Club from 1920 to 1962. It includes the constitution and by-laws of the Club and the names of all the members at three different periods, 1923, 1944, and 1961. It also has a list of the officers and a list of the members who have died. It includes a brief account of Boy Scout Troop 5. Although there are some blanks due to the fact that the records have not all been preserved, yet the monograph is a valuable contribution to the history of the Church.

SECTION XV
The State Assumes Partial Responsibility for Expansion

We must now revert to the main theme of this period of the history of the Columbia Methodist Church, namely, provision for more room for its membership, and especially for the growing student body using its services. The three annual conferences in the state to which appeals had been made for help had responded by making annual conference appropriations to support an effective worker among the students and by appointing a permanent Commission to make a continuing study of the needs of the Church in Columbia.

This Commission soon concluded that there must be a more suitable church plant in Columbia, as well as wise guidance for student activities, and so reported to the annual conferences. It was recognized that something must be done, but what would be a good program of action and how much would it cost? As to the expense the Commission in its first meeting on May 4, 1916, before the United States had entered World War I, discussed this problem all the afternoon, and finally came to the conclusion that $150,000 should provide an adequate plant for the activities of the local Church and care for the social and religious needs of the students. In its second meeting in the same year the Commission proposed that Columbia ought to raise $50,000 of the total amount; about fifty of the leading members of the local Church met with the Commission that same evening and agreed unanimously that the Broadway Church would shoulder its share of the costs. This was presented to the next Quarterly Conference on November 24, 1916, and approved. But no definite plans were yet made for the actual financial campaign to raise money within or away from Columbia.

Soon, the country was engulfed in war. Male students left their studies in large numbers to join the armies and navies of their government or to assist in furnishing supplies for the war campaign. The Commission held two meetings during the war years, but its discussions were chiefly on the amount of temporary support needed for the student work at Columbia, and how it should be divided among the three annual conferences.[102]

---

[102] Because of the transfer of Halberstadt to Cape Girardeau in 1918, and finding that not all of the money which had been appropriated by

Congregational Leaders Through This Period

J. M. Baker

Judge J. A. Stewart

Mrs. Blanche H. Stephens

George H. Beasley

J. W. Schwabe

Perhaps it was because of the lessened demand for space in the church building during the war that the new minister, S. W. Hayne, proposed some sort of an enlargement of the Broadway Church rather than an entire new building on another location. The Commission, however, declined that rather easy solution, and it was hoped that a financial campaign could be launched as soon as the war was over. In a meeting of the Commission on June 9, 1919, the question of enlargement of the Broadway Church building rather than of the erection of a new Church was thoroughly discussed again, but for the second time the Commission voted to adhere to its former decision.

A new complication, however, had already appeared. The General Conference of 1918, under the driving stimulus of the Layman's Missionary Movement, had voted to celebrate the centennial of the organization of a missionary department in the Methodist Episcopal Church in America by raising $30,000,000 for the cause of missions. In the same General Conference it was reported that the educational institutions of the Church were in dire financial straits and it was voted to wage a campaign for $18,000,000 for the schools and colleges belonging to the Church, and $10,000,000 for its two universities at Atlanta and Dallas respectively. To avoid confusion between these two financial campaigns, the centenary program was to have the right of way for the first two years of the next quadrennium, while the educational campaign was to have the right of way during the last two years. These two great efforts to raise money, which were to be carried on in every Southern Methodist Church in the land, would make much more difficult the raising of money for building purposes in local communities. But the Columbia Church itself, though faced with the erection of a new church building, pledged over $18,000 for the Centenary Campaign and nearly as much for the Educational Campaign.

In this same meeting of the Commission, June, 1919, still another complex problem presented itself. A committee of women representing the Woman's Missionary Council appeared and proposed that there be included in the plans of the Commis-

---

the three conferences had been used, the Commission voted to use $125 for the publication and distribution of a weekly paper among the Methodist students and families in Columbia, provided the local congregation met the balance of the expense. Thus began the publication of the *Broadway Church Herald,* later called the *Methodist Foundation Herald,* which was continued for several years. There is a partial file of this paper in the library of the State Historical Society in Columbia.

sion the building of a $100,000 residence hall for Methodist women attending the University of Missouri. Student housing at the University, especially for women, was very short at that time (as indeed it usually has been during the entire history of the University). The building of women's residence halls at educational centers by church groups was no new thing. It had been done successfully in other southern university towns. The women's arguments seemed convincing, and to make their proposal more acceptable, they agreed to pay $75,000 of the estimated cost of the $100,000 residence hall if the Methodists of Missouri would pay $25,000 and furnish the site. This seemed to the members of the Commission a good proposition. They decided, therefore, to change the campaign for $150,000 to $300,000 of which $75,000 was already pledged by the Woman's Council.[103]

In a long meeting of the Commission on March 4, 1920, the members took under consideration the great increase in costs of building materials as a result of the war. In making new estimates, therefore, as to the amount of money which would be needed it concluded that from $450,000 to $500,000 should be raised. But the Commission decided to go ahead with its plans because the situation in the Church at Columbia was becoming desperate. The attendance of students at the University in the year 1919-1920 was over a thousand more than the preceding year, and the year after that more than a thousand more than that year.

Meanwhile under the guidance and inspiration of the student secretary from 1919 to 1923, E. H. Newcomb, the Methodist students had entirely reorganized their church work and had established M S O, the Methodist Student Organization as it was known until the union of the Northern and Southern Churches

---

[103] In the long run this was probably an unwise decision. Though indeed a fine location for the residence hall was secured and a splendid building erected accommodating nearly 90 women, yet its management soon found that the rooms could not be reserved for "Methodist girls," and the building named Hendrix Hall for Mrs. Adam Hendrix, mother of Bishop E. R. Hendrix, became simply a dormitory for the women students of the University. The Woman's Council, a few years later, reviewing the situation, decided it would be wise to withdraw from the business of maintaining dormitories at state university centers. The Council hoped to sell the building to the University, but the latter did not have the money at that time to purchase it. It was sold for $80,000, much less than it had cost, to a group of Columbia doctors for offices and was named the Professional Building. The Methodist Foundation had paid out as its share of the building and site $43,000 of its funds needed so desperately a few years later.

in 1939. At the beginning of every semester new officers were elected and teams organized to include hundreds of the Methodist students in definite activities. In the fall of 1920 the men students undertook themselves to add a large room to the Broadway Church; the original church building had no basement under the chapel and the students, with the consent of the official board, appeared at the church one Saturday morning with picks and shovels and began excavation under the chapel. An advisory committee of the board was appointed to oversee the work and to raise money for some of the expenses. Eventually a room as large as the chapel was constructed with a cement floor and cement walls and lighted by electricity. It was reported in the board meeting of December 2, 1920, that the improvement cost $2,834.82. This included, however, new chapel lights as well as lights in the basement room, new chairs for both the chapel and the basement room, and construction of the stairway to the basement. M S O habitually carried out a financial campaign among its members every year to raise funds for its own activities.[104] A committee from M S O appeared in the Church board meeting of October 7, 1920, and offered to contribute toward the Church expenses 20% of all the money they raised for their organization. This was gratefully accepted by the stewards.

Up to this time there had been years of discussion but little positive action. But the year 1921 was the turning point in the movement to build a great church plant in Columbia. On April 4, 1921, the Commission met in Centenary Church in St. Louis where Dr. O. E. Goddard appeared on request as a representative of the General Board of Missions. When it was suggested that a large appropriation for this project from the General Board would act as a go-ahead signal, he replied that he could make no positive answer without action first by the Board, but that he believed the members were friendly to such undertakings. He indicated that there was a fund of $5,000,000 which had been appropriated originally for the Church's war work in the armies in Europe, but that since the war had come to an end rather suddenly and sooner than expected the most of this fund was unexpended, and that now the Board might use a portion of the

---

[104] For instance, during the conference year of 1921-1922, the total fund raised by the students amounted to $3,922.45 of which $803 went to the church building fund. See *Methodist Foundation Herald,* September 9, 1922.

fund for work in state schools. He advised the Commission to petition formally for an appropriation from that fund. The petition thereupon was drawn up and a committee named to meet with the Board in Nashville early in May.

The Commission instructed its committee to present to the Board at Nashville the following schedule of funds which it hoped to receive:

Woman's Missionary Council	$ 75,000
The Broadway Church in Columbia	50,000
Three Conference Boards of Missions	30,000
The General Board of Church Extension	50,000
Three Conference Boards of Church Extension	15,000
General Board of Missions	250,000
Private subscriptions	30,000
	$500,000 [105]

In a meeting of the Broadway Church board of stewards, May 12, 1921, there was a long discussion of the building program. Randolph, one of the committee sent to Nashville, had returned and reported to the board a favorable attitude in the General Board of Missions, though as yet they would make no definite promise of financial aid. Randolph felt sure, however, that aid would be forthcoming. The general discussion among the stewards was so optimistic that, on suggestion of Randolph, a committee was authorized for the selection of a site "located as nearly as possible at the center of the town and student population."

The Annual Conference met that year in Hannibal on August 31.[106] The president of the Conference was Bishop W. B.

---

[105] This was of course too sanguine. The Woman's Council found that it could contribute no more than $66,666 but the officers of the conference missionary societies in Missouri waged a campaign among their auxiliaries for a contribution of five dollars from each local member, and thus secured enough not only to offset the reduced amount from the Council but to provide greater costs for the building than had been foreseen and to furnish the hall. The General Boards of Missions and of Church Extension never were able to furnish as large an amount as had been anticipated, neither were the conference boards.

[106] The Missouri Annual Conference was one of the first of the annual conferences to choose delegates to the next General Conference of 1922. In its election of lay delegates Mrs. Stephens was chosen on the first ballot and became the first woman delegate ever elected to a Southern General Conference. The *Broadway Methodist Herald* of October 1, 1921, said that the Columbia Church felt great pride in the fact that the first woman to be elected a delegate to a General Conference should come from its own membership.

Murrah, but Bishop W. F. McMurry and Dr. R. L. Russell, representing respectively the General Boards of Church Extension and of Missions, were present to make a formal proposal for financial aid to the Commission, which in turn reported to the Conference. McMurry was a native Missourian and understood the situation at Columbia better than any other member of the College of Bishops. The proposal suggested that it would take at least $400,000 to erect the buildings necessary at Columbia, though as it turned out this estimate was far too low. The Board of Missions and the Board of Church Extension each would contribute $50,000 on condition that the Woman's Council would contribute $75,000 and that $225,000 would be provided by Columbia and the state of Missouri at large. The proposal suggested that not less than $100,000 should come from Columbia and Boone County, but this amount was to be credited with the sale price of the Broadway Church building. The report was approved by the State Commission, which made the additional suggestions that the work start at once, and that Bishop McMurry be asked to head the "General Building Committee." This was then approved by the Annual Conference.

Columbia Methodist Pastors, 1913-1930

Charles C. Grimes, 1913-1917

S. W. Hayne, 1917-1919

Joseph D. Randolph, 1919-1923

Mavin T. Haw, 1923-1927

M. N. Waldrip, 1927-1930

Section XVI
Construction of the Missouri Methodist Church

When the news of the action of the Annual Conference at Hannibal was received in Columbia, there was great excitement and rejoicing, not unmixed with dubiousness about the ability to raise locally such a large sum as $100,000. The board of stewards had to agree first of all that it would accept the difficult task. Perhaps this was the most important question coming before the board in a generation. After a long discussion in the meeting of October 4, 1921, during which it was emphasized that the sale price of the old church, said to be worth $35,000, would be included in the $100,000,[107] a motion to approve the financial campaign was carried unanimously by a standing vote. There followed the appointment of certain committees to set up the campaign, and during the next three months there were almost constant meetings of committees, the board, or special called sessions of the Quarterly Conference.

Perhaps the most disturbing and divisive question, though actually not the most important, was that of the location of the new church. A committee on sites had been appointed the previous spring, but because at that time this did not seem to be a pressing matter, nothing had been done. Now in October a new committee on sites of eight members with Schwabe as chairman was appointed. News of the impending purchase had circulated among holders of desirable locations, and prices seemed to become exorbitant; at a board meeting in November at which Bishop McMurry was present, two of the discouraged members of the committee proposed that the Broadway Church be retained and rebuilt with additions. The Bishop expressed himself vigorously against that proposal. He wanted a location within two blocks south of Broadway where there would be room for a commodious auditorium, a religious education section, and headquarters for student activities, a building in which the town, the Church and the state would take pride; if the members of the Broadway Church did not want such a plant, he said he might as well take the train and go home! But he warned that in that case the

---

[107] Only $6,500 was eventually realized from the sale of the Broadway Church.

Methodist Episcopal Church would build a great church in Columbia and the southern Church would sink into insignificance. That ended finally the talk of remodeling the Broadway Church.

After another month the committee on sites proposed the choice of three locations, all on the south side of Locust Street between Eighth and Hitt Streets. The location finally chosen after two long sessions of the Quarterly Conference was known as the Trimble property, between Ninth and Tenth Streets, for which $37,500 was paid. In later years there was still some question as to whether this had been the best choice.

Another committee of seventeen members was appointed to secure subscriptions for the building fund. Robert E. L. Hill was general chairman of this committee, but James W. Schwabe was in actual charge of the financial campaign. At first it was expected to begin this canvass immediately, but for one reason or another the work was delayed until the following spring. The subscriptions were to be made for three or five years, as the subscriber preferred, with annual payments. It was reported in the next Annual Conference of September, 1922, that $47,000 had been subscribed in Columbia.

A third important committee, named in October, 1921, became known as the building committee, and had general charge of the entire project. It lasted until the erection of the church was completed in 1930 though its membership was modified from time to time. There was a larger directive body which came to be known as the general building committee in distinction from the Columbia members who were called the local building committee. The general building committee consisted of Bishop McMurry, who was chairman and who represented the Board of Church Extension; Dr. R. L. Russell, author of the phrase, "Missouri Methodist Foundation," who represented the General Board of Missions; Dr. Ivan Lee Holt, who represented the St. Louis Annual Conference; L. D. Murrell, a layman from Marshall who represented the Southwest Missouri Annual Conference; and F. F. Stephens who represented the Missouri Annual Conference. Added to these were always the presiding elder of the Fayette District and the pastor of the local Church whoever they might be at the time.

Whenever the general building committee met in Columbia it was always understood that the members making up the local committee would join and complete the general committee, but

W. B. NOWELL, SR.
Local Chairman

MANUEL DRUMM,
Chairman Finance

F. F. STEPHENS,
Secretary-Treasurer

J. T. McMULLAN

Others who have been members of the Building Committee from time to time: F. A. Dalton, J. T. Prichett, B. D. Sipple, J. D. Randolph, Mrs. F. F. Stephens, J. A. Stewart, O. B. Wilson, M. T. Haw.

S. R. BARNETT

F. B. MUMFORD

E. B. McDONNELL

J. J. PYLES

Local Building Committee—Missouri Methodist Church

the local group which decided many small matters had its own officers also. Stephens was secretary of both groups and, as first named, when the chief problems concerned the building of the residence hall, Mrs. Stephens was chairman of the local committee. Other members of the local group as named in October, 1921, were O. B. Wilson, P. H. Ross, F. B. Mumford, and J. D. Randolph, ex-officio. Wilson and Ross afterwards moved from town and their places on the committee were taken in November, 1923, by J. J. Pyles and W. B. Nowell, and the latter was then elected chairman of the local committee. It later became desirable to enlarge the local membership of the committee and at different times J. T. McMullan, Manuel Drumm, F. A. Dalton, E. B. McDonnell, and S. R. Barnett were added. Drumm became chairman of a sub-committee on finance and was the driving force in the committee until his death in 1930. Dalton withdrew his membership from the committee and from the Church April 23, 1928, to join his wife in another church.

The building of the residence hall started first and progressed more rapidly than that of the Church. This was because it had a large percentage of the total cost already guaranteed in 1921. The women realized, however, before starting construction that the building plus the furnishings would cost more than the projected $100,000. They brought this matter to the attention of the general building committee and it was suggested that they put on a campaign in the three Woman's Conference Missionary Societies in the state. This was done and a donation was sought of five dollars from each active member in the state. Enough was raised thereby to offset the decreased contribution from the Woman's Missionary Council, $66,666 instead of $75,000, greater costs than they had expected in the building operation, and the furnishings for the entire hall. A board of control was established with Mrs. R. H. Emberson as chairman, Mrs. J. C. Handy, vice-chairman, Mrs. W. M. Alexander, secretary, and Mrs. Stephens, treasurer, and with seven other women representing the three annual conferences and the Woman's Missionary Council. The membership of the board of control, like that of the building committee, was changed afterwards from time to time.

A member of the committee on sites of the Foundation, Judge Stewart, discovered a splendid location for the hall known as the Mitchell property on the north side of University Avenue, between Ninth and Hitt Streets and within one block of the

CONSTRUCTION OF THE METHODIST CHURCH

University Library. This was purchased in December, 1922, for $18,000, supplied by the Foundation. A St. Louis firm of architects, Jamieson & Spearl, which had drawn the plans and specifications for many of the University buildings, was employed as architect for the hall. Ground was broken in April, 1924, and the cornerstone was laid September 11, with addresses by President Brooks of the University, Bishop McMurry, and Mrs. J. W. Downs of Nashville, Tennessee. The building was completed, furnished, and opened for students in September, 1926.

The most distressing problem facing the Foundation from the start was the collection of sufficient funds. Not only did the cost of the building site for the Church have to be provided, but the cost of the site of the residence hall as well, and in addition $25,000 for the building of the hall. These three expenditures made over $80,000 which had to be raised before any funds could be applied toward the building of the Church. The general boards advanced $40,000 on the first costs but this left $40,000 to be raised locally and in the state. Even before the first unit of the church building, the ground floor, was constructed, the Quarterly Conference on request of the building committee borrowed $45,000 from a local bank, mortgaging the real estate owned by the Church in Columbia; thirty members of the Church gave as additional security their personal notes for $500 each. But this financial transaction caused dissatisfaction in the board of trustees of the Broadway Church and led to the resignation of two members.

On recommendation of Bishop McMurry, who had been General Secretary of the Board of Church Extension before his election as Bishop and president of that Board after he became Bishop, Dr. A. J. Baylor, head of the architectural department of the Board of Church Extension, was employed to draw the plans and specifications. The first draft was received in Columbia in February, 1924. They were studied carefully in several sessions of the building committee and were submitted to different groups in the local Church for study and criticism. The location of the kitchen and the placing of kitchen equipment were referred to the officers of the Woman's Missionary Society; the plans for the Sunday School unit were gone over carefully by Marvin T. Haw, the pastor, who was himself a specialist in Sunday School work and who secured many suggestions from the General Sunday School Board of the Church in Nashville. The placing of the Church on the building lot was a source of considerable discussion and disagreement, but Haw insisted that room be left on the east end of the lot for a parsonage and this necessitated placing the front line of the foundation six feet from the west sidewalk. Finally, on December 29, 1924, it was decided to secure bids for the construction of only the ground floor and to cover it with a temporary roof.

The bids for this construction, exclusive of heating, lighting, and furniture, were opened on May 14, 1925, and ranged from $72,287 to $85,818. The low bid was made by the Phillips Construction Company of Columbia to whom the construction was let, but even then a decision had not been made as to whether the outside facing of the walls should be brick or stone. On a roll call vote in the committee with the clerical members all voting in favor of brick, and the lay members divided, the committee voted in favor of brick. Later when the superstructure was added, this was changed to Indiana Bedford limestone.

A local supervisor, Harry S. Bill, architect in the art department of the University, was employed to watch the work from day to day. The treasurer at his own request was placed under bond to the amount of $20,000, and the chairman of the local building committee, also at the request of the treasurer, had to approve any accounts before they were paid. The name selected by the Quarterly Conference on August 10, 1925, to be placed on the cornerstone was "Missouri Methodist Church, A. D. 1925." To this was added the scripture verse, "Jesus saith unto him, I am the way, the truth, and the life." In a called session of the Quarterly Conference on October 9, the date of October 20 was set as the time for laying the cornerstone of the new building. The University Glee Club under the direction of Herbert Wall, professor of voice in the University, was present and sang two numbers. Bishop McMurry gave the chief address in which he said among other things, "The Church would not be fulfilling its duty to the youth of Missouri without providing such a building. The Gospel should go along with education, and we want to preach a great Gospel in a great building." [108]

There were numerous articles placed in the cornerstone, including the Bible, the *Methodist Hymnal*, the *Discipline* for 1922, copies of the Columbia daily newspapers of October 20, 1925, Minutes of the 1924 annual conferences of the state, list of the membership of the Broadway Methodist Church, directory

---

[108] *Columbia Missourian*, October 20, 21, 1925.

Missouri Methodist Church
Cornerstone Laying, October 20, 1925

of the Columbia Telephone Company, and numerous other articles and publications. A church dinner celebrating the event that night was attended by 450 members and friends.

The first service held in the chapel of the new Church in the southeast corner of the building was a vesper service on Sunday evening, May 31, 1926, under the direction of the students with the student director, G. S. Nichols, presiding. He said in an address that it was quite fitting that the first meeting should be in charge of the students since the whole Missouri Methodist Foundation movement was conceived to furnish them with the proper religious environment.

The Missouri Annual Conference met in Columbia the following September, and though the official sessions were held in the Broadway Church, the women of the Church had moved all their dining and kitchen equipment to the new Church and meals for the delegates were served there. And from that time on, many services of one kind or another were held there, though the Sunday morning services were still held in the Broadway building. During the following winter the Church suffered a great loss in the tragic death on January 14, 1927, of James W. Schwabe. At the next Quarterly Conference the members stood in silent prayer in memory of him. He had been very active as a member of the official board since his election to that body in 1909.

In September, 1927, Mr. Haw had completed his quadrennium as pastor of the Broadway Church. He had been a diligent worker and was noted for his pastoral calling on the members. He reported at the end of his first year that he made 1007 pastoral calls during the year, and his later years were just as busy with such work. He was also very much interested in the organization and development of the Sunday School and during the hour of Sunday School activities he usually passed about from one division to another to make encouraging remarks.

He was succeeded in 1927 by Marion Nelson Waldrip who came from a pastorate in Kansas City and had been a noted pulpit orator. In his first sermon in Columbia he emphasized the necessity for the Church to complete the superstructure of the Missouri Methodist Church. He himself, however, while urging the local officials to resume building, furnished little other assistance except that he was a devotee of decorative art in church buildings and to him was due the planning of the magnificent windows of the Church when it was completed. Many of the win-

CONSTRUCTION OF THE METHODIST CHURCH

dows of the Broadway Church had been beautiful reproductions of classical pictures, presented as memorials by different persons or church organizations. It was seriously proposed to move them to the new Church, but they simply did not fit with the style of art glass windows adopted for the sanctuary of the new Church and there were no other window openings for them. It is possible that they might have been worked into the windows of the chapel, but when the chapel was first built those windows were still needed in the Broadway Church. One thing which might have been moved but was not, was the marble slab commemorating the donors of the McAlester Chapel in the Broadway Church. It has since disappeared.

After the completion of the ground floor and despite the urging of the new pastor, Dr. Waldrip, several months elapsed before building operations on the superstructure began. It was almost as if the membership was waiting to catch its breath before starting on the next lap. Actually, however, during that period of seeming inactivity, frequent meetings of the building committee, usually with Bishop McMurry present, were held. The most pressing and insistent problem discussed was the financial one, how to cancel the debt already contracted for building the ground floor, and how to secure the funds to continue the building operations. Various outside fund-raising organizations offered their services but their terms were so onerous that the committee refused to employ them. Many of those who had made subscriptions could not or would not meet their payments, and indeed one subscriber who had paid his pledge asked to have the money returned! Even the Board of Church Extension, because apparently it had made commitments beyond its income, asked to have its subscription of $50,000 reduced, and after some correspondence the building committee reduced the amount by $5,000. It was not until February 7, 1928, that the treasurer of the Foundation fund reported that he had repaid the last of the money borrowed from the local bank to build the first unit, the ground floor of the Church. The mortgages on the church property held in Columbia were then released, and the thirty $500 notes given by local members of the Church as additional security to the bank were returned to the makers. This left the church free from debt, but with no funds to continue the building operation.

In the meantime the officials of the Broadway Church had been thinking for the past five years of incorporating the Church. It was finally done in the spring of 1928, in accordance with the provisions of the *Discipline* at that time which made all the members of the Quarterly Conference directors in the corporation, and required a meeting of the directors at least once a year with a majority present. This was usually accomplished by calling a meeting following the Fourth Quarterly Conference. The first president of the corporation was Joseph D. Randolph, who was presiding elder of the Fayette District at that time. One member of the official board, misunderstanding the purpose of the corporation, and thinking it made the members of the board individually responsible for the debts of the Church, resigned from the board. The purpose was precisely the opposite.

If the Broadway Church building at that time could have been sold at its estimated value, and all of the services of the Church could have been transferred to the ground floor of the new building, it might have encouraged the building committee to proceed at once, but no offers could be received for the purchase of the old Broadway Church. The canvassing for funds over the state had almost stopped; the salaries and expenses of agents who were employed to do this work almost ate up the returns from many new subscriptions, and it became the judgment of the committee that not much could be secured by combing over the state for small additional subscriptions.

At this point Bishop McMurry suggested that an attempt be made to secure a large loan from a bonding and loan company in St. Louis, but it was found that such a loan would require more security than could be furnished locally. To get this security it was proposed to ask the three annual conferences in the state to approve the loan and to pledge their full faith and credit for its repayment. This was a most important step in the building of the new Church, for without the loan the Church could not have been built for many years. The great depression of the thirties and the coming of World War II would have delayed building for at least eighteen years.

Resolutions authorizing negotiations for a loan of one hundred ninety-seven thousand dollars ($197,000) of first mortgage 5½% serial gold bonds maturing in installments commencing with the year 1930 and ending with the year 1938 were introduced into each of the three annual conferences in the state in 1928 and, with the support of the Bishop, were passed.[109] The

---

[109] For the complete text of the resolutions see *Minutes, Missouri Annual Conference,* 1928, pp. 62-63.

CONSTRUCTION OF THE METHODIST CHURCH

resolutions told of the incorporation of the Church in Columbia, in the board of directors of which the three annual conferences had representatives. The corporation had acquired a new location for the Columbia Church and had erected thereon, at a cost of about eighty-five thousand dollars ($85,000) the first story of a great church building. The completion of this structure would require approximately two hundred twenty-five thousand dollars ($225,000) more. The Church in Columbia owned also property on Broadway having an estimated conservative value of sixty thousand dollars ($60,000) (!) The resolutions continued that Bishop McMurry had made application to Messrs. Bitting and Company of St. Louis for a loan of one hundred ninety-seven thousand dollars ($197,000) to be secured by a first mortgage on both of the properties in Columbia. This loan could be carried through if the three conferences would pledge their full faith and credit to the repayment of the loan. It was resolved, therefore, in each annual conference to approve the loan, to be secured by a first mortgage on both Columbia properties, and that each conference pledge its full faith and credit to the repayment of the loan, principal and interest. It was under these circumstances that the three conferences of the state pledged themselves to the repayment of nearly two hundred thousand dollars of borrowed funds for the building of the Missouri Methodist Church.

In the meantime Bishop McMurry had been elected president of Central College at Fayette in 1924, and had assumed the great work of reorganizing its curriculum, raising its standards and expanding its campus. In connection with the erection of new buildings for Central College, he came into contact with John Epple of the Epple Construction Company. In the spring of 1928 the Bishop asked Epple to make a rough estimate of the amount necessary to complete the construction of the Missouri Methodist Church according to the preliminary plans and specifications as already drawn. After studying the plans Epple reported to the committee on May 14, 1928, that exclusive of the art glass, organ, furniture, and the architect's fees, it would cost approximately $207,000. This was not a bid but a fairly accurate estimate as far as it could be made with the preliminary plans. The committee then voted to have all the plans and specifications completed as soon as possible to get them ready for contractors to make bids for the construction. The plans as finally completed were distributed to five construction firms who were asked to have their proposals in the hands of the committee by June 22. On that date the bids were all received and referred to the architect for comparison after figuring various alternatives, deductions, and additions. The committee had already discussed with Bitting and Company the problem of a loan, for it was necessary to have such a loan before the contract was let. A week later with all the members of the general committee present, it took up in order such questions as the character of the roof material, the material to be used for window mullions, conduits for electric wiring, and floor finishing for the sanctuary and the Sunday School portion of the building. After all of these and similar questions were decided, it was voted to offer a contract to the lowest responsible builder contingent upon completing negotiations with the loan company, for without such a loan the work could not proceed. The architect figured all of the alternatives which had been made, and it was found that the lowest bid was from the Epple Construction Company, $219,000. The bids of the other contractors ran up to $240,200.

Construction began as soon as the negotiations for the loan, authorized by the annual conferences, were completed, and continued through the next year. The building committee was in frequent session to settle questions as they arose.[110] It was noticeable that after the contract was let, the most of the meetings of the committee were of the local members only. By the time of the great market crash of October 29, 1929, ushering in the depression of the thirties, the most of the building had been completed; the contracts for the organ, the art glass windows, the lighting fixtures, the pews and other furniture had been made and the most of these things had been installed. The church building was about ready to be turned over to the church corporation by the end of the year 1929, and the first public services were held in the sanctuary on the first Sunday of 1930, though the Sunday morning services had been held in the social hall below the sanctuary since the first of the preceding September. By the time of the use of the sanctuary, the great depression was in full swing, though the great depth to which it would go was not recognized for several months. For the next few years the history

---

[110] There were ninety-six recorded meetings for which the minutes were kept before the completion of the Church.

of the Church was a history of desperate efforts to meet the ordinary running expenses, without paying any interest on the debt or without reducing the debt. The Church sadly needed the money-raising ability of James W. Schwabe, who, as already mentioned, had died on January 14, 1927.

The Missouri Methodist Church
John Epple, Builder

Section XVII
The Church Through the Great Depression

It will be noticed from the preceding section of this history that the final occupation of the new church building and the commencement of the Great Depression of the thirties occurred at approximately the same time. It had been known by the membership of the building committee and by the church membership generally that when the Church was occupied, a debt would be left to be paid in future years, but it could not have been known under what difficult circumstances the debt would become due. The decade of the twenties had been a rather prosperous period over the country, and if a start in raising funds had been made immediately after the historic Hannibal session of the Annual Conference in 1921, by a professional fund-raising organization, it is possible that adequate funds could have been secured long before the end of the decade, but from first to last the conduct of the financial campaign had been in the hands of amateurs, trained for other professions, and had never been sufficiently pressed.

The difficulties in raising the necessary amount of money for the Missouri Methodist Foundation enterprise had been increased by the addition of the project for building a residence hall for women attending the University. Yet the great need for a new and larger church and religious education building had never abated, and the Church officials had pressed ahead with that part of the building program after the residence hall was completed, even though no funds were available.

On the day when the congregation first occupied the sanctuary, January 5, 1930, the public service had been concluded by a general appeal for new subscriptions; members of the official board had been stationed in the aisles in different parts of the sanctuary with pencils and subscription forms to wait upon those who were willing to make or to increase subscriptions. This public appeal for money in a worship service was embarrassing to the stewards, but it helped a bit to relieve the financial strain. Yet far from enough was raised to wipe out the indebtedness. During subsequent months small partial interst payments were made, but it was at that time that the national financial crisis gradually became more rather than less severe. In May, 1930, it was proposed to start another great campaign over the state for addi-

Congregational Leaders Through This Period

Manuel Drumm

J. E. Hawkins

Mrs. Laura Evans

Cecil Coffman

tional funds, and the pastor in his report to the Quarterly Conference of May 1 announced that Manuel Drumm, from his sickroom, had assumed the leadership for this great effort. But it was just two weeks later that Drumm died suddenly of heart failure, and nothing more was heard about this campaign. The last meeting of the building committee ever held had been at his home, January 20, 1930, at which there were discussions of a new organization to wage a campaign for the Foundation in the state. His death was almost an irreparable loss to the financial stability of the Church at that particular time in its history. Not only was he a local preacher and devoted to the highest interests of the Church, but he was also a most successful businessman, and local and state business leaders had the highest confidence in his judgment. He had been a moving force in the successful effort of 1928 to go ahead with the building operations, and his judgment was usually the last word in any disputed question. The Church would sorely miss his counsel.

In less than a year after the passing of Manuel Drumm, the death angel struck again. Mrs. Blanche H. Stephens died suddenly from a brain stroke on February 17, 1931. In the Quarterly Conference of February 23, the pastor noted: "It is proper at this place to make special recognition of the life and labors of Mrs. F. F. Stephens. Her duties as president of the Woman's Missionary Council made her the woman of largest influence in the whole Church. Southern Methodism has lost a great leader whose vision will be greatly missed. Tributes have come from many quarters of the country. They testify to the large service she has rendered. This Church has been honored to have one of its members elevated to so high a place in the Church and nation." Bishop McMurry came to Columbia to preach her funeral sermon.

Bishop McMurry himself died in St. Louis January 17, 1934. It is certainly not too much to say that without his impelling leadership the Missouri Methodist Church would never have been built. His funeral services, attended by many friends from Columbia, were held in the Centenary Church in St. Louis on January 19.

Before the hard times of the thirties had passed, two other leaders in the Foundation movement died. On June 28, 1934, W. B. Nowell, chairman of the local building committee through several years, passed away. Mr. Nowell had become a member of the board of stewards for the first time on September 6, 1889 and had continued to serve the Church faithfully for the next forty-five years. Two years later, on March 17, 1936, James Marion Baker died. His chief interests through all his life had been his family, his business, and his Church. He was an honored and faithful member of the board for over fifty years and, at one time or another, had been a member or chairman of all its committees and had held every official position on the board. He was probably better versed in the various activities of the Church through all those years than any other member. It was chiefly, however, through his kindly spirit, his temperate language and wise advice when disputed questions came before the board, his generosity, and his utter faithfulness to all the interests of the Church that he made his influence felt. To all of the other members of the board, the memories and influence of this leader were both an inspiration and a benediction.

The Missouri Annual Conference of 1930 met in Columbia in September. The new Bishop for Missouri, A. Frank Smith, just elected to the episcopal office at the Southern General Conference in Dallas,[111] realized the need for a change of pastors in Columbia and appointed in the place of Waldrip, Frank C. Tucker, formerly of Mexico. The Church was most fortunate in Tucker's appointment. He was a courageous, optimistic, friendly man, radiating hopefulness and good will everywhere he went.

Something of Dr. Waldrip's pride in having been pastor of the Missouri Methodist Church when it was built appears in an interview which he gave to a newspaper reporter when he left Columbia in 1930. In the interview, not published until May 26, 1933, he said: "I was sent here to do a specific work. It is completed now, and it is time for me to leave. I have put in not only three years' time on the building of the Missouri Methodist Church, but also a great amount of money in beautifying it. It is the finest in the Midwest and I believe there is nothing finer in the United States. This Church in another place would have cost a million dollars instead of six hundred thousand, the actual cost. I was sent from Kansas City to help in this work, and I am glad it is completed." [112]

[111] Other bishops elected at this General Conference were Arthur J. Moore and Paul B. Kern. No bishops were elected in the General Conference of 1934 at Jackson, Mississippi, but in the last General Conference of the Methodist Episcopal Church, South, held in Birmingham, the following were elected: Ivan Lee Holt, W. W. Peel, Clare Purcell, C. C. Selecman, J. L. Decell, W. C. Martin, and W. T. Watkins.

[112] *Columbia Missourian,* May 26, 1933. Dr. Waldrip's estimate as to what the Church would have cost in another place was his own, and his statement as to its actual cost was an unofficial guess.

At this Annual Conference of 1930 a report was presented from a special committee of presiding elders on the debt situation in the Columbia Church. That portion of the bonded debt of $197,000, coming due September 1, 1930, had not been and could not be paid, either as to principal or interest. Because of the default, the bondholders might be forced to sell the new building to secure payment. To prevent this disaster to the Church, it was proposed to call upon the three annual conferences to fulfill the obligations which they had assumed in 1928. Randolph, now filling the office of presiding elder of the Mexico District, and with his time fully occupied, was to be director of this new campaign, to serve without salary. The following November was set aside to make this collection throughout the state, but without any adequate program for the campaign and with an already overworked man appointed as director, very little was raised at that time.

In June, 1931, the Bishop called a meeting in Fayette of the presiding elders of the entire state, together with some leading laymen, to discuss the Columbia situation. They agreed to try to secure from Bitting and Company a new issue of bonds to be substituted for the old 1928 bonds, but to bear the same rate of interest, five and one-half per cent. Enough additional was to be borrowed to satisfy the unpaid interest on the 1928 bonds. Bitting and Company agreed to this new proposition, and the proportion of the share of each of the three conferences of the entire debt was fixed, and each conference was made responsible for its share. The three conferences approved this plan at their following annual meetings, and it was supposed that in this way a beginning at last would be made in the payment of the Bitting debt. The new bonds were issued as of March 1, 1932.[113] For the sake of the record, it should be added that there was a second mortgage of $100,000 against the new church building, held by the Board of Church Extension of the Methodist Episcopal Church, South, as a result of the contribution of the General Church Boards toward the building fund. This was a formal debt which would not have to be repaid if the Church were never sold.

In the meantime the Columbia congregation was having its full share of financial troubles. In the first report, mentioned above, made to the Annual Conference of 1930 about the debt

---

[113] Recorder's Office, Boone County Courthouse, Book 190, p. 622.

situation of the Missouri Methodist Church, reference was made to a "floating indebtedness" borne by the Columbia congregation of $100,000. This was in addition to the debt of $197,000 owed to the customers of the Bitting house in St. Louis, and since this was the part of the indebtedness for which the local congregation was responsible, it caused more anxiety to the local membership than the bonded indebtedness. It had arisen for the most part from contracts with various corporations to supply such equipment and church furniture as pews, stained glass windows, floor coverings, and especially the Skinner pipe organ. A considerable amount was also still due to the general contractor.

In the attempt to secure funds to meet this indebtedness, following the collapse of the fund-raising campaign proposed in May, 1930, a third mortgage bond was issued by the Church. This mortgage was for $88,000 and bore interest of seven per cent. The bonds were issued in various denominations from $100 to $1,000. Very few of these bonds were ever sold. Only a few of the members of the local Church purchased them. The records in the Recorder's Office show that J. A. Stewart held five bonds valued at $4,000; C. C. and Beulah Coffman, one at $500; F. F. Stephens, five at $1,500; J. J. Pyles, two at $200; J. M. Baker, two at $200; E. B. McDonnell, eight at $800; Mrs. Corinne Arnold, one at $100; and O. D. Gray, one at $100. In most cases the holders of these bonds eventually gave them to the Church. A large share of the remaining bonds of this issue was used as additional security for funds borrowed from Columbia banks. This issue of third mortgage bonds was not the solution for the payment of the floating indebtedness. The creditors would not accept the bonds, and the members of the Church would not or could not buy them to a sufficient amount.

The legal situation of the Church at this time was complicated. Had the creditors brought suit, it would have been, in the first place, against Bitting and Company, who held the prior mortgage; moreover, it was questionable whether the companies which had sold the various furnishings to the church could sue for the recovery of those materials, because it would have to be determined in each case whether the materials had entered into the church edifice and thus had become a part of the building and subject to the Bitting mortgage. The pastor and the finance committee kept working on the problem, and in the Church Bulletin of April 10, 1932, they published a "Plan for Paying Debt on the Missouri Methodist Church." This plan, in reviewing the history of the building project, emphasized that the project had included both the building of Hendrix Hall (the residence hall for women) and the Missouri Methodist Church. The former, costing $175,000, had been completed and deeded free of debt to the Woman's Missionary Council. The latter had been completed by January, 1930, at a cost, in round numbers, of $435,000, plus the cost of the lot. In addition, the cost of the state campaign to secure funds had been about $41,000, and the paving on Locust Street cost $2,000. This made a total expenditure of $653,000. In round numbers, $550,000, including the money borrowed through the Bitting firm, had been raised and expended, or its expenditure earmarked for supplies. This left $103,000 plus about $9,000 interest charges, making a floating debt of about $112,000. The plan of April 10, 1932, listed the creditors as follows:

	Principal	Interest
American Seating Co.	$20,000.00	$2,300.00
Blackwell-Wielandy Co.	3,450.00	410.64
Board of Church Extension	500.73	
Epple Construction Co.	11,647.72	1,685.12
Guth Electric Co.	3,150.00	33.65
Jacoby Art Glass Co.	4,100.00	340.30
Skinner Organ Co.	31,000.00	3,538.71
Columbia Banks	26,082.50	230.45
Lamar and Whitmore	450.00	36.00
Second Mortgage Bonds	3,100.00	237.32
	$103,480.95	$8,812.19

The plan called for the payment of one-third of the accrued interest on the floating indebtedness as of May 15, 1932, about $3,500, and in September, 1932, and annually thereafter for eleven years, an addition of $11,147 to the annual budget. This would keep up the interest and gradually reduce the principal until it was paid in 1943. It was emphasized that the first deadline to meet was the payment on May 15. "Failing in this, our plan fails."

This was just at the depth of the national depression, and it proved impossible to meet that first deadline; therefore, the whole plan of April 10 failed. Two months later, on June 15, 1932, out of patience with the Missouri Methodist Church, two of its chief creditors, the Skinner Organ Company and the American Seating Company, filed suits against the Church totaling $54,700. The organ company asked for the return of the organ with $1,000 damages or the payment of its bill of

$34,700,[114] while the seating company asked for the payment of three promissory notes amounting to $20,000. Despite the courageous spirit of the pastor, the morale of the Church fell to a low ebb. But the directors of the church corporation employed a local attorney, Lakenan M. Price, and when the cases came up for trial in the October, 1932, term of court, both were continued at the defendant's request, and again in 1933 they were continued.

The complex financial situation of the Columbia Church during these years was disconcerting and indeed discouraging. There was the Bitting debt of $197,000, which the three annual conferences of the state, under pressure of the Bishop, had guaranteed, but which was always in the background as a threatening mortgage on all the property of the Church in Columbia. There was also the "floating indebtedness" just described. Finally there were the regular running expenses of the Church as fixed in the annual budgets. The minutes of the monthly meetings of the official board during the years of the Great Depression bear mute evidence of the struggle to maintain the financial integrity of the Church. Collections dropped in amount immediately after the great stock market crash. It seemed as if money almost disappeared from circulation. One of the sermons preached on a Sunday morning was on the subject of "Money," and though its qualities were described, it was not brought forth from hiding.

Waldrip's last annual salary, fixed while the sun of prosperity still shone over the land, was $5,200, but it is doubtful whether he ever received it all. Tucker's salary for the year 1930-1931 was fixed at $5,000, but the treasurer's report at the end of the year indicated he had been paid $400 less. As Tucker began his second year, 1931-1932, the budget was severely cut, and the pastor even agreed to assume himself the payment of the parsonage rental, but at the end of the year the annual budget lacked $5,000, of which $1,750 was due the minister. Starting bravely Tucker's third year with a budget of $18,500, of which $8,000 was for interest, the board faced deficits by the end of the first month. Reviewing the situation in a called meeting in December,

---

[114] The Missouri Methodist congregation will forever owe a debt of gratitude to James T. Quarles, dean at that time of the College of Fine Arts of the University, and organist and director of the choir of the Methodist Church for nearly a generation. Without any commission he was the architect for the fine Skinner organ installed, and he was scandalously underpaid for his services through the years.

the stewards voted to check back from the building fund to the budget fund all that had been set aside for interest and to reserve nothing more for interest until further orders. In March, 1933, finding the unpaid bills mounting each month, the board at Tucker's own request reduced his annual salary by $500.

In the following May, for what were regarded as valid reasons, it was voted by the Quarterly Conference to ask the Circuit Court to dissolve the corporation of the Missouri Methodist Church. It was on the ground that the Church was insolvent and unable to meet its obligations. The Court was asked to deliver the property into the hands of the officers of the church corporation for the benefit of its creditors.[115] Another suit was pending at the same time to determine whether the organ could be reclaimed by the Skinner Organ Company or its successor, or whether it had become a part of the church building and was subject to the real estate mortgage. Judgment in the latter case was given later in favor of the organ company, but it did not remove the organ.

The members of the Church were thunderstruck when they read in the newspaper about the suit for dissolution. They were not sure whether the Church would be open for services the following Sunday, but the pastor of the Church, Frank Tucker, gave a reassuring interview to a newspaper reporter the next day. He emphasized that the suit would not affect the ecclesiastical body of the Church and that its work would be carried on as before. The action for dissolution on the ground of insolvency, he said, was for the purpose of protecting the interests of all the creditors on an equal basis. It was told to the reporter that several courses of action were open to the church corporation under the supervision of the Circuit Court, but that, pending arrangements with the creditors, the work of the pastor and the congregation would be carried on as usual. The pastor said also that the building itself and its equipment were not readily saleable and that it was probable that the corporation and the creditors might reach an agreement for amortization of the debt over a long period when economic conditions would be more favorable.[116]

While the suit for dissolution was under advisement by the

---

[115] The president of the corporation at that time and through the entire period of the depression was Lindsay A. Nickell, businessman of Columbia. His advice was of great value through many crises. The suit for dissolution was filed May 26, 1933, and was dismissed October 6, 1933. Records of the Circuit Court, Boone County, Book 55, p. 130.

[116] *Columbia Missourian,* May 27, 1933.

Columbia Methodist Pastors, 1930-1957

Frank C. Tucker, 1930-1934

Robert C. Holliday, 1934-1942

J. Wilson Crichlow, 1942-1947

A. G. Williamson, 1947-1952

Hugh O. Isbell, 1952-1957

Court, efforts for some adjustments of the debt were redoubled between the officers of the Church and the creditors. On Sunday morning, August 6, 1933, the pastor announced that an agreement had been made with six of the creditors, namely, the American Seating Company, the Blackwell-Wielandy Company, the Board of Church Extension, the Epple Construction Company, the Guth Electric Company, and the Jacoby Art Glass Company, by which each was to be paid a reduced amount of its claim against the Church. Under the prevailing financial conditions at that time, it is probable that the creditors were glad to make such a settlement. The total principal and interest owing to these companies as of April 10, 1932, when the plan of that date had been published in the Church Bulletin, was $47,578.16. It was now agreed that the debts would draw no interest for a period of ten years, and a moratorium on law suits against the Church was arranged for this period. The Church was therefore relieved from any immediate danger from these companies.

As to the Skinner Organ Company, which was not included in the list of companies which had made the agreement just mentioned, a separate plan was adopted involving the payment of an annual rental by the Church of $1,000. Although the Church was usually behind on these payments, occasionally by a great effort it would bring itself up to date with the payments. After the end of the Tucker quadrennium that plan was continued, and the Church did not seem to be so hard-pressed as before.

SECTION XVIII
Methodism Becomes a United Church

During the worst of the period of hard times in the thirties, three of the Methodist denominations of the country were moving rapidly toward unification. It would require a full volume to describe adequately this historic development. Suffice it to say here that Methodism in America had been originally a single denomination in which through the years certain divisions had occurred. The group which came to be known as the Methodist Protestant Church had split from the main body in 1830 mainly because of its opposition to the subordination of the laity in the government of the Church, and to the growing authority exercised by the episcopacy; recent legislation in the General Conferences of the two other leading branches of Methodism, however, in the opinion of many of the leaders of the Methodist Protestant Church had corrected those tendencies.

The other great division, that of 1844, had been over questions of church government and slavery;[117] fundamental changes in the civil government of the United States as a result of the Civil War had wiped away the historic causes for the disputes of the antebellum period. But it took some time, as noted in previous sections of this work,[118] for the bitterness between the northern and southern churches to be reduced to the point where they could even consider friendly relations. The gradually growing friendliness, however, led finally to a very definite plan for union which came before the southern General Conference in Oklahoma City in 1914. The Conference of that year adopted a declaration containing these words, "The Methodist Episcopal Church, South, regards the unification of the Methodist Episcopal Church, the Methodist Protestant Church, and the Methodist Episcopal Church, South, by the Plan proposed by the Joint Commission on Federation, as feasible and desirable," but did not officially adopt that plan. Instead, the Conference proposed to continue consideration of union by the work of a Commission on Unification, conditioned upon similar action by the Methodist Episcopal Church.

---

[117] See p. 35 *et seq.*
[118] See p. 97.

In the southern General Conference of 1918 all that was done was to reappoint the Commission on Unification, and during the two following years the Commission developed a plan of union by the formation of regional conferences, but the northern church in its General Conference of 1920 failed to act favorably upon that plan. It proposed instead that a *convention* of the two churches be established to set up a new plan. The southern General Conference at Hot Springs in 1922 rejected the plan of a convention, but reappointed the Commission with instructions for the Bishops to call a special session of the southern General Conference should the Joint Commission in the meantime produce and ratify by a two-thirds majority a new plan of union. Such a plan was proposed by the Commission and was endorsed by a two-thirds majority of the northern General Conference in the spring of 1924, and a special session of the southern General Conference was convened in July, 1924, in Chattanooga. There the new Plan of Union was endorsed by more than two-thirds of the delegates, but since before becoming effective it had to be approved by a three-fourths majority of the members of the annual conferences, it was submitted to them, where during the subsequent year it received a majority vote but failed to receive the necessary three-fourths vote.

This left matters about where they had been for several years past. The southern General Conference of 1926 at Memphis seemed to be more conservative, but it did appoint a special Committee on Research and Investigation. No new plan was developed during the following quadrennium. The southern General Conference of 1930 at Dallas had no specific proposition, therefore, before it, but appointed a new Commission on Interdenominational Relations and Church Union "with instructions to cultivate a spirit of fraternity with the Methodist Episcopal Church looking toward the ultimate union of these two great branches of Episcopal Methodism." That Commission recommended to the southern General Conference of 1934 the continuation of definite efforts to make and agree upon plans for the union of the three Churches represented, including here the Methodist Protestant Church.

Much progress was made during the next year, and in 1935 the Joint Commission drew up and published in all the church papers a plan it recommended. This Plan was approved by the other two Methodisms in 1936 by large constitutional majorities. Union of the three Methodisms was finally, therefore, up to the Methodist Episcopal Church, South. Since the Plan had to to be acted upon by both the General Conference and the southern annual conferences, it was sent first by the College of Bishops to the annual conferences in 1937 for action. It was a rather tense time for Methodists throughout the country, but this time the southern annual conferences, voting separately as they met during the year, ratified the current Plan of Union by a vote of 8,897 to 1,247. The twenty-third General Conference of the Methodist Episcopal Church, South, meeting in what proved to be its last quadrennial session on April 23 to May 5, 1938, in Birmingham, Alabama, finally approved the Plan by a vote of 434 to 26.[119] In order to settle any question as to the ecclesiastical constitutionality of the action taken by the General Conference, this whole question was immediately referred to the Judicial Council of the Church, and in a long and elaborate opinion it upheld in every particular its legality.

The Plan of Union as thus adopted provided for a "Uniting Conference" to be held within twelve months at a place chosen by a Joint Commission on Entertainment and a time fixed by the Bishops. The place selected was Kansas City and the time April 26, 1939. The purpose of this Conference was to harmonize the three *Disciplines* of the uniting bodies rather than to pass new legislation. This Conference was composed of 900 delegates of whom 400 came from the Methodist Episcopal Church, 400 from the Methodist Episcopal Church, South, and 100 from the Methodist Protestant Church. These delegates were to be chosen by the annual conferences in the same manner as they had chosen delegates to their respective general conferences, and the ministerial and lay members were to be in equal number.[120] The Conference was in session from April 26 to May 10, in which time it performed the work laid out for it to do, and voted its acceptance of a new *Discipline*.[121]

In Columbia there had been little cause in the first place for disunion. Columbia, indeed, was in that part of Missouri called "Little Dixie," and from the early days until the Civil War

---

[119] It should be noted that two Bishops, Warren A. Candler and Collins Denny, submitted a statement to be placed in the Minutes of the Conference, voicing their opposition to the union of the three Methodisms. Both had already been retired as effective Bishops.
[120] The delegates from the Missouri Conference were, clerical, R. C. Holliday, Frank C. Tucker, D. K. Pegues and J. D. Randolph, and lay, F. F. Stephens, J. M. Woods, W. H. Utz, Jr., and P. M. Marr.
[121] See Appendix VI, p. 221.

many of its inhabitants held one or two or more slaves as household servants, but whether they held slaves or not, Methodists were all welcomed into the local Church. The Columbia Methodist Church since the separation in 1845 had belonged to the Methodist Episcopal Church, South, and no northern Methodist Church had been organized there, but communicants coming from that Church joined the one Methodist Church in Columbia and were generally happy and satisfied with their church relations.

Union, therefore, made little change in the Columbia Church except for a few changes in nomenclature, such as District Superintendent for Presiding Elder, Woman's Society of Christian Service for Woman's Missionary Society, and Wesley Student Organization for Methodist Student Organization. There was no change in theology or church government.

SECTION XIX
Final Settlement of the Building Debts and Dedication of the Missouri Methodist Church

The Broadway Church building had been on the market for sale immediately after all its religious services had been moved to the new church building on Locust Street, in September, 1929. But for the next few years during the depression period no religious denomination dared to expand its program and its financial liabilities by undertaking the purchase of the Broadway building. Through all these years the building was appraised in the annual reports to the Missouri Conferences as being worth $35,000. Indeed, in a report one year, it was said to be worth $60,000. Finally, in 1943, an agreement was made with the Church of God (Holiness) to purchase the building for $5,000 plus "other valuable considerations." This latter inducement was the former building of the Church of God, which was taken by the Missouri Methodist Church and eventually sold to the Church of the Nazarene for $1,500, so that the Missouri Methodist Church finally received $6,500 for the sale of the Broadway Church. This amount, small as it was, made possible an agreement reached through negotiations of the associate minister, Rev. H. D. Tucker, with officials of the reorganized Skinner Organ Company by which the organ company gave final title to the Church for the ownership of the organ in exchange for the money from the sale of the church. This solved one of the disagreeable debt problems faced by the board through the years since the completion of the building of the Church.[122]

A new agreement was made in 1944 by the same creditors who had agreed in 1933 not to press for a settlement for ten years and to charge no interest in the meantime. The new agreement specified that the creditors would accept a partial payment of their former claims and cancel approximately 75 per cent of their remaining claims against the Church. Although this was in the midst of World War II, the pastor and official board felt that this was a good opportunity to retire nearly $50,000 of the indebtedness. A whirlwind campaign to raise $12,500 was waged for the next few weeks, and a "victory dinner" was held

---

[122] See *Missouri Methodist Church Messenger,* May 27, 1943, and January 6, 1944.

in the social hall of the church May 31, 1944. The records of L. D. Johnston, church treasurer at that time, show that $2,152.25 was paid to the John Epple Construction Company on April 15; $5,959.50, to the American Seating Company; $851.25, to the Guth Electric Company; and $1,040.32, to the Blackwell-Wielandy Company on April 17; and $1,500, to the Jacoby Art Glass Company; and $152, to the Board of Church Extension on May 22. With these payments out of the way, there was left to pay $24,000 of the second mortgage bonds, much of which was held by local members of the Church, who afterwards donated the bonds to the Church. The other bonds were absorbed from year to year into the annual budget.

During these years the Annual Conference had not been able to make the payments on the Bitting debt to which they had agreed in 1932. In 1935, with no interest having been paid, a revised substitute agreement was made with Bitting and Company, and through them with the other bondholders, for a third issue of bonds. According to this new agreement, the interest on the bonds was reduced to three per cent. This new agreement was ratified by all the holders of the former bonds, and new three per cent bonds were issued as agreed upon. Times were better financially by 1935, and the conferences were able to meet their obligations. On December 11, 1943, the old Church (Broadway) was released from the mortgage of November 1, 1935, so that it could be sold to the Church of God (Holiness), free of encumbrances. The latter religious denomination had commenced holding its services in the old Broadway Methodist Church building on May 10, 1943. The conferences continued to reduce the Bitting indebtedness, and it was announced in 1947 that the last of those bonds had been paid.

The load of debt with which the Missouri Methodist Church struggled during the thirties probably caused more hardship to the pastors of the Church than to any other persons. Frank C. Tucker had remained as pastor until 1934 when his quadrennium of services was over. The prohibition against the appointment of a preacher for more than four years was still in effect, but there was a special provision in the *Discipline* that when a majority of the presiding elders of a conference should concur by ballot, the bishop might appoint a preacher to a pastoral charge for more than four consecutive years. The official board of the Columbia Church asked the Bishop for the reappointment of Tucker under this provision. "We appreciate him for his zeal,

FINAL SETTLEMENT OF DEBTS, AND DEDICATION

courage, and sacrificial service to our Church, for his understanding and brotherly spirit, for the inspiration of his sermons, and for his faithfulness as a pastor." The Bishop, however, decided to transfer him to the Francis Street, St. Joseph, Church, and he was succeeded by Robert C. Holliday.

Both Holliday's father and his grandfather had been members of the Missouri Conference, though neither had been pastor of the Columbia Church. Holliday came to Columbia from the presiding eldership of the Mexico District. At the end of his four years in Columbia, the Church at large was about ready for one of the great events in its history, described in the previous section of this history, reunion with the Methodist Episcopal Church and with the Methodist Protestant Church. Holliday's standing among the pastors of the Annual Conference is shown by his having been elected leader to the Uniting Conference of the clerical delegation. The *Discipline* of the new united Church did not have any provision limiting the pastor to a period of four years. Holliday therefore was continued in Columbia until 1942, the first minister in the history of the Columbia Church to serve for more than four years. He was reappointed for a ninth year, but was transferred on October 10, 1942, soon after the Annual Conference of that year, to the St. Louis Conference, and was assigned to the district superintendency of the Cape Girardeau District, exchanging assignments with J. Wilson Crichlow who came to Columbia as pastor.

Crichlow was a man of great ability, and was especially able in raising the percentage of giving among the members of the congregation. He was also most fortunate in the lovely, able, and devoted wife who shared with him the difficulties and sorrows of a church in time of war, World War II. It was in Crichlow's pastorate, and with the help of the associate pastor, Mr. Tucker, that the church finally extricated itself from the floating indebtedness.[123] Crichlow then was transferred back to the St. Louis Conference and appointed assistant secretary of the Board of Pensions with a special assignment to raise the endowment for the greater support of the retired preachers of Methodism and their widows and dependents. It was at that time, and out of debt, that the Missouri Methodist Church was finally ready for dedication.

The final release of the Bitting mortgage was on July 2, 1947,

---

[123] P. 183-184.

showing that all due on the Bitting bonds had been fully paid. The dedication ceremonies were held just before the Annual Conference of 1947, which convened that year in Columbia. The Church dedication was held before a packed congregation on Sunday morning, September 7, in the cathedral-like structure. Bishop Ivan Lee Holt presided, and introduced Bishop A. Frank Smith, who delivered a sermon on "Grace of Christian Practice." This was followed by the reading of the Church canticle and the actual dedication ritual conducted by Bishop Holt. The Bishop related briefly the history of Methodist Churches in Columbia, of which this was the fourth successive one. Its cornerstone had been laid in 1925 while Marvin T. Haw was pastor. The building had been completed in 1930, but it had taken seventeen years to free the Church from the debt. It was at the conclusion of the Annual Conference that Crichlow was transferred to the St. Louis Conference. His successor in Columbia was the Rev. A. G. Williamson.

Missouri Methodist Church
Locust Street Entrance

The Sanctuary

John and Charles Wesley
from the center panels of The Methodist Window

The Pulpit

The Lectern

The Altar

The Altar
Cross

Contemporary Ministerial Leadership

Bishop Eugene M. Frank
Bishop of the Missouri Area
1956—

Monk Bryan, Pastor
1957—

Section XX
The Church Looks to the Future

The preceding section of this history could be the concluding section, for it told of the final success of the Missouri Methodist congregation and of the three annual conferences of the state in extricating themselves from the building debt and in participating in the dedication of the church building according to the ritual of the Methodist Church. But to stop here would seem to leave the Church suspended in mid air, like the Acropolis in Athens as one sees it at night with the flood lights from below lighting it up, a glorious vision suspended in the sky but after all only a glorious vision of the past. The history of the Missouri Methodist Church did not stop with its dedication, and will not stop as long as the present changes into the past. At the risk, therefore, of forsaking his role as a historian, and because he wishes to try to leave with his readers, in this era of transition, an understanding of the church's expanding present and possible future, the author attempts to explain some immediate past events as they relate to the future.

It must be remembered that the problem of finding more room for the activities of the Methodist Church in Columbia faced the Broadway Methodist Church almost as soon as it was built. That church building had been erected to care for the needs of that day, but with the rapid growth of Columbia and the student body after 1905, the building would have needed to be enlarged or suburban churches erected. The latter program had been tried first, and Wilkes Boulevard Church was organized, followed at a later time by the organization of the Community Methodist Church, on West Broadway in 1957. Even now (in 1964) plans are being made for another suburban church in the northeastern part of the expanding city, and perhaps before many years have passed similar outlying churches will rise in other suburbs.

But it was the rapid growth of the University student body in the first three decades of the twentieth century, many of whom wished to attend services in the Broadway Methodist Church, which forced the attention of Methodist leaders in the state upon Columbia, and this led finally to the building of the Missouri Methodist Church. Various workers mentioned heretofore had been employed from time to time in the pastoral care of the students, but the first to organize them effectively was a layman, Ernest H. Newcomb, director from 1919 to 1923. He was followed from year to year during the twenties by other such workers.

During the same years the Disciples' Bible College of Missouri was expanding its offerings by persuading other denominations to support a teacher and thus share in its instructional work. The first such Methodist teacher was Lawrence E. Murphy in 1924-25, followed in 1925-27 by Miss Helen E. Stafford, and then in 1928 by Walter A. Hearn. His financial support came from the General Board of Education and the conference boards of education of the Church. Hearn continued his very excellent religious teaching for a generation, and when he retires in 1965, he will be succeeded in the expanded Missouri School of Religion by another such Methodist teacher, Harley H. Zeigler. In the period from 1932 to 1936 when money was scarce and it was difficult to secure appropriations for both a director of the Methodist Student Organization and a teacher in the Bible College, Hearn assisted by his wife, Olive W. Hearn, took over both positions. Then, for a period of two and a half years, the offices of teacher and director were separated, but from February, 1939, to September, 1948, Mr. and Mrs. Hearn were co-directors of the student work, while Hearn kept up his teaching in the Bible College. In September, 1948, Warren L. Briggs was secured as director and was continued until 1958 when he was succeeded by E. Lee Wilhelm, and in 1961, by Robert W. Younts. This appointment of a full-time administrative director of students in denominational groups has become the common practice in state schools across the nation. There are now several such directors in Wesley Foundations in Missouri.

On the other hand, the various activities once carried on in the headquarters of these denominational buildings seem to be falling off in interest among the students. Apparently, it is one of those changes taking place in this era of transition for which no person or official can be held responsible. It may be explained partially by the changing living habits of the students who room and board in the many large student dormitories rising so rapidly on the campus. In addition, there are now on the campus a Student Union Building and the Student Commons, something the University did not have thirty or forty years ago. Students find worthwhile recreations in these campus buildings that were

THE CHURCH LOOKS TO THE FUTURE

not in existence formerly. One of the problems of the future will be to find new ways of holding the loyalty of the students to the churches of their youth.

One of the results in the changes in student living has been a re-assessment of the plans for a new Wesley Foundation building. Only the second floor of the educational unit of the Church was set apart for their activities. Believing this would furnish far less room than the students needed, plans were made for the purchase of land adjoining the Church where a fine Wesley Foundation building would be erected. The land was purchased, but now under changed conditions, is the building needed? If erected, would it be used by the students?

Another building problem is before the Church, but it also leads from the past, into the present and future. The long-standing policy of the local Church had been to rent a home as a parsonage. But in 1947, when World War II had come to an end rather suddenly, the Federal Government decided to give each returning soldier who wished it, a college education, and these "G.I." soldiers were flooding colleges all over the land. College administrations had to increase very rapidly their instructional staffs. As a result it became almost impossible to rent a suitable house in Columbia for a parsonage. But just at that time a member of the faculty, E. C. Phillips, who lived at 202 Thilly Avenue, and who was also a member of the official board of the Church, was retiring, and offered to sell his home on liberal terms to the Church. It was bought and Dr. Williamson became its first occupant.

This property was used as a parsonage by Williamson and by his successor. But in the spring of 1957, the board decided to buy a new house for a parsonage, and a two-family house at 1015 Prospect Avenue was purchased. It proved to be unsatisfactory for a parsonage, and the board passed a resolution that this was only a temporary solution of the parsonage question. Finally, in 1962 a lot was purchased at the corner of Sunset and Westover Streets, and it was voted at a church conference on November 10, 1964, to proceed with the construction of a parsonage at this location. This, it is expected, will solve the parsonage problem for the Columbia Church for some years to come.

During the depression very little had been done to keep the physical plant of the church building in good repair. It was nearly twenty years after its occupancy before anything was

McMurry Chapel

spent for its upkeep, and any householder knows that his home cannot be left for twenty years without expenditures for upkeep; neither can a church building. The roof was leaking, and the gutters were falling from the building. Downspouts were clogged, and the window sills and mullions were rotting. The most necessary repairs began during the pastorate of Isbell and were continued under Bryan. The walls of the sanctuary and many rooms in the educational unit were repainted. The great organ was taken apart, rebuilt, and enlarged at a cost of $31,000; and the carillon, previously installed in the northwest steeple of the building, was moved to the swell chamber which is located behind the organ case. New floor coverings were laid in the social hall and in other parts of the building, and the beautiful transcept windows in the sanctuary and the great Wesley window in the rear of the Church were taken down and releaded.

In 1951-1952, Mr. and Mrs. John A. Epple financed the entire reconstruction of the chapel in the southeast corner of the educational unit at a cost of about $50,000. With a new Hammond organ, the gift of Mrs. S. P. Cresap, widow of a former minister, the chapel was dedicated in memory of Bishop McMurry as the McMurry Chapel, October 27, 1952.

Another interior building change was made when the Sunday School rooms of the kindergarten department were moved from the south end of the educational unit over the chapel and placed on the ground floor near the north end of the educational unit. There, in case of fire, the little children could be removed without danger or loss of lives. The rooms vacated by them were then built over into a group of adjacent and well-equipped church offices which could be heated in winter or cooled in summer by the same furnace and air conditioner which serve the chapel.

Before reorganization of the three Methodist denominations in 1939, the Missouri Methodist Church had no regular clerical or business staff to assist the minister. For a short period during the pastorates of Holliday and Crichlow, H. D. Tucker had served as associate minister. After the dedication of the Church in 1947, the constantly widening scope of the program of the Church, the growing size of the membership with the consequent increased financial income, made it necessary and possible to add gradually several new officials to the church staff. In 1957, Miss Janet Isbell was employed as Director of Religious Education; she served until 1962 when she was followed by Mrs. Charmione Jones, who served for two years. In the fall of 1964, Miss Kay

France became the Director of Religious Education. In 1958, Bert Powell was secured as Associate Pastor, followed three years later by Jerry Statler. In 1958, there was also added a Superintendent of Maintenance, Harry P. Anglen, and in January, 1961, Ray E. Rice became Director of Administration. Other members of the local ministerial staff may be added as they are needed in the future.

During its recent history, as indeed throughout the time of its existence, the Columbia Church has suffered periods of sorrow caused by the deaths of some of its most faithful members. But, characteristic of a living and vital church organization, the ranks have always been filled by efficient and devoted men and women stepping forward to take the place of those who have gone on before. Mention should be made of Mrs. Beulah C. Coffman, who for fifteen or twenty years has served with fidelity and faithful and accurate ability as church treasurer. Mention should also be made of Miss Talitha Gisler who served as an incomparable church secretary for a long period during the mid-century years.

For a half century or more, since its development as one of the leading Churches of the Annual Conference, the Columbia Church always fostered a good program of music for its religious services. A member of the University faculty, who had been organist and choir master for the Church for twenty-two years, Dean James T. Quarles, reached the age of retirement at the University in 1948 and was leaving Columbia. The Church decided to continue, if possible, that satisfactory connection with the music department of the University, and after a short interval, secured in 1953 as organist and choir master, Perry G. Parrigin, Professor of Organ in the University; he began at that time a ten-year period of admirable service for the Church. He was followed in 1963 by Miss Patricia Whitmarsh of Christian College. The Church has been emphasizing in recent years the formation of choirs of different ages of children to build up the music potential of the church membership.

Early in the pastorate of Monk Bryan, to interest members of the Church in financing special projects in its future development, a committee on Wills and Legacies was appointed, with Dean Glenn A. McCleary of the School of Law of the University as chairman. This committee made several reports to the board and finally developed a "Foundation of the Missouri Methodist Church of Columbia." This was incorporated under the laws of the State of Missouri. Persons may become members of the Foundation by the payment of $25 to its funds or by indicating future giving by will, legacy, bequest, trust, or insurance policies, and by signing the charter. The funds of the Foundation do not enter the regular funds of the church organization, but are invested and held inviolably for the purposes designated by the givers. There are at the present time only fifteen or twenty members of the Foundation, though it is not known how many persons have left legacies in their wills for designated purposes to the Foundation. The present officers of the Foundation consist of E. M. Funk, president, Talitha Gisler, secretary, and Jerome Twitty, treasurer.

The Church's activities and influence outside of Columbia have greatly enlarged. It has always, except during the dark years of the depression, paid its full appropriations for the conference and general missionary activities of the Church, but the support by the Church of special representatives in the mission field began in 1962 with the assumption of the $7,500 responsibility for the salary and support of Mr. and Mrs. Wilson T. Boots in Argentina. Following his transfer on account of illness, the Church has undertaken the support of Mr. and Mrs. Robert Hanson, ministering to the activities of the Protestant church in Salzburg, Austria. It is expected that the mission work of the Church will grow and expand.

Outside of Columbia within the Missouri Area, a reorganization of the territorial divisions and of the administration of the Church has taken place. The last session of the old Missouri Conference was the 123rd, held in St. Louis in October, 1939, just after the Uniting Conference of the Church at large in Kansas City. This session was under the presidency of Bishop Ivan Lee Holt, just elected to the bishopric in 1938. Without any substantial change in its territory, there followed immediately at that time the organization of the first session of the Missouri Annual Conference of the new Methodist Church, with its membership from the three former Methodist organizations in that territory. John C. Broomfield, formerly of the Methodist Protestant Church, became presiding bishop of the Missouri Area, and served in that capacity for a quadrennium. Bishop Holt then was returned to the presidency of the Missouri Area and served for three quadrenniums until 1956, when he was followed by Bishop Eugene M. Frank. This was the Twenty-Third Session of the reorganized Church after the union of the three branches of Methodism in 1939.

In the meantime, in the last few sessions of the Missouri Annual Conference, the meeting place had been regularly in Fayette, and the time had been changed from September to June. (See App. IV.) The college buildings of Central College were used to lodge and board the ministers and lay delegates and to provide meeting places for committees and boards. This change in meeting place was one of the reasons for having the conference become a spring rather than a fall annual conference. It led to a reorganization of the financial year in all the individual churches in the conference. This change took place in 1956, the last year of the presidency of Bishop Holt.

In 1961, a rather massive territorial reorganization took place in the Missouri Area. There had been three conferences in this Area for many years, but it was now reorganized into two conferences, the Missouri East Conference and the Missouri West Conference. The names of the three former conferences disappeared with their twenty-third annual meeting, and a new numbering of the sessions began. Although this did not change essentially the internal organization of the individual churches, it did shift to a considerable extent the boundary lines of the former Districts. The north and south line dividing the two annual conferences cut between Columbia and Fayette, thus shifting Columbia from its connection for the past century with the Fayette District to the Jefferson City District.

The reasons for this reorganization of the Missouri Area are said to have been chiefly the following: the former three annual conferences in the state were relatively weak in comparison with other annual conferences over the nation. The reduction of the organizational structure by one-third, two conferences instead of three, would allow a more efficient use of man power and of money spent in church machinery. Two conferences with a larger number of churches with any given relative strength would facilitate the transfer of ministers in making the wisest and best annual appointments. It is probable that more changes in the organizational structure will come in the future.

It has been said that the union of the three branches of Methodism in 1939 made few changes immediately in the organization of the local churches, except that there were a few changes in nomenclature.[124] The purpose of the Uniting Conference had

---

[124] See page 182.

Left to right, first row, Mrs. M. C. Swaney, Mr. C. Swaney, Mass Dance Koon, Mrs. Z., Jay Faut Ronn, E. M. Funk, Bert Powell; second row, Arthur Ausherman, Mrs. Lawrence Hepple, Mrs. Fred Miller, Miss Talitha Gisler, Mrs. Herman Fritz, Waldo Powell; third row, Ted Jones, William Taft, Mrs. Anna Evans, Mrs. Kenneth Zenge, Miss Evalyn True, Franklin Gafke, William Kasmann; fourth row, Earl Byers, Mrs. Earl Byers, Warren Briggs, Mrs. Warren Briggs, Mrs. C. C. Coffman, Mrs. Byron Osborne, Frank Rucker, Fred Meinershagen; fifth row, Don Bird, Allen Baker, Harold Johnson, O. V. Wheeler, Quentin Schenk.

201

not been to pass new church legislation, but to harmonize the *Disciplines* of the united churches. Changes began to appear, however, in the subsequent sessions of the General Conference meeting quadrennially. These cannot be catalogued here, but notice should be taken of the structural changes in the local churches which were provided by different General Conferences.

Under the guidance of Pastor Monk Bryan the administration of the Columbia Church has been kept in line with the changing laws of the Church. The incorporation of the Church in 1928, for instance, was done in accordance with the *Discipline* of the Methodist Episcopal Church, South, then in effect. The entire membership of the Quarterly Conference at that time were directors of the corporation. As revised by the General Conference, the directors of an incorporated Church consisted of nine members who were also the board of trustees. The former board of stewards became the Official Board under the revised law, and various commissions succeeded the former board committees. All local churches must have a board of trustees, but in an incorporated church, this board becomes the board of directors with similar powers to those exercised by a board of trustees in an unincorporated church.

This section of the history should include a short statement about the three pastors of the Church since its dedication. They all have been able and active men in the ministry, beloved by their parishioners, and with a strong influence extended outward not only on the local Church but through the conference and beyond. Aaron G. Williamson, appointed pastor at the time of its dedication, was born in Lincoln, Nebraska, and received his education in various colleges and in the Boston School of Theology. He held pastorates in Kansas and in Oklahoma City; in the latter place he rendered a great service in developing the Methodist Oklahoma City University. His strenuous service in that work undermined his health and compelled him to curb his activity. He moved from the Oklahoma Conference to the Missouri Conference and became pastor of Francis Street Church, St. Joseph, from which place he came to Columbia in 1947. While serving as pastor in Columbia, he was active in civic life. He was president for one year of a Columbia service club and for another year was president of the United Fund drive during which the fund was quickly and fully subscribed. His health failed completely, however, and he retired from the ministry in 1951 by orders of his physician and moved to Okla-

Some recent laymen active in the Church

Dale Summers

Don Bird

L. D. Johnston

Leeon Smith

H. R. Mueller

Herman A. Lehwald
District Superintendent
1963—

Jerry D. Statler
Associate Minister
1962—

Walter A. Hearn
Professor, Missouri School
of Religion, 1928-1965

Jyles Whittler
Custodian, 1932—

homa City. After a series of heart attacks, he died March 20, 1955, in Oklahoma City.

Hugh O. Isbell, who followed Williamson, was born in Birmingham, Alabama, November 15, 1898. On the death of his parents, he moved to Texas to be raised by an uncle; during his school and college days he received many medals for all-around citizenship and scholarship. He graduated from Southern Methodist University with an A.B. degree and from the Perkins School of Theology with a B.D. degree. He joined the St. Louis Annual Conference in 1924 and served various pulpits in that conference. He married Miss Norma Wagner of Jackson, Missouri, and they had two daughters, Janet and Margie. He transferred to the Southwest Missouri Conference for different assignments and was then moved to the Missouri Conference in 1951 and appointed pastor of the Missouri Methodist Church. He was a trustee of Southern Methodist University and of the Missouri Bible College, and was president for one year of the Missouri Council of Churches. Central College honored him with a degree of Doctor of Divinity in 1955. It was during his pastorate that some major renovations of the church building were begun. He was loved by his parishioners for his gentle character and for the devotional quality of his sermons. He became seriously ill in February, 1957, and after a major operation, from which he seemed to be recovering satisfactorily, he died suddenly of heart failure on March 2, 1957. His death was the first in the history of the Columbia Church of the active pastor and created poignant grief among the members of the Church. His funeral sermon was preached by Bishop Frank.

Monk Bryan, who was moved from the Maryville, Missouri, Methodist Church to succeed Isbell, was born in Blooming Grove, Texas, June 25, 1914. He had a distinguished ministerial ancestry. He graduated from Baylor University in 1935 and from the Perkins School of Theology in Dallas in 1938, and then did a year of post graduate work at Drew Theological Seminary. He married Corneille Barker Downer, whose father was Dr. James W. Downer of Baylor University. They have three children, Lucy Corneille, Robert Monk, and James Johnson. Bryan has served pastorates in the Central Texas Conference and the St. Louis Conference before coming to the Maryville Church in the Missouri Conference. He has served as delegate to many important national and international meetings. He is at present president of the Missouri Council of Churches. He is noted for the strong character of his sermons and for his administrative ability.

The Church has in recent years attracted to its membership many able and active men and women. Under a plan adopted in 1956-1957 under which members of the official board cannot serve longer than three successive years, new blood is constantly infused into the life system of the Church. Thus, the Church goes on "from strength to strength," and the Missouri Methodist Church has become, indeed, the Cathedral of Missouri Methodism.

Appendix I
Church Statistics—Continuation of Table on Page 106

Conference Year	Pastor	Salary of Pastor	No. Church Members	Baptisms	S.S. Members	W.M.S. Members	W.M.S. Amt. Raised	Total Church Collections
1930	Tucker	$ 5,200	1146	2	1100	252	$4,491	$ 46,787
1931	Tucker	5,000	1155	5	1008	174	4,444	22,331
1932	Tucker	5,000	979	5	1168	155	5,655	24,170
1933	Tucker	4,000	987	8	976	132	3,061	16,520
1934	Holliday	4,000	1002	13	607	118	2,088	15,730
1935	Holliday	3,500	1009	10	693	112	2,228	18,714
1936	Holliday	3,500	1015	10	801	123	3,592	20,056
1937	Holliday	4,000	1041	13	791	109	3,645	29,812
1938	Holliday	4,000	1048	13	781	*	2,364	20,708
1939	Holliday	4,000	1061	12	754	121	2,581	18,056
1940	Holliday	4,000	961	14	708	120**	2,626	18,514
1941	Holliday	5,800(2)	1055	45	714	123	2,089	18,900
1942	Holliday	5,800(2)	1124	18	768	118	1,533	20,286
1943	Crichlow	5,800(2)	1196	50	806	126	1,142	18,563
1944	Crichlow	6,300(2)	1243	40	792	131	1,608	30,756
1945	Crichlow	5,950(2)	1150	46	750	202	1,276	27,714
1946	Crichlow	4,500	1275	50	774	106	3,865	29,917
1947	Crichlow	5,000	1336	59	824	129	4,088	38,570
1948	Williamson	8,385(2)	1347	97	834	154	4,175	39,369
1949	Williamson	6,000	1424	48	903	183	5,127	31,832
1950	Williamson	6,000	1404	31	923	302	3,067	29,959
1951	Williamson	6,000	1418	42	958	196	2,680	33,308
1952	Isbell	6,000	1552	51	1032	209	4,063	78,209
1953	Isbell	6,500	1616	46	1616	257	4,526	41,957
1954	Isbell	6,500	1659	48	1277	330	2,912	38,608
1955	Isbell	6,500	1703	40	1289	341	3,062	46,005
1956	Isbell	4,667	1726	39	1411	355	3,605	33,494
1957	Bryan	7,230	1768	40	1106	346	6,519	66,593

APPENDIX I—continued

Conference Year	Pastor	Salary of Pastor	No. Church Members	Baptisms	S.S. Members	W.M.S. Members	W.M.S. Amt. Raised	Total Church Collections
1958	Bryan	7,750	1804	29	1804	366	4,561	67,712
1959	Bryan	8,000	1730	49	1485	326	3,324	73,525
1960	Bryan	10,770(2)	1765	51	1273	338	5,093	88,904
1961	Bryan	8,800	1685	56	1531	350	7,029	97,896
1962	Bryan	11,800(2)	1794	54	1427	352	5,350	106,482
1963	Bryan	14,200(2)	1863	37	1205	364	1,262	108,458
1964	Bryan	8,750	1885	20	1102	362	2,328	78,511

* Left vacant in Conference Statistics.
** Name changed to W.S.C.S.

APPENDIX II

Broadway Church Pastors and Officers (1904-1930)

Year	Pastor	Pres. Bd. Stewards	Pres. WMS	S. S. Supt.	Pres. Meth. Brotherhood (After 1920 Men's Club)
1904-05	S. P. Cresap	J. A. Stewart	*	C. J. Walker	*
1905-06	C. M. Bishop	*	*	C. J. Walker	*
1906-07	C. M. Bishop	J. A. Stewart	*	C. J. Walker	*
1907-08	C. M. Bishop	*	*	C. J. Walker	*
1908-09	C. M. Bishop	*	Mrs. M. A. Dearing	C. J. Walker	*
1909-10	C. M. Aker	J. A. Stewart	Mrs. M. A. Dearing	C. J. Walker	F. F. Stephens
1910-11	C. M. Aker	J. A. Stewart	Mrs. W. B. Nowell	C. J. Walker	J. M. Hughes
1911-12	C. M. Aker	J. A. Stewart	Mrs. Turner McBaine	W. T. Cross	W. H. Hays
1912-13	C. W. Tadlock	*	*	*	F. B. Mumford
1913-14	C. C. Grimes	*	*	F. F. Stephens	*
1914-15	C. C. Grimes	*	*	W. H. Rusk	*
1915-16	C. C. Grimes	*	*	A. C. Bush	*
1916-17	C. C. Grimes	J. M. Baker	Mrs. F. F. Stephens	F. F. Stephens	*
1917-18	S. W. Hayne	J. M. Baker	Mrs. F. F. Stephens	F. F. Stephens	*
1918-19	S. W. Hayne	*	Mrs. R. H. Emberson	M. A. Larey	*
1919-20	J. D. Randolph	F. B. Mumford	Mrs. R. H. Emberson	M. A. Larey	*
1920-21	J. D. Randolph	F. B. Mumford		F. F. Stephens	T. S. Townsley
1921-22	J. D. Randolph	F. F. Stephens	Mrs. J. A. Stewart	P. H. Ross	A. J. Meyer
1922-23	J. D. Randolph	F. F. Stephens	Mrs. F. E. Moore	P. H. Ross	H. F. Grinstead
1923-24	M. T. Haw	S. R. Barnett	Mrs. C. D. Rodgers	I. B. Jackson	Howard Groves
1924-25	M. T. Haw	S. R. Barnett	Mrs. J. A. Stewart	I. B. Jackson	E. L. Morgan
1925-26	M. T. Haw	J. J. Pyles	Mrs. E. L. Morgan	E. E. Windsor	A. A. Jeffrey
1926-27	M. T. Haw	*	Mrs. E. L. Morgan	J. F. Nicholson	J. T. McMullan
1927-28	M. N. Waldrip		Mrs. A. B. Woods	J. F. Nicholson	O. S. Thompson
1928-29	M. N. Waldrip	F. F. Stephens	Mrs. A. B. Woods	A. S. Emig	C. W. Furtney
1929-30	M. N. Waldrip	F. F. Stephens	Mrs. A. B. Woods	A. S. Emig	B. E. Miller

* Records have been lost where there are blanks.

Appendix III
Some Church Officials, Missouri Methodist Church, 1930-1965*

Year	Pastor	Pres. Off. Board	Pres. WMS (After 1940 WSCS)	S. S. Supt.	Pres. Men's Club
1930-31	Frank C. Tucker	F. F. Stephens	Mrs. A. B. Woods	A. S. Emig	B. E. Miller
1931-32	Frank C. Tucker	F. F. Stephens	Mrs. A. B. Woods	A. S. Emig	J. E. Blackmore
1932-33	Frank C. Tucker	J. E. Blackmore	Mrs. F. E. Moore	A. S. Emig	B. J. Carl
1933-34	Frank C. Tucker	F. F. Stephens	Mrs. T. A. Ewing	A. S. Emig	H. R. Mueller
1934-35	R. C. Holliday	J. E. Blackmore	Mrs. T. A. Ewing	A. S. Emig	C. C. Coffman
1935-36	R. C. Holliday	J. E. Blackmore	Mrs. T. A. Ewing	A. S. Emig	J. M. Neukomm
1936-37	R. C. Holliday	E. A. Trowbridge	Mrs. E. A. Renfrow	A. S. Emig	Wm. Dalton
1937-38	R. C. Holliday	E. A. Trowbridge	Mrs. E. A. Renfrow	A. S. Emig	E. C. Ringer
1938-39	R. C. Holliday	E. A. Trowbridge	Mrs. A. S. Emig	A. S. Emig	H. E. Johnson
1939-40	R. C. Holliday	Ed Roberson	Mrs. A. S. Emig	A. S. Emig	Horace Wren
1940-41	R. C. Holliday	Ed Roberson	Mrs. J. O. Martin	E. Garrison	E. R. Garrison
1941-42	R. C. Holliday	Ed Roberson	Mrs. I. G. Morrison	E. Garrison	M. L. Stuart
1942-43	J. W. Crichlow	Ed Roberson	Mrs. I. G. Morrison	H. D. Tucker	M. L. Rummans
1943-44	J. W. Crichlow	Ed Roberson	Mrs. I. G. Morrison	H. D. Tucker	G. D. Jones
1944-45	J. W. Crichlow	J. I. Gordon	Mrs. H. E. Johnson	Paul Mourning	Paul Mourning
1945-46	J. W. Crichlow	J. I. Gordon	Mrs. H. E. Johnson	Paul Mourning	M. C. Swinney
1946-47	J. W. Crichlow	H. R. Mueller	Mrs. H. E. Johnson	George D. Jones	Byron Cosby
1947-48	A. G. Williamson	H. R. Mueller	Mrs. Dale Summers	George D. Jones	Dale Summers
1948-49	A. G. Williamson	A. A. Jeffrey	Mrs. Dale Summers	George D. Jones	George Mansur
1949-50	A. G. Williamson	A. A. Jeffrey	Mrs. Bert Hopper	L. D. Murphy	Chester Young
1950-51	A. G. Williamson	A. A. Jeffrey	Mrs. Bert Hopper	Earl E. Deimund	Walter Baird
1951-52	Hugh O. Isbell	A. A. Jeffrey	Mrs. S. Valentine	L. J. Murphy	Earl Byers
1952-53	Hugh O. Isbell	A. A. Jeffrey	Mrs. Earl Byers	L. J. Murphy	Corl Leach
1953-54	Hugh O. Isbell	H. E. Johnson	Mrs. Earl Byers	Earl E. Deimund	C. D. Mitchell
1954-55	Hugh O. Isbell	H. E. Johnson	Mrs. C. E. Klingner	L. J. Murphy	R. E. Rice
1955-56	Hugh O. Isbell	Frank W. Rucker	Mrs. R. E. Rice	L. J. Murphy	Fred Miller
1956-57	Hugh O. Isbell	Frank W. Rucker	Mrs. M. C. Swinney	Donald Bird	John Brox
1957-58	Monk Bryan	L. G. Townsend	Mrs. M. C. Swinney	Donald Bird	Neil Freeland

1958-59	Monk Bryan	L. G. Townsend	Mrs. M. C. Swinney	Donald Bird	Joe Edmondson
1959-60	Monk Bryan	Ernest M. Funk	Mrs. M. C. Swinney	Burton Leach	Ernest M. Funk
1960-61	Monk Bryan	Ernest M. Funk	Mrs. Ernest M. Funk	Burton Leach	Clovis Jones
1961-62	Monk Bryan	Allen Baker	Mrs. Ernest M. Funk	Floyd Townsend	Loren Gafke
1962-63	Monk Bryan	Allen Baker	Mrs. L. G. Townsend	Floyd Townsend	Burton Leach
1963-64	Monk Bryan	J. E. Covington	Mrs. L. G. Townsend	Floyd Townsend	Harold Hedrick
1964-65	Monk Bryan	J. E. Covington	Mrs. Harold Hedrick	Floyd Townsend	Allen Baker

* A confusing difficulty of this table is that some of the organizations begin their year with January and some begin with the church year which in turn varies.

APPENDIX IV

Sessions of Missouri Conference

1—From Its Formation in 1816 to the Church Division of 1844

No.	Date	Presiding Bishop	Place of Conference	Presiding Elder (Mo. Dist.)	Circuit Rider (Boonslick)
1	Sept. 1816	William McKendree	Shiloh Meet. House, Ill.	Jesse Walker	Joseph Piggott
2	Oct. 1817	Robert R. Roberts	Bethel Meet. House, Ill.	Jesse Walker	J. Scripps and Wm. Townsend
3	Oct. 1818	William McKendree	Vincennes, Ind.	Jesse Walker	Alex. McAllister
4	Sept. 1819	Enoch George	McKendree Chapel, Mo.	Jesse Haile	J. Scripps and J. Harris
5	Sept. 1820	Robert R. Roberts	Shiloh Meet. House, Ill.	S. H. Thompson	J. Scott (*Cedar Creek Ct.*)
6	Oct. 1821	Robert R. Roberts	McKendree Chapel, Mo.	S. H. Thompson	Samuel Bassett
7	Oct. 1822	Robert R. Roberts	St. Louis, Mo.	David Sharp	David Chamberlin
8	Oct. 1823	William McKendree	St. Louis, Mo.	David Sharp	W. W. Redman and Joseph Edmonson
9	Oct. 1824	William McKendree	W. Padfield, Ill.	Jesse Haile	William W. Redman
10	Aug. 1825	Robert R. Roberts	New Tennessee, Mo.	John Dew	Benj. S. Ashby
11	Sept. 1826	Robert R. Roberts	McKendree Chapel, Mo.	Andrew Monroe	(Omitted)
12	Sept. 1827	Joshua Soule	St. Louis, Mo.	Andrew Monroe	James Bankson
13	Sept. 1828	Joshua Soule	Fayette, Mo.	Jesse Greene	N. T. Talbot
14	Sept. 1829	Joshua Soule	Potosi, Mo.	Jesse Greene	W. Crane & W. W. Redman
15	Sept. 1830	Robert R. Roberts	St. Louis, Mo.	A. McAllister	J. C. Berryman
16	Sept. 1831	Robert R. Roberts	McKendree Chapel, Mo.	Joseph Edmondson	G. W. Teas & W. A. H. Spratt
17	Sept. 1832	Joshua Soule	Pilot Grove	Jesse Greene	
18	Sept. 1833	Joshua Soule	Mtn. Spring, Ark.	Jesse Greene	W. W. Redman
19	Sept. 1834	Robert R. Roberts	Bellevue	Jesse Greene	Robert H. Jordan (*Col. Ct.*)
20	Sept. 1835	Robert R. Roberts	Arrow Rock	Jesse Greene	J. F. Young & R. S. Reynolds
21	Sept. 1836	Robert R. Roberts	St. Louis (*Col. Dt.*)	Andrew Monroe	Robert H. Jordan & C. Smith
22	Sept. 1837	Joshua Soule	St. Louis	Andrew Monroe	William Ketron & J. L. Forsyth
23	Sept. 1838	Joshua Soule	Boonville	Andrew Monroe	J. F. Young & Samuel Grove
24	Oct. 1839	Thomas A. Morris	Fayette	William Patton	D. Fisher & D Sherman
25	Sept. 1840	Beverly Waugh	St. Louis	William Patton	Benj. R. Johnson
26	Oct. 1841	Thomas A. Morris	Palmyra	Jesse Greene	Benj. R. Johnson
27	Sept. 1842	Robert R. Roberts	Jefferson City	Jesse Greene	Asa McMurtry (*Col. & Rochept. Ct.*)
28	Sept. 1843	J. O. Andrew	Lexington	Jesse Greene	Walter Prescott

212

2—From Formation of M. E. Church, South, 1844 to 1880

No.	Date	Presiding Bishop	Place of Conference	Presiding Elder (Columbia District)	Preacher
30	Oct. 1845	Joshua Soule	Columbia	William Patton	William M. Rush
31	Sept. 1846	Robert Payne	Hannibal	Andrew Monroe	Z. N. Roberts
32	Sept. 1847	William Capers	Glasgow	Andrew Monroe	Z. N. Roberts
33	Oct. 1848	James O. Andrew	Weston	Andrew Monroe	John Cotton
34	Sept. 1849	Robert Payne	Fulton	Andrew Monroe	P. M. Pinckard
35	Oct. 1850	(None present)	Canton	Jacob Lanius	P. M. Pinckard
36	Sept. 1851	William Capers	Fayette	Jacob Lanius	R. P. Holt & E. K. Miller
37	Oct. 1852	Robert Payne	St. Joseph	E. M. Marvin (*St. Chas. Dist.*)	B. H. Spencer (*Columbia Station*)
38	Sept. 1853	James O. Andrew	Palmyra	E. M. Marvin	B. H. Spencer
39	Sept. 1854	H. H. Kavanaugh	Brunswick	M. G. Berryman	J. S. Todd
40	Sept. 1855	John Early	Richmond	Andrew Monroe (*Fayette Dist.*)	A. P. Linn (*Col.-Nashville Ct.*)
41	Sept. 1856	G. F. Pierce	Louisiana	P. M. Pinckard	S. W. Coke (*Columbia Station*)
42	Sept. 1857	James O. Andrew	Glasgow	P. M. Pinckard	William Penn (*Columbia Circuit*)
43	Sept. 1858	John Early	Chillicothe	W. G. Caples	Benj. F. Johnson
44	Sept. 1859	Robert Payne	St. Joseph	B. H. Spencer	W. G. Miller (*Columbia Station*)
45	Sept. 1860	H. H. Kavanaugh	St. Charles	Edwin Robinson	W. G. Miller & Jos. Dines (*Col. Ct.*)
46	Sept. 1861		Glasgow	Edwin Robinson	William F. Bell
	No session held in 1862 because of the War, and no bishops present in 1861, 1863, or 1864.				
47	Oct. 1863		Fulton	Edwin Robinson	R. H. Jordan & J. S. Smith
48	Sept. 1864		Mexico	Horace Brown	R. H. Jordan & Thompson Penn
49	Aug. 1865	H. H. Kavanaugh	Hannibal	Andrew Monroe	J. R. Taylor & R. A. Claughton
50	Sept. 1866	D. S. Doggett	Richmond	Andrew Monroe	Thomas DeMoss & Henry D. McEwin
51	Sept. 1867	E. M. Marvin	Macon City	D. A. Leeper	J. P. Nolan (*Columbia Station*)
52	Sept. 1868	H. H. Kavanaugh	Weston	W. A. Mayhew	T. J. Gooch
53	Sept. 1869	G. F. Pierce	Chillicothe	W. A. Mayhew	M. B. Chapman
54	Sept. 1870	H. N. McTyeire	Columbia	W. A. Mayhew	John D. Vincil

213

Appendix IV, part 2—continued

No.	Date	Presiding Bishop	Place of Conference	Presiding Elder (Columbia District)	Preacher
55	Sept. 1871	D. S. Doggett	Palmyra	William Penn	John D. Vincil
56	Sept. 1872	G. F. Pierce	Mexico	William Penn	John D. Vincil
57	Sept. 1873	Wm. Wightman	Carrollton	W. M. Newland	W. H. Lewis
58	Sept. 1874	John C. Keener	St. Joseph	J. H. Pritchett	W. H. Lewis
59	Oct. 1875	John C. Keener	Glasgow	J. H. Pritchett	W. H. Lewis
60	Sept. 1876	H. N. McTyeire	Hannibal	W. M. Rush	George W. Horn
61	Sept. 1877	E. M. Marvin	Fulton	W. M. Rush	George W. Horn
62	Sept. 1878	D. S. Doggett	Macon City	W. M. Rush	George W. Horn
63	Sept. 1879	W. N. Wightman	Louisiana	W. M. Rush	H. B. Watson
64	Sept. 1880	John C. Keener	Richmond	B. H. Spencer	H. B. Watson

3—From 1881 to 1916

No.	Date	Presiding Bishop	Place of Conference	Presiding Elder (Fayette Dist.)	Preacher (Columbia Station)
65	Sept. 1881	G. F. Pierce	Moberly	B. H. Spencer	H. B. Watson
66	Sept. 1882	J. C. Granbery	Plattsburg	J. A. Mumpower	E. K. Miller
67	Sept. 1883	A. W. Wilson	Chillicothe	J. A. Mumpower	E. K. Miller
68	Sept. 1884	Linus Parker	Shelbina	J. A. Mumpower	Chaney Grimes
69	Sept. 1885	J. C. Granbery	Columbia	J. A. Mumpower	M. B. Chapman
70	Sept. 1886	H. N. McTyeire	St. Joseph	J. H. Ledbetter	J. A. Beagle
71	Sept. 1887	E. R. Hendrix	Mexico	J. H. Ledbetter	J. A. Beagle
72	Sept. 1888	E. R. Hendrix	Gallatin	J. H. Ledbetter	J. H. Jackson
73	Sept. 1889	J. C. Granbery	Palmyra	J. H. Ledbetter	J. H. Jackson
74	Sept. 1890	J. S. Key	Fayette	E. K. Miller	J. H. Jackson
75	Sept. 1891	R. K. Hargrove	Maryville	E. K. Miller	J. H. Jackson
76	Sept. 1892	C. B. Galloway	Montgomery City	E. K. Miller	T. E. Sharp
77	Sept. 1893	A. G. Haygood	Monroe City	E. K. Miller	T. E. Sharp
78	Sept. 1894	E. R. Hendrix	Carrollton	J. R. A. Vaughan	T. E. Sharp
79	Sept. 1895	W. W. Duncan	Macon	J. R. A. Vaughan	W. F. Packard
80	Sept. 1896	C. B. Galloway	Hannibal	J. R. A. Vaughan	W. F. Packard
81	Sept. 1897	O. P. Fitzgerald	Albany	J. R. A. Vaughan	J. H. Glanville
82	Aug. 1898	W. A. Candler	Memphis	John Anderson	M. H. Moore
83	Aug. 1899	J. C. Granbery	Fayette	John Anderson	M. H. Moore
84	Aug. 1900	J. C. Granbery	Fulton	R. H. Cooper	M. H. Moore
85	Sept. 1901	W. A. Candler	St. Joseph	R. H. Cooper	M. H. Moore
86	Sept. 1902	A. W. Wilson	Chillicothe	R. H. Cooper	S. P. Cresap
87	Sept. 1903	C. B. Galloway	Mexico	R. H. Cooper	S. P. Cresap
88	Aug. 1904	E. R. Hendrix	Columbia	R. H. Cooper	S. P. Cresap
89	Aug. 1905	E. R. Hendrix	Palmyra	B. D. Sipple	C. M. Bishop
90	Aug. 1906	J. S. Key	Carrollton	B. D. Sipple	C. M. Bishop
91	Aug. 1907	J. S. Key	Moberly	B. D. Sipple	C. M. Bishop
92	Aug. 1908	H. C. Morrison	Hannibal	A. B. Culbertson	C. M. Bishop
93	Sept. 1909	W. A. Candler	Savannah	A. B. Culbertson	C. M. Aker
94	Aug. 1910	Collins Denny	Plattsburg	A. B. Culbertson	C. M. Aker

215

Appendix IV, part 3—continued

No.	Date	Presiding Bishop	Place of Conference	Presiding Elder (Fayette Dist.)	Preacher (Columbia Station)
95	Aug. 1911	Collins Denny	Columbia	A. B. Culbertson	C. M. Aker
96	Sept. 1912	E. D. Mouzon	Shelbina	A. C. Johnson	C. W. Tadlock
97	Sept. 1913	E. E. Hoss	St. Charles	A. C. Johnson	C. C. Grimes
98	Sept. 1914	E. R. Hendrix	St. Joseph	A. C. Johnson	C. C. Grimes
99	Sept. 1915	E. R. Hendrix	Chillicothe	A. C. Johnson	C. C. Grimes
100	Aug. 1916	E. R. Hendrix	Fayette	Charles O. Ransford	C. C. Grimes

4—From 1917 to Uniting Conference of 1939

No.	Date	Presiding Bishop	Place of Conference	Presiding Elder (Fayette Dist.)	Preacher (Columbia Station)
101	Sept. 1917	E. R. Hendrix	Richmond	C. O. Ransford	S. W. Hayne
102	Sept. 1918	W. B. Murrah	Fulton	C. O. Ransford	S. W. Hayne
103	Sept. 1919	W. B. Murrah	Mexico	C. O. Ransford	Jos. D. Randolph
104	Sept. 1920	W. B. Murrah	Liberty	W. M. Alexander	Jos. D. Randolph
105	Aug. 1921	W. B. Murrah	Hannibal	B. D. Sipple	Jos. D. Randolph
106	Aug. 1922	W. F. McMurry	Moberly	B. D. Sipple	Jos. D. Randolph
107	Sept. 1923	W. F. McMurry	St. Joseph	B. D. Sipple	Marvin T. Haw
108	Sept. 1924	W. F. McMurry	Richmond	B. D. Sipple	Marvin T. Haw
109	Sept. 1925	W. F. McMurry	Chillicothe	J. D. Randolph	Marvin T. Haw
110	Sept. 1926	W. F. McMurry	Columbia	J. D. Randolph	Marvin T. Haw
111	Sept. 1927	W. F. McMurry	St. Joseph	J. D. Randolph	M. N. Waldrip
112	Sept. 1928	W. F. McMurry	Shelbina	R. C. Holliday	M. N. Waldrip
113	Sept. 1929	W. F. McMurry	Salisbury	R. C. Holliday	M. N. Waldrip
114	Sept. 1930	A. F. Smith	Columbia	R. C. Holliday	Frank C. Tucker
115	Aug. 1931	A. F. Smith	Mexico	G. A. Shadwick	Frank C. Tucker
116	Sept. 1932	A. F. Smith	Fulton	G. A. Shadwick	Frank C. Tucker
117	Aug. 1933	A. F. Smith	Hannibal	John L. Taylor	Frank C. Tucker
118	Sept. 1934	J. M. Moore	Moberly	John L. Taylor	Robt. C. Holliday
119	Sept. 1935	J. M. Moore	Chillicothe	John L. Taylor	Robt. C. Holliday
120	Sept. 1936	J. M. Moore	Richmond	H. H. Brower	Robt. C. Holliday
121	Sept. 1937	J. M. Moore	St. Joseph	H. H. Brower	Robt. C. Holliday
122	Sept. 1938	W. T. Watkins	Excelsior Springs	H. H. Brower	Robt. C. Holliday
123	Oct. 1939	Ivan Lee Holt	St. Louis		Robt. C. Holliday

5—From United Methodism, 1939, to Reorganization of the Missouri Area, 1961

No.	Date	Presiding Bishop	Place of Conference	District Superintendent (Fayette Dist.)	Preacher (Mo. Meth. Church)
1	Oct. 1939	Ivan Lee Holt	St. Louis	H. H. Brower	R. C. Holliday
2	Sept. 1940	John C. Broomfield	Cameron	H. H. Brower	R. C. Holliday
3	Sept. 1941	John C. Broomfield	Brookfield	H. H. Brower	R. C. Holliday
4	Sept. 1942	John C. Broomfield	Hannibal	H. H. Brower	J. Wilson Crichlow
5	Sept. 1943	John C. Broomfield	St. Joseph	C. B. Galatas	J. Wilson Crichlow
6	Oct. 1944	Ivan Lee Holt	Columbia	C. B. Galatas	J. Wilson Crichlow
7	Sept. 1945	Ivan Lee Holt	Chillicothe	C. B. Galatas	J. Wilson Crichlow
8	Sept. 1946	Ivan Lee Holt	St. Joseph	C. B. Galatas	A. G. Williamson
9	Sept. 1947	Ivan Lee Holt	Columbia	C. B. Galatas	A. G. Williamson
10	Sept. 1948	Ivan Lee Holt	St. Joseph	C. B. Galatas	A. G. Williamson
11	Sept. 1949	Ivan Lee Holt	Cameron	W. B. Morgan	A. G. Williamson
12	Sept. 1950	Ivan Lee Holt	St. Joseph	W. B. Morgan	Hugh O. Isbell
13	Sept. 1951	Ivan Lee Holt	Maryville	W. B. Morgan	Hugh O. Isbell
14	Sept. 1952	Ivan Lee Holt	St. Joseph	W. B. Morgan	Hugh O. Isbell
15	Sept. 1953	Ivan Lee Holt	Brookfield	W. B. Morgan	Hugh O. Isbell
16	Sept. 1954	Ivan Lee Holt	Columbia	W. B. Morgan	Hugh O. Isbell
17	Sept. 1955	Ivan Lee Holt	Moberly	M. L. Koch	Hugh O. Isbell
18	Sept. 1956	Ivan Lee Holt	St. Joseph	M. L. Koch	Hugh O. Isbell
19	June 1957	Eugene M. Frank	Fayette	M. L. Koch	Monk Bryan
20	June 1958	Eugene M. Frank	Fayette	A. Sterling Ward	Monk Bryan
21	June 1959	Eugene M. Frank	Fayette	A. Sterling Ward	Monk Bryan
22	June 1960	Eugene M. Frank	Fayette	A. Sterling Ward	Monk Bryan
23	May 1961	Eugene M. Frank	Fayette	*	*

From Organization of the Missouri East Conference, 1961 to 1964

No.	Date	Presiding Bishop	Place of Conference	District Superintendent (Jefferson City District)	Preacher
1	May 1961	Eugene M. Frank	Fayette	M. G. Joyce	Monk Bryan
2	June 1962	Eugene M. Frank	Fayette	M. G. Joyce	Monk Bryan
3	May 1963	Eugene M. Frank	Fayette	H. A. Lehwald	Monk Bryan
4	May 1964	Eugene M. Frank	Fayette	H. A. Lehwald	Monk Bryan

* Conclusion of organization of the Missouri Conference. No appointments made.

No.	Date	Place	Bishops Elected in Each Conference
1.	May 1, 1846	Petersburg, Va.	Joshua Soule and J. O. Andrew held over from M. E. Church; Wm. Capers and Robert Paine elected
2.	May 1-31, 1850	St. Louis, Mo.	Henry B. Bascom
3.	May 1-31, 1854	Columbus, Ga.	G. F. Pierce, John Early, H. H. Kavanaugh
4.	May 1-31, 1858	Nashville, Tenn.	(None elected)
5.	May, 1862		(Not held because of War)
5.	April 4-May 3, 1866	New Orleans, La.	Wm. M. Wightman, E. M. Marvin, D. S. Doggett, H. N. McTyeire
6.	May 4-26, 1870	Memphis, Tenn.	John C. Keener
7.	May 1-26, 1874	Louisville, Ky.	(None elected)
8.	May 1-24, 1878	Atlanta, Ga.	(None elected)
9.	May 3-25, 1882	Nashville, Tenn.	A. W. Wilson, Linus Parker, J. C. Granbery, Robert K. Hargrove
10.	May 5-25, 1886	Richmond, Va.	Wm. W. Duncan, C. B. Galloway, E. R. Hendrix, J. F. Key
11.	May 7-26, 1890	St. Louis, Mo.	A. G. Haygood, O. P. Fitzgerald
12.	May 3-21, 1894	Memphis, Tenn.	(None elected)
13.	May 5-23, 1898	Baltimore, Md.	W. A. Candler, H. C. Morrison
14.	May 7-26, 1902	Dallas, Tex.	Coke Smith, E. E. Hoss
15.	May 3-21, 1906	Birmingham, Ala.	J. J. Tigert, Seth Ward, James Atkins
16.	May 4-21, 1910	Asheville, N.C.	Collins Denny, John C. Kilgo, W. B. Murrah, R. J. Waterhouse, E. D. Mouzon, James H. McCoy, W. R. Lambuth
17.	May 6-25, 1914	Oklahoma City, Okla.	(None elected)
18.	May 2-18, 1918	Atlanta, Ga.	John M. Moore, W. F. McMurry, U. V. W. Darlington, H. M. Dubose, W. N. Ainsworth, James Cannon, Jr.
19.	May 3-22, 1922	Hot Springs, Ark.	W. B. Beauchamp, J. E. Dickey, Sam R. Hay, H. M. Dobbs, H. A. Boaz
			Special Session
19.	July 2-4, 1924	Chattanooga, Tenn.	(None elected)
20.	May 5-20, 1926	Memphis, Tenn.	A. J. Moore, P. B. Kern, A. F. Smith
21.	May 7-24, 1930	Dallas, Texas	(None elected)
22.	April 26-May 8, 1934	Jackson, Miss.	Ivan Lee Holt, W. C. Martin, W. W. Peele, C. Purcell, C. C. Selecman, W. T. Watkins
23.	April 23-May 5, 1938	Birmingham, Ala.	

Few Bishops had been chosen in the Methodist Episcopal Church before the Division of 1845. Thomas Coke and Francis Asbury were chosen in 1784, Richard Whatcoat in 1800, William McKendree in 1808, Enoch George and Robert R. Roberts in 1816, Joshua Soule in 1820 but refused to accept election at that time; Soule reelected in 1824 along with Elijah Hedding; J. O. Andrew and John Emory in 1832, Beverly Waugh, Wilbur Fiske and Thomas A. Morris in 1836, and L. L. Hamline and E. S. Janes in 1844.

Appendix VI
The Declaration of Union
The Preamble

WHEREAS, The Methodist Episcopal Church, The Methodist Episcopal Church, South, and The Methodist Protestant Church did through their respective General Conferences appoint Commissions on Interdenominational Relations and Church Union; and

WHEREAS, these Commissions acting jointly did produce, propose and present to the three churches a Plan of Union; and

WHEREAS, these three churches, each acting separately for and in its own behalf, did by more than the constitutional majorities endorse and adopt this Plan of Union, in accord with their respective constitutions and Disciplines, and did effect the full consummation of union in accordance with the Plan of Union; and

WHEREAS, these three churches in adopting this Plan of Union did authorize and provide for a Uniting Conference with certain powers and duties as therein set forth; and

WHEREAS, The Uniting Conference duly authorized and legally chosen in accordance with the Plan of Union is now in session in the city of Kansas City, Mo.:

The Affirmation

NOW, THEREFORE, we, the members of the Uniting Conference, the legal and authorized representatives of The Methodist Episcopal Church, The Methodist Episcopal Church, South, and The Methodist Protestant Church, in session here assembled on this tenth day of May, 1939, do solemnly in the presence of God and before all the world make and publish the following Declarations of fact and principle:

The Declarations

I.

The Bishop: The Methodist Episcopal Church, The Methodist Episcopal Church, South, and The Methodist Protestant Church are and shall be one United Church.

The Delegates: We do so declare.

II.

The Bishop: The Plan of Union as adopted is and shall be the constitution of this United Church, and of its three constituent bodies.

The Delegates: We do so declare.

III.

The Bishop: The Methodist Episcopal Church, The Methodist Episcopal Church, South, and The Methodist Protestant Church had their common origin in the organization of the Methodist Episcopal Church in America in 1784, A.D., and have ever held, adhered to and preserved a common belief, spirit and purpose, as expressed in their common Articles of Religion.

The Delegates: We do so declare.

IV.

The Bishop: The Methodist Episcopal Church, The Methodist Episcopal Church, South, and The Methodist Protestant Church, in adopting the name "The Methodist Church"

	for the United Church, do not and will not surrender any right, interest or title in and to these respective names which, by long and honored use and association, have become dear to the ministry and membership of the three uniting Churches and have become enshrined in their history and records.
The Delegates:	We do so declare.

V.

The Bishop:	The Methodist Church is the ecclesiastical and lawful successor of the three united Churches, and through which the three Churches as one United Church shall continue to live and have their existence, continue their institutions, and hold and enjoy their property, exercise and perform their several trusts under and in accord with the Plan of Union and *Discipline* of the United Church; and such trusts or corporate bodies as exist in the constituent Churches shall be continued as long as legally necessary.
The Delegates:	We do so declare.

VI.

The Bishop and **the Delegates:** To the Methodist Church thus established we do solemnly declare our allegiance, and upon all its life and service we do reverently invoke the blessing of Almighty God. Amen.

INDEX

Abolition movement appears, 35
Ainsworth, Bishop W. N., 140, 219
Aker, Cecil M., pastor, 105n, 160, 119-123, 131, 133, 133n, 209, 215, 216
   Picture, 132
Aker, Grover C., 120-121, 122
Alexander, W. M., 217
Alexander, Mrs. W. M., 156
Allen, Professor and Mrs. E. A., 98
American Seating Company, 173, 177, 184
   Files suit against church, 173, 174
American Colonization Society, formation of, 35
Ames, Bishop Edward R., 63
   Heads movement to seize southern Church property, 65
Anderson, John, 215
Anderson, W. G., 95
Anderson, W. H., 58
Anderson, W. T., 83n, 108, 109, 116
Andrews, Bishop James O., 50, 212, 213, 219
   Possesses slaves, 37
   Suspended from office of bishop, 37
Anglen, Harry P., 198
Annual Conferences, first establishment of, 21
Architects
   Matthews and Clark, 109
   Jamieson and Spearl, 157
   Baylor, A. J., 157
Arkansas Conference, organized, 33
Arnold, Mrs. Corinne, 172
Asbury, Francis, 19, 21, 23, 24, 24n, 219
   Picture, 20
Ashby, Benjamin S., pastor, 212
Ashby, Thomas, 39
Atkins, Bishop James, 113, 219
Austin, Samuel, 33n

Baird, Walter, 210
Baker, Allen, 211
   Picture, 201
Baker, Hugh E., 108
Baker, James M., 95, 101, 108, 109, 170, 172, 200
   Picture, 146
Baltimore Conference joins southern church, 64
Bankson, James, pastor, 212
Barnett, S. R., 156, 209
   Picture, 155
Baptist Church Building, 44, 103
Baptists need Church, 32
Bascom, Bishop Henry B., 51, 150n, 219
Bassett, Samuel, pastor, 212
Bayley, Alonzo V., 107
Bayley, Mrs. Alonzo V., 107n
Baylor, A. J., 157
   Drew plans for Missouri Methodist Church, 157
Beagle, J. A., pastor, 86, 215
Beasley, Edward F., 108, 116, 117
Beasley, George H., 91, 101, 102, 108n, 117
   Picture, 146
Beauchamp, Bishop W. B., 140, 219
Bell, William F., pastor, 58, 213
Bennett, Belle H.
   Makes plea for laity rights for women, 119, 137
Berry, Harvey G., 44
Berryman, J. C., pastor, 212
Berryman, M. G., 49, 213
Bible College of Missouri, 131
Bird, Don, 210, 211
   Picture, 201, 203
Bishop, Charles M., pastor, 106, 113, 116-119, 120, 209, 215
   Picture, 132
Bishop, none present in Missouri Conference, 57
Bitting and Company, St. Louis, 172, 173, 174, 184

Loan funds for building project, 163, 164
　Replace bonds with new issue, 171
　3rd issue of bonds, 184
　Bonds paid, mortgage released, 185-186
Blackmore, J. E., 210
Blackwell-Wielandy Company, 173, 177, 184
Boaz, Bishop H. A., 140, 219
Boone County, formation of, 29
Boone County, History of 1882
　Names of few early Methodists mentioned, 33
Boonslick Circuit, 24, 25
Boots, Wilson T. and Nora, 199
Boy Scouts, 143
Bowling, C. W., 101, 109
Bowling, Charles B., 109
Bowling, Mrs. James D., 102, 109
　Picture, 94
Boyce, James R., 44
Boyle, Joseph, 37, 39
Brady, George, 123
Briggs, Warren L., 194
　Picture, 201
Briggs, Mrs. Warren L.
　Picture, 201
Broadway Church
　See: Building, Broadway Church
Brooks, Stration D., 157
Broomfield, Bishop John C., 199
　Picture, 130
Brossart, Mr. and Mrs. J. F., 113
Brower, H. H., 217, 218
Brown, Horace, 61, 213
Brown, John E., 113
Browning, Wesley, 37, 39
Brox, John, 210
Bryan, Era, 7
Bryan, Gid J., 7
Bryan, Monk, pastor, 7, 197, 198, 205-206, 207, 208, 210-211, 218
　Picture, 192, 201
Bryan, Mrs. Monk
　Picture, 201
Budd, James Thomas, 122
Building, Broadway Church, 43n
　To be built, 109
　Building committee, 109

Matthews and Clark, Architects, 109
　Cornerstone ceremony, 110
　Dedication ceremony, 110
　Memorial windows, donors, 111
　Chapel, 111
　Cost of church reported, 111
　Picture, 114
　McMurry, opposes expansion, 153
　Sold, 153n, 183
Building, Columbia Churches
　First building, 44-45
　Picture, 42
　Second building, 80n, 81
　Third building, 83
　Picture, 81
　Fourth building
　　See: Building, Broadway Church
　Fifth building
　　See: Building, Missouri Methodist Church
Building, Missouri Methodist Church
　Financial Campaign, 147-151
　Presented to Missouri Annual Conference, 150
　General building committee, 154
　Local building committee, 156, 164
　Picture, 155
　Committee on site, 153
　Building fund committee, 154
　Site chosen, 154
　First plans, 157
　A. J. Baylor, Architect, 157
　Contract for ground floor, 158
　Cornerstone laying, 158, 160
　Picture, 159
　Local supervisor, Harry Bill, 158
　Selection of name, 158
　First chapel service, 160
　Contract for super-structure, 164
　Construction completed, 164, 186
　First service, 164, 167
　Building debt problems, 162, 167, 169, 193
　　Mortgage, 161
　　First mortgage bonds, 162

Bitting and Company, 163
Great depression, 167, 169, 173, 174
Second state-wide campaign, 168, 169
Indebtedness
  Floating, 172, 173, 174, 184
  Second mortgage, 171, 172
  Third mortgage, 172, 185, 186
  "Plan for paying debt," 172-173
  Suits filed against church, 173-175, 175n
  Pastor's salary partially paid, 174, 175
  Suit filed for dissolution of church, 175-176
  Settlement with creditors, 177
  Debt retired, 183, 184, 185
  New agreement, 183, 184
  Victory dinner, 183-184
Building, need for improvement
  Congregation outgrows Broadway Building, 145
  Costs set, 145
Bush, A. C., 109
Byers, Earl, 210
  Picture, 201
Byers, Mrs. Earl, 210
  Picture, 201

Camp meetings, 23
Candler, Bishop Warren A., 97, 181, 215, 219
  Picture, 127
Cannon, Bishop James, Jr., 140, 219
Capers, Bishop William, 51, 213, 219
Caples, W. G., 49, 57n, 58, 213
Carl, B. J., 210
Carryer, Dr. J. W., 101
Catholics, Growth in Columbia, 104
Casteel, Judge B. J., 140n
Cedar Creek Circuit, 29
  Camp meetings, 31
Central Methodist College, 71, 89, 163, 200
Chamberlin, David, pastor, 212
Chapman, M. B., pastor, 77, 79, 86, 99, 213, 215
Chandler, Thomas, 38

Christian Church Building, 103-104
Church Conference, Local, 69
Church Division, middle forties, 47
Church Workers in State Universities, Conferences, 134
Civil War, 55-58
Clark, Marshall, 143
Claughton, R. A., pastor, 67, 213
Coffey, M. W., 101
Coffman, A. B., 117, 122
  IXL, 118
Coffman, Beulah C. (Mrs. C. C.), 172, 198
  Picture, 201
Coffman, Cecil C., 143, 172, 210
  Picture, 168
Coke, S. W., pastor, 213
Coke, Bishop Thomas, 19, 21, 23, 219
Cole, Dr. J. B., 117
Colored Methodist, 24
Colored Methodist Episcopal Church of America, 76
Columbia, District formed, 33
  Name disappears, 34
Columbia church members unknown, 33
Columbia Church
  Point on Cedar Creek Circuit, 31
  Made a "station," 48
Columbia, Circuit, organized, 31, 32
Columbia-Rocheport Circuit, formation of, 36
"Columbia Tigers" organized, 60
Community Methodist Church, 193
Confederate Force invades Missouri, 60
Congor, C. H., 108, 109
Cooper, George A., 91
Cooper, R. H., 215
Cope, S. W., pastor, 49
Cosby, Byron, 210
Covington, Joe E., 211
Cotton, John, pastor, 213
Craig, H. M., 142
Crane, W., pastor, 212
Cresap, Dr., S. P., pastor, 106, 107, 109, 113, 116, 209, 214

225

Appreciation to, 111
　Picture, 132
Cresap, Mrs. S. P., 197
Crichlow, J. Wilson, pastor, 185, 186, 197, 207, 210, 218
　Picture, 176
Crosby, James E., 143
Cross, W. T., 209
Crouch, E. W., 109
Culbertson, A. B., 215, 216
Culver, Paul M., 140n
Cunningham, David, 44
Curry, C. F., 113

Dalton, F. A., 155, 156
Dalton, William, 210
Dameron, Mrs. Sarah, 110
Daniels, Turner R., 33n, 44
Darlington, Bishop U. V. W., 140, 219
Dearing, Mrs. M. A., 209
Dearing, Mrs. M. E., 101
Dearing, Milton, M., 101
Decell, Bishop, J. L., 170n
Deimund, Earl E., 143, 210
DeMoss, Thomas, pastor, 71, 72n, 73, 213
Denny, Bishop Collins, 119, 215, 216, 219
　Picture, 128
　Opposes laity rights for women, 138
　Opposes Union of Methodism, 181n
Depression, Great, 167, 169, 173, 174, 183
Dew, John, 212
Dickey, Bishop J. E., 140, 219
Dines, Joseph, pastor, 49, 57, 58, 213
Dines, Tyson, 58
Director, Church, 105n
　First ever published, 101-102
Disciples' Bible College, 194
Discipline, remains same for both churches, 51
　Expunge "slave trade," 51, 52
District Superintendent
　New name for Presiding Elder, 21n, 182
Division of Churches between

Boonslick and Columbia, Circuit unknown, 33
Dobbs, Bishop H. M., 140, 219
Doggett, Bishop David S., 68, 213, 214, 219
Douglas, J. B., 95
Downs, Mrs. J. W., 157
Drumm, Manuel, 141n, 168
　Importance on Building project, 156, 169
　Picture, 155
DuBose, Bishop H. N., 140, 219
Duncan, Bishop William W., 97, 219

Early, Bishop John, 21, 213, 219
Edmondson, Joseph, pastor, 31n, 211, 212
Elwang, W. W., Presbyterian pastor, 110
Emberson, Mrs. R. H., 138, 156, 209
Emig, A. S., 209-210
Emig, Mrs. A. S., 210
Emory, Bishop John, 219
Enoch, Bishop George, 24n, 25, 219
Episcopal Church Building, 104
Episcopal Districts, 105n
Epple, Mr. and Mrs. John A., 197
Epple, John, 163, 197
　Makes estimate of building cost, Missouri Methodist Church, 163
　Picture, 166
Epple Construction Company, 163, 164, 172, 173, 177, 184
Epworth League, 90, 91, 92
Epworth League, Columbia Church, 91
Evans, Mrs. Anna
　Picture, 201
Evans, F. D., 83, 95, 101, 109, 111
Evans, Mrs. Laura E., 117
　Picture, 168
Exhorters, 77n
Ewing, Mrs. T. A., 210

Federal Council of Churches, 115-116, 116n
Financial Problems, Columbia, Church, 83-84

226

Financial systems, 78
Fisher, David, pastor, Columbia Circuit, 36, 212
Fiske, Bishop Wilbur, 219
Fitzgerald, Bishop O. P., 97, 215, 219
Forsyth, James L., pastor, Columbia Circuit, 36, 212
France, Kay, 197-198
Frank, Bishop Eugene M., 199
   Picture, 196
Franklin, Missouri, 25
Fraternal relations, North and South, 97-98, 179
Freeland, Neil, 210
Fritz, Herman
   Picture, 201
Fritz, Mrs. Herman
   Picture, 201
Funk, Ernest M., 199, 211
   Picture, 201
Funk, Mrs. Ernest M., 211
Furtney, C. W., 209

Gafke, Franklin
   Picture, 201
Gafke, Loren, 211
Galatas, C. B., 218
Galloway, Bishop Charles B., 97, 110, 215, 219
   Picture, 127
Garrison, E. R., 210
General Conference
   1784, Christmas Conference, 19, 27, 219
   1792, 21
   1796, 21
   1800, 21, 23, 219
   1804
   1808, 23, 27, 219
   1812
      First delegated, 23
   1816, 24, 27, 219
   1820, 219
   1824, 219
   1832, 219
   1836, 33, 219
   1844, 37, 38, 219
   1845, Convention of, 37, 38
      Delegates to, 37
   1846, 40, 51, 53, 219
   First M. E. Church, S., 38
   1848, Methodist Episcopal Church, 50, 63
   1850, 47, 51, 219
   1854, 43 51, 219
   1858, 43, 51, 52, 53, 68, 77, 219
   1862, 73
      Cancelled, 58, 219
   1866, 56n, 64, 66, 68, 69, 70, 75, 76, 219
      Great importance of, 68
      Discussed without action name of church, 68-69
      Introduces lay representation, 69
      Episcopal Districts established, 105n
      Lay representation, Annual and General Conference, 136
   1870, 69n, 97, 136, 219
   1872, M. E. Church, 97
   1874, 97, 98, 219
   1878, 89, 97, 219
      Established Woman's Foreign Missionary Society, 124
   1882, 219
      Proposes change of church name, 96
   1886, 97, 219
      Authorized organization of Woman's Department Board of Church Extension, 124
   1890, 90, 97, 219
   1894, 91, 97, 219
   1898, 97, 214, 219
   1902, 113, 124, 215, 219, 326, 329
      Recommends withdrawal from staffing high schools, 115
      Deaconess, office of, established, 115
   1906, 113, 219
   1910, 119, 125, 139, 219
      Laity rights for women refused, 119, 137
      Established office of lay leader, 140
   1914, 125-126, 135, 141
      Bishops oppose laity rights for women, 137
      Bishops appointed for quad-

rennium to specific areas, 139-140
Plan of Union, 179
1918, 139, 140, 141, 147, 180, 219
  Approve laity rights for women, 138
1920, M. E. Church
  Refused plan of Union, 180
1922, 138, 140, 219
  Rejects Northern Convention plan, 180
1924, Special Session, 219
  Endorses plan of Union, 180
1926, 180, 219
1930, 170, 170n, 219
1934, 180, 170n, 219
1938, 170n, 219
  Last meeting of Southern Conference, 181
George, Bishop Enoch, 25, 212
Gibson, Maria L., 89n
Gisler, Talitha, 198, 199
  Picture, 201
Glanville, John, 37
Glanville, J. H., pastor, 86, 215
God, Church of, 183, 184
Goddard, Dr. O. E., 149
Gooch, T. J., pastor, 76, 77, 213
  Picture, 82
Gordon, J. I., 210
Granbery, Bishop John C., 97, 105, 215, 219
Gray, O. D., 172
Greene, Jesse, 32, 36, 37, 39, 212
Gribble Family, 99
  Gribble, Lois, 99
  Gribble, Alta, 99
Grimes, Chaney, pastor, 86, 95, 134n, 215
  Picture, 93
Grimes, Charles C., pastor, 106, 134, 136, 209, 216
  Picture, 152
Grinstead, H. F., 209
Grinstead, L. R., 143
Grove, Samuel, pastor, Columbia Circuit, 36, 212
Groves, Howard, 209
Growth of church membership rapid, 29, 32
Guitar, John and Emily, 32

Gutekunst, Fred, 136
Guth Electric Company, 173, 177, 184

Haile, Jesse, 25, 212
Halberstadt, W. L., 135, 136, 145n
Hamline, Bishop L. L., 219
Handy, Mrs. J. C., 156
Handy, Reverend J. C., 135
Hanes, C. O., 142n
Hanson, Robert and Mazelle, 199
Hargrove, Bishop Robert K., 97, 215, 219
Harrell, G. W., Jr., 101, 108, 109
Harris, John, pastor, Boonslick Circuit, 25, 212
Haw, Marvin T., pastor, 106, 138, 155, 158, 160, 186, 209, 217
  Picture, 152, 157
Hawkins, J. Emmett, 138, 139, 142n
  Picture, 168
Hay, C. M., 140n
Hay, Bishop Sam R., 140, 219
Hayes, Mrs. Juliana, 89
Haygood, Bishop A. G., 97, 215, 219
Hayne, Stanley W., pastor, 106, 136, 142, 209, 217
  Proposes enlarging Broadway Church, 147
  Picture, 152
Hays, W. H., 123, 209
Haystack Prayer meeting, 140, 140n
Hearn, Olive W. (Mrs. Walter A.), 194
Hearn, Walter A., 194
  Picture, 204
Hedding, Bishop Elijah, 219
Hedrick, Harold, 211
Hedrick, Mrs. Harold, 211
Henderson, G. W., 83
Hendrix, Mrs. Adam, 89, 148n
Hendrix, Bishop Eugene R., 89n, 97, 111, 140, 148n, 215, 219
  First President, Federal Council of Churches, 116
  Picture, 127
Hendrix Hall
  See Women's Residence Hall

Hepple, Mrs. Lawrence
  Picture, 201
Hill, A. Ross
  President, University of Missouri, 123
Hill, Robert E. L., 154
Holliday, Robert C., pastor, 181n, 185, 197, 207, 210, 217, 218
  Picture, 176
Holt, Bishop Ivan Lee, 154, 170n, 199, 200, 217, 218, 219
  Picture, 130
  Presides, Dedication of Missouri Methodist Church, 186
Holt, Richard P., pastor, 41, 213
Hopper, Mrs. Bert, 210
Horn, George W., pastor, 84, 86, 87, 214
Horner, John P., 95, 96, 99
  Picture, 94
Horner, Mrs. John P., 99
Hoss, Bishop E. E., 113, 216, 219
  Picture, 129
Hughes, J. M., 123, 209

Indebtedness, Missouri Methodist Church
  Floating, 172, 173, 174, 184
  Second mortgage, 171, 172
  Third mortgage bonds, 172, 185, 186
  "Plan for paying debt," 172, 173
  Suits filed against church, 173, 174, 175, 175n
  Suit filed for dissolution of church, 175, 176
  Settlement with creditors, 177
  Debt retired, 183, 184, 185
  Pastor's salaries partially paid, 174, 175
  New agreement with creditors, 183, 184
  See Building, Missouri Methodist Church
Isbell, Hugh O., pastor, 197, 205, 207, 210, 218
  Picture, 176
Isbell, Janet, 197
  Picture, 201

Jackson, I. B., 209

Jackson, J. H., pastor, 86, 87, 89, 98, 99, 100, 101, 105, 215
  Picture, 93
Jacoby Art Glass Company, 173, 177, 184
Jameson, James M., 38
Jamieson and Spearl, Architects, 157
Janes, Bishop E. S., 219
Jeffrey, A. A., 143, 209, 210
Jewell, William, 32, 44
  Picture, 30
Johnson, A. C., 216
Johnson, Benjamin F., pastor, 49, 213
Johnson, Benjamin R., pastor, Columbia Circuit, 36, 212
Johnson, Harold E., 210
  Picture, 201
Johnson, Mrs. Harold E., 210
Johnson, Thomas, 37
Johnston, L. D., 184
  Picture, 203
Jones, Charmione (Mrs. Donald), 197
Jones, Clovis, 211
Jones, George D., 210
Jones, Ted
  Picture, 201
Jordon, Robert H., pastor, 31, 31n, 32, 36, 60, 61, 212, 213
Joyce, M. G., 219

Kasmann, William
  Picture, 201
Kavanaugh, Bishop H. H., 49, 51, 213, 219
Keener, Bishop John C., 97, 214, 219
Kern, Bishop Paul B., 170n, 219
Ketron, William, pastor, Columbia circuit, 36, 212
Key, Bishop Joseph F., 97, 215, 219
  Picture, 128
Kilgo, Bishop John C., 119n, 219
Klingner, Mrs. C. E., 210
Koch, M. L., 218
Krummel, J. A., 91

Laity rights for women, 88, 108n, 119, 137

General Conference, 119
  Bishops oppose, 137
  Memorial, Woman's Missionary Council, 137
  Approved, General Conference, 138
Lambuth, Bishop W. R., 119n, 219
Larey, M. A., 209
Lathrop, Dr. John H., 32
Laws, S. S., President, University of Missouri, 96n
Lawson, Judge Martin E., 140n
Lay Activities, Board of, 140, 141
Lay leader, office of, 140
  Missouri Conference list, 140n
  Columbia Church, 141n
Lay representative, 69
  First election of laymen, 77
Laymen, Prominent, 203
Laymen's Association, Conference, 90
Laymen's Missionary Movement, 140, 141, 147
Leach, Burton, 211
Leach, Corl, 210
Ledbetter, J. H., 215
Leeper, D. A., 76, 213
Leftwich, W. M., 55
Lehwald, Herman A., 218
  Picture, 204
Lewis, W. H., pastor, 83, 86, 87, 214
Limbaugh, Rush H., 133
Lincoln, Abraham, 57
Linn, A. P., pastor, 49, 213
Little Dixie, 181
Lockwood, B. M., 101, 102
Lockwood, W. D., 91
Louisiana Purchase Treaty of 1803, 19
Lynn, John H., 37
Lyons, James M., 95

Mansur, George, 210
Marr, P. M., 181n
Martin, Mrs. J. O., 210
Martin, T. T., 143n
Martin, Bishop W. C., 170n, 219
Marvin, Bishop Enoch M., 43, 43n, 48, 49, 56n, 68, 104, 213, 214, 219

Picture, 82
Matthews and Clark of Saint Louis, Architects, Broadway Church, 109
Matthews, Charles, 101, 109
Matthews, Mrs. Eliza, 33n
Matthews, Milton S., 33n, 44, 56n
Maupin, W. D., 95, 101
Maupin, W. T., 95
  Picture, 94
Mayhew, W. A., 76, 77, 80, 213
Meinershagen, Fred
  Picture, 201
Membership loss, as a result of division in 1845, 40
Men's Club
  T. T. Martin, author of history of Club, 143n
  Boy Scouts, 143
  See Methodist Brotherhood
Methodism, Division of, 179, 182
Methodism, Unification of
  Plan of Union, 179, 180, 181
  Special session, General Conference, 180
  General Conference, approved Plan of Union, 181
  Judicial Council of the Church, 181
  Uniting Conference, Kansas City, 181
  New nomenclature, 182, 200
  Declaration of Union, 220, 221
Methodist Brotherhood of Columbia
  Organized, 120, 123
  First officers elected, 120
  Re-organized into Men's Club, 142, 143
Methodist Episcopal Church, South, 38, 78, 96, 137
  Organized, 58
Methodist preaching in Boone County Courthouse during the 20's, 31
Methodist Student Organization, 148, 149, 182
Methodists and Baptists cooperate in the building of the Union Church, 52
  See Union Church

230

Meyer, A. J., 143, 209
Middle Period, 47
Miller, B. E., 142n, 209, 210
Miller, E. K., pastor, 41, 86, 87, 112, 213, 215
    Picture, 93
Miller, M. F., 143
Miller, Mrs. Fred
    Picture, 201
Miller, W. G., pastor
49, 57, 58, 213
Mills, Samuel J., 140n
Ministerial Trials, 78, 79
Minutes, Missouri Annual Conference
    Begins publication of, 85
Missions, Board of
    After Civil War, 75
Missouri Annual Conference, 35
    Meets in Columbia, 38
    Decides to "go South," 38
Missouri Annual Conference
    1816, 212
        Formation of, 24
    1817 to 1818, 212
    1819, 212
        First held in Missouri, 25
    1820, 25, 29, 35, 212
    1821 to 1833, 212
    1834, 31, 212
    1835, 33, 35, 212
    1836, 33, 36, 212
    1837, 212
    1838, 36, 212
    1839, 36, 212
    1840, 36, 212
    1841, 212
    1842, 34, 36, 212
    1843, 212
    1844, 36, 37, 212
    1845, 38, 40-43, 213
    1846, 40, 213
    1847, 40, 213
    1848, 40, 213
    1849 to 1851, 213
    1852, 34, 43, 213
    1853, 48, 213
    1854 to 1857, 213
    1858, 53n, 213
    1859, 213
    1860, 49, 57, 76, 213
    1861, 57, 58, 213
    1862, 213
        Cancelled, 58
    1863, 60, 80n, 213
    1864, 60, 213
        Oath prescribed for members of Conference, 60-61
        Conference refuses to take oath, 61
    1865, 65, 67, 69, 213
        Its report on "State of the Church," 66
    1866, 69, 70, 70n, 71, 96, 213
    1867, 72, 73, 75, 77, 78, 213
    1868, 76, 213
    1869, 77, 78, 213
    1870, 79, 86, 213
        Held in new Presbyterian Church, 79
    1871, 85, 214
    1872 to 1877, 214
    1878, 89, 214
    1879 to 1880, 214
    1881 to 1882, 215
    1883, 85n, 215
    1884, 215
    1885, 96, 215
    1886 to 1887, 215
    1888, 100, 215
    1889, 215
    1890, 90, 100, 215
    1891, 215
    1892, 90, 215
    1893, 91, 215
    1894, 92, 215
    1895 to 1897, 215
    1898, 107n, 215
    1899, 92, 215
    1900, 105, 107, 215
    1901 to 1903, 215
    1904, 111, 112, 215
    1905, 80n, 215
    1906 to 1908, 215
    1909, 119, 215
    1910, 215
    1911, 123, 216
    1912 to 1913, 216
    1914, 135, 216
    1915 to 1916, 216
    1917 to 1920, 217
    1921, 150, 151, 217

Financial budget for new church plant, 150
1922, 154, 217
1923 to 1925, 217
1926, 160, 217
1927 to 1929, 217
1930, 170, 217
  Reviews debt situation, Missouri Methodist Church, 171
1931, 217
1932, 107n, 217
1933, 217
1934, 184, 217
1935 to 1938, 217
1939, 217
  Last session, 199
1940 to 1941, 218
1942, 185, 218
1943 to 1961, 218
Missouri Area
Reorganized, 199, 200
Missouri Circuit, 23
Missouri Compromise, 28, 35
Missouri Constitution, 1865
  Oath required of clergy, 64
Missouri East Annual Conference, 200
  1961 to 1964, 218
Missouri Methodist Church
  Laying Cornerstone, 159
  Dedication of, 186, 193
  Picture, 187
  Holt, Ivan Lee, Presiding Bishop, dedication, 186
  Smith, A. Frank, Bishop gives sermon, 186
  Sanctuary, picture, 188
  Methodist Window, picture, 189
  Pulpit and Lectern, picture, 190
  Altar and Cross, picture, 191
  McMurry Chapel, picture, 196
Missouri Methodist Church Building
  See building, Missouri Methodist Church
Missouri Methodist Church, Inc, 161, 162, 163
  Incorporated, 161-162
Missouri Methodist Foundation, 154, 156, 157, 167, 169

Missouri West Annual Conference, 200
Mitchell, C. D., 210
Mitchell, D. T., 117
Mitchell, Mrs. D. T., 117
Mitchell, Josephine, 117
Monroe, Andrew, 36, 37, 39, 44, 58, 60, 61, 67, 212
  Picture, 30
Moore, Bishop Arthur J., 170n, 219
Moore, Mrs. F. E., 209, 210
Moore, Bishop John M., 140, 217, 219
  Picture, 130
Moore, Matthew H., pastor, 86, 101, 104, 105, 106, 107, 120, 215
  Picture, 132
Morgan, E. L., 209
Morgan, Mrs. E. L., 209
Morgan, W. B., 218
Morris, Bishop Thomas A., 212, 219
Morrison, Bishop H. C., 97, 215, 219
  Picture, 128
Morrison, Mrs. I. G., 210
Mount Zion Methodist Church, burned September, 59, 73
Mourning, Paul, 210
Mouzon, Bishop E. D., 119n, 216, 219
  Picture, 128
Mueller, H. R., 210
  Picture, 203
Mumford, F. B., 108, 123, 134, 142, 142n, 156, 209
  Picture, 155
Mumpower, J. A., 95, 215
Murphy, L. D., 210
Murphy, L. J., 210
Murphy, Lawrence E., 194
Murrah, Bishop W. B., 119n, 140, 150, 151, 217, 219
  Picture 129
Murrell, L. D., 154
Music, 76
  Instrumental, not common in church services, 77

McAlester, Dr. Andrew W., 99, 109

232

Picture, 94
McAlester, B., 44, 83, 95, 99, 101
  Picture, 94
McAlester, Mrs. B., 99
McAlester Family, 111
McAllister, Alex, pastor, Boonslick Circuit, 212
McAnally, David Rice, 47, 59
McAnally, David Rice, Jr., 48n, 96, 98
McBaine, Turner, 109
McBaine, Mrs. Turner, 125, 138, 209
McCleary, Glenn A., 198
McCoy, Bishop James H., 119n, 219
McDonald, Mrs. Witten, 89
McDonnell, E. B., 142n, 156, 172
  Picture, 155
McDonnell, Ed, 117
McDonnell, Emmett, 117
McEwin, Henry D., pastor, 71, 213
McKendree Chapel
  Picture, 22
McKendree, Bishop William, 23, 24, 212, 219
McMullan, J. T., 156, 209
  Picture, 155
McMurry, Bishop W. F., 80n, 113, 140, 150, 157, 161, 162, 163, 169, 217, 219
  Important to Columbia Church, 115
  Ex officio, Chairman, Building Committee, 115
  Picture, 129
  Heads "General Building Committee," 151, 154
  Opposes expansion, Broadway Church, 153
  Cornerstone laying, Missouri Methodist Church, 158
  McMurry Chapel, Missouri Methodist Church, 197
McMurry, Wilson S., 38
McMurtry, Asa, pastor Columbia Circuit, 36, 212
McTyeire, Bishop Holland N., 24, 68, 78, 79, 213, 214, 215, 219

Nairn, S. W., 116
National Council of Churches, 116n

Nazarene, Church of, 183
Neukomm, J. M., 210
Newcomb, Earnest H., 136, 148, 194
Newland, W. M., 214
Nichols, G. S., 160
Nicholson, J. F., 209
Nickell, Lindsay A., 175n
  IXL, 123
  Organization of teen-age boys, 118
Nineteenth Amendment, U.S. Constitution, 137
Nolan, J. P., pastor, 72, 75, 76, 213
  Picture, 42
Norwood, Emma
  See Vincil, Mrs. John D.
Norwood, Frank, 91
Nowell, W. B., 95, 99, 101, 108, 134, 156, 169-170
  Picture, 155
Nowell, Mrs. W. B., 209
Nutt, Fauntleroy, 44

Orr, J. C., 95, 99
Osborne, Mrs. Byron
  Picture, 201

Packard, W. F., pastor, 86, 215
  Picture, 93
Paine, Bishop Robert, 51, 213, 219
Palmyra Conference, 65
Parker, Bishop Linus, 97, 215, 219
Parrigan, Perry G., 198
Parsonage, 73, 117, 195
Patton, William, 36, 37, 38, 39, 212, 213
Payne, Moses U., 32, 33, 99
  Picture, 30
  Memorial window for, 111
Peele, Bishop W. W., 170n, 219
Pegues, D. K., 181n
Penn, Thompson, pastor, 61, 213
Penn, William, pastor, 49, 213, 214
Perkins, J. T., 101, 108, 109
Phillips, Construction Company of Columbia, 158
Phillips, E. C., 195
Phillips, Thomas, 33n
Pierce, Bishop George F., 51, 213, 214, 215, 219

233

Piggott, Joseph, 24, 25, 212
Pinckard, Patrick N., pastor, 41, 47, 49, 59, 67, 213
Plan of Union, Methodism, 179, 180, 181
Powell, Bert, 198
　Picture, 201
Powell, Waldo
　Picture, 201
Prescott, Walter, pastor, 36, 212
Presbyterian Church Building, 32, 103
Presbyterian Church, 79
Presiding Elder
　Becomes District Superintendent, 21n, 182
Price. E. M., 108
Price, Lakenan M., 174
Pritchett, J. H., 214
Pritchett, J. T., 155
Probationers, 50
Publishing House ownership referred to U. S. Courts, 50
Purcell, Bishop Clare, 170n, 219
Pyles, J. J., 156, 172, 209
　Picture, 155

Quarles, James T., 174n, 198
Quarterly Conference Records, 92
　First Extant record, 92, 95

Randolph, Joseph, D., pastor, 106, 136, 138, 142, 150, 155, 156, 162, 171, 181n, 209, 217
　Picture, 152
Ransford, Charles O., 216, 217
Read, President Daniel, 79
　University of Missouri
Redman, W. W., pastor, 38n, 212
　Picture, 30
Reed, Mrs. W. L., 125
Reese, A., 95
Renfrow, Mrs. E. A., 210
Resolution to join Southern Methodist Church, 38
Revival meetings, 98
Reynolds, R. S., pastor, 31, 212
Rice, Ray E., 198, 210
Rice, Mrs. R. E., 210
Riggans, Dr. G. W., 83, 95, 96
Riley, T. J., 117

Ringer, E. C., 210
Roberson, Ed, 210
Roberts, Bishop Robert R., 24n, 212, 219
Roberts, Z. N., pastor, 213
Robinson, Edwin, 49, 57, 60, 213
Rodgers, Mrs. C. D., 209
Ross, P. H., 156, 209
Rucker, Frank W., 210
　Picture, 201
Rummans, M. L., 210
Rush, William M., pastor, 67, 213, 214
Rusk, W. H., 142n, 209
Russell, R. L., 151, 154

St. Louis Christian Advocate, 47, 67, 71, 72, 73n, 74
　Authorized under conditions, 47
　Suspended by Federal authorities, 59
　Editor imprisoned, 59
　Prints letters about difficulties of Columbia Church, 71, 72
Schenk, Quentin
　Picture, 201
Schwabe, James W., 120, 122, 141n, 146, 153, 165
　Charge of financial campaign, building fund, 154
Scott, James, pastor, Cedar Creek Circuit, 29, 212
Scripps, John, pastor, Boonslick Circuit, 25, 212
Searcy, Reverend B. P., 108n
Searcy, Mary, 91n, 108n
Sebastian, C. B., 101
Selecman, Bishop C. C., 170n, 219
Sessions, Missouri Annual Conference, 105n, 212
Shadwick, G. A., 217
Shaefer, J. M., 101
Shannon, James, 96n
Sharp, T. E., pastor, 86, 99, 104, 215
　Picture, 93
Sharp, David, 212
Sherman, Daniel, pastor, 36, 212
Shiloh Meeting House
　Picture, 22
Shore, Mr. and Mrs. Ben R., 117
Shore, Margaret, 117

234

Sipple, B. D., 113, 155, 215, 217
Sites, Committee on
  See Building, Missouri Methodist Church
Skinner, Organ Company, 183
  Files suit against church, 173, 174, 175, 177
Slaveholding, common practice among early settlers, 28
Slaveholding, strict rules against, 27
Slavery question divides the Church, 35
  Missouri Annual Conference, 35
Smith, Bishop A. Frank, 7, 170, 171, 217, 219
  Picture, 129
  Sermon dedication of Missouri Methodist Church, 186
Smith, Condley, pastor, 31, 36, 212
Smith, Bishop Coke, 113, 219
Smith, James S., pastor, 60, 213
Smith, Jesse H., 136
Smith, Leeon
  Picture, 203
Smith, Rosa, 91
Smith, Dr. S. D., 123, 142n, 142
Smoke, Captain and Mrs. S. A., 111
Soule, Bishop Joshua, 43, 50, 212, 213, 219
Spanish influenza epidemic, 136
Spencer, Berry H., pastor, 43, 48, 49, 56n, 58, 67, 213, 214
  Picture, 42
Spratt, W. A. H., pastor, 212
Stafford, Helen E., 194
Stanton, Edwin, M., 63
Statistics, Church, Columbia, 33n, 86, 106, 207-212, 218, 219
Statler, Jerry, 198
  Picture, 204
Stephens, Mrs. Blanche H. (Mrs. F. F.), 125, 138, 155, 156, 169, 209
  Picture, 146
  First woman delegate, Southern General Conference, 150n
Stephens, Louise I., 9
Stephens, Frank F., 7, 117, 120, 122, 134, 135, 142, 154, 156, 172, 181n, 209, 210
  Picture, 6, 155

Stephenson, Mrs. W. T., 138
Stewards, Board of, Columbia Church
  Duties, 108, 138
Stewart, Mrs. J. A., 209
Stewart, John A., 108, 109, 118, 120, 134, 142, 155, 156, 172, 209
  Picture, 146
Stuart, M. L., 210
Student Problems, Committee on, Board of Stewards, 134
Suburban churches, 193
Sunday School, Broadway Church, 118, 131
Summers, Dale, 210
  Picture, 203
Summers, Mrs. Dale, 210
Superannuates
  Support of, 78
  5% plan, 78
Swinney, M. C., 210
  Picture, 201
Swinney, Mrs. M. C., 210, 211
  Picture, 201
Switzler, William F., 33n, 112

Tadlock, Charles W. pastor, 105, 106, 133, 134, 209, 216
  Picture, 132
Taft, William
  Picture, 201
Talbot, N. T., pastor, 212
Taylor, John L., 217
Taylor, John R., pastor, 67, 213
Teas, G. W., pastor, 212
Tennessee Conference, 24
Thompson, O. S., 209
Thompson, Samuel H., 23, 29, 212
Tigert, Bishop J. J., 113, 219
Todd, J. S., pastor, 49, 213
Townsend, Floyd, 211
Townsend, L. G., 210
Townsend, Mrs. L. G., 211
Townsend, William, pastor, 212
Townsley, T. S., 209
Travis, John, 23
Treaty of Peace, 19
Trowbridge, E. A., 143, 210
True, Evalyn
  Picture, 201

Trustees, Board of
  Duties, 107, 108
Tucker, Frank C., pastor, 170, 174, 175, 177, 181n, 184, 207, 210, 217
  Reassuring interview, 175
  Picture, 176
Tucker, H. D., Associate pastor, 183, 184, 185, 197, 210
Twitty, Jerome, 199

Union Church, 36, 38, 43, 99
  Used for public meetings, 32
Union, Declaration of, Appendix VI, 220, 221
Uniting Conference, 181, 199
University of Missouri
  Fire destroys building, 100, 101, 103
Utz, W. H., Jr., 181n

Valentine, Mrs. S., 210
Vandeventer, C. I., 58, 67
Vaughan, J. R. A., 215
Vesser, John W., 113, 116
Vincil, John D., pastor, 60, 61, 65, 80, 80n, 83, 86, 111n, 213, 214
  Picture, 82
Vincil, Mrs. John D., 80n

Waldrip, Marion N., pastor, 106n, 160, 161, 170, 174, 209, 217
  Picture, 152
Walker, Senator Charles J., 117, 134, 209
Walker, Jesse, 25, 212
Walker, William, 108, 109
Wall, Herbert, 158
Ward, A. Sterling, 218
Ward, Bishop Seth, 113, 219
Waterhouse, Bishop R. J., 119n, 219
Waterman, Nathaniel, 38
Watkins, Mrs.   , 89
Watkins, Bishop W. T., 170n, 217, 219
  Picture, 130
Watson, H. B., pastor, 86, 90, 214, 215
Waugh, Bishop Beverly, 212, 219
Wesley, Charles, 23
Wesley Foundation, 194, 195
Wesley, John 23

Picture, 18
  Quotation from, 19
Wesley Student Organization, 182
Wesleys, Mission to America, 19
Westlake, Thomas W., 101
Whatcoat, Bishop Richard, 21, 23, 219
Wheeler, O. V.
  Picture, 201
Whitmarsh, Patricia, 198
Whitsides, J. M., 120
Whittler, Jyles
  Picture, 204
Wightman, Bishop William M., 68, 214, 219
Wilhelm, E. Lee, 194
Wilkes Boulevard Church, 193
  Established, 122
Williams, President Walter, University of Missouri, 91
Williamson, A. G., pastor, 186, 195, 202, 205, 207, 210, 218
  Picture, 176
Wills and Legacies, Committee Organized "Foundation of the Missouri Methodist Church of Columbia," 198, 199
  Officers, 199
Wilson, Bishop A. W., 97, 215, 219
  Picture, 127
Wilson, O. B., 155, 156
Windsor, E. E., 142n, 209
Windows, Stained glass, Missouri Methodist Church, 25n, 160, 161
Winter, William Hauser, 37
Wolff, Theodore, H., 38n
Woman's activities in Church work, 88, 89
Woman's Missionary Council, 125, 137
Woman's Missionary Society
  Becomes Woman's Society of Christian Service, 182
Woman's Missionary Society, Columbia, Church, 90, 142
Woman's Missionary Society, Missouri Conference, 89
Woman's Missionary Society, M. E. Church, S., 89, 138
Woman's Missionary Society, Missouri Conference, 125

Woman's Parsonage and Home Mission Society, 124
  See Woman's Missionary Council
Woman's Society of Christian Service, 182
Women members, Columbia, Church, 73, 89, 108n
Women's Residence Hall, Hendrix Hall, 147, 148, 156, 167, 173
  Built, 156, 157
  Cornerstone laid by Bishop McMurry, 157
"Women's Rights," 108n
Woods, Mrs. A. B., 209, 210
Woods, J. M., 181n
World War I, 136, 145, 149
Wren, Horace M., 143, 210

Yochum, William, 120, 123
Young, Chester, 210
Young, J. F., pastor, 31, 36, 212
Younts, Robert W., 194
Youth Societies, 99, 100

Zeigler, Harley H., 194
Zenge, Mrs. Kenneth
  Picture, 201
Zumbrunnen, A. C., 134